THE Taste of Home
RECIPE BOOK
Second Edition

Editor: Julie Schnittka
Associate Editors: Ann Kaiser, Faithann Stoner
Assistant Editor: Kristine Krueger
Food Editor: Mary Beth Jung
Assistant Food Editor: Coleen Martin
Test Kitchen Assistants: Judith Scholovich, Sherry Smalley
Art Directors: Ellen Lloyd, Vicky Wilimitis
Illustrations: Jim Sibilski
Photography: Scott Anderson, Mike Huibregtse,
Erickson Photography (p. 9), Pamela Siefken (p. 11)
Prop Stylist: Anne Schimmel

© 1996, Reiman Publications, L.P.
5400 S. 60th St., Greendale WI 53129
International Standard Book Number: 0-89821-213-8
Library of Congress Catalog Card Number: 95-72659

PICTURED ABOVE: Sky-High Strawberry Pie (recipe on p. 11).

PICTURED ON FRONT COVER. Clockwise from top: Baked Ham with Cumberland Sauce, Norwegian Parsley Potatoes and Asparagus with Sesame Butter (recipes on p. 9).

Spend a Full Year with the Best Cooking in the Country!

WHAT DOES it take to be ranked by families coast to coast as the *very* best food magazine in the country? You're holding the answer right in your hands.

This second edition of *The Taste of Home Recipe Book* brings you the best of the best from the pages of North America's most popular cooking publication—with 3 million subscribers and still growing! It's the single source of *over 350* down-home country-style selections published in *Taste of Home* during its historic second year.

This colorful photo-filled collection gives you a tantalizing taste of what makes *Taste of Home* so refreshingly different from all other food magazines:

● *Taste of Home* is the only publication edited by 1,000 everyday cooks—*cooks just like you*—from every state plus every Canadian province. Throughout the year, these field editors share recipes for their families' favorite meals. We've included six of them here, as you'll see when you turn to page 6, including Ruth Andrewson's Honey-Glazed Chicken, Spiced Carrot Strips, Paprika Potatoes and Fruit 'n' Nut Cherry Pie. It's a meal she prepares often in her Leavenworth, Washington kitchen.

● "My Mom's Best Meal" takes readers back in time and taste as fellow cooks recall fantastic foods—and fond memories—from their childhood. For instance, when Linda Gaido of New Brighton, Pennsylvania prepares Mom's Roast Beef, Oven-Roasted Potatoes, Country Green Beans and Baked Apple Slices (recipes on page 27), she tastefully pays tribute to a mother whose reputation for mouth-watering roasts is still unrivaled in the family.

● A bounty of budget meals proves that you don't have to sacrifice flavor in order to be frugal. Take the breakfast created by Marsha Ransom of South Haven, Michigan—Hearty Egg Scramble, Ambrosia Fruit and Jellied Biscuits (recipes on page 34) cost just 94¢ a plate!

● Complete Meals in Minutes make great cooking quick and easy...because they go from start to serving in *30 minutes or less*! For an example of such express eating, check out Quick Chicken Cacciatore (a fast-to-fix main meal from Marcia Hostetter of Canton, New York)...Mini Blue Cheese Rolls (Myrtle Albrecht's been making them for 30 years in Cameron Park, California)...and No-Cook Coconut Pie (a no-fuss favorite from Concordia, Missouri cook Jeanette Fuehring). The recipes for this speedy Italian supper can be found on page 36.

● In the Potluck Pleasers section (see page 52), cooks share an appealing assortment of most-requested recipes—from hearty starters and savory side dishes to meaty main meals and delectable desserts—that are guaranteed to add special flair to the buffet at your next get-together.

You'll also find dozens of dishes that are perfect if you're cooking for a crowd—or just for yourself or the two of you. And there are plenty of other irresistible ideas for snacks, soups, salads and side dishes, along with main meals, breads and dessert.

What's more, we've made this cookbook as practical and easy-to-use as the food that's in it. Each recipe is complete on a page...there's no need to turn the page in mid-making to finish a dish.

With that, please dig in...and begin enjoying an entire year's worth of the best cooking in the country from the best cooks in the country!

CONTENTS

TO ORDER ADDITIONAL COPIES of *The Taste of Home Recipe Book, Second Edition*, send your name and address, along with $12.99 each (plus $2.50 shipping/insured delivery) to Country Store, Suite 3613, 5925 Country Lane, Greendale WI 53129. Specify item number 20286. For credit card orders, call toll-free 1-800/558-1013. The first edition of *The Taste of Home Recipe Book* is also available. Specify item number 19550 when ordering.

OUR EDITORS' FAVORITE MEALS

1,000 great country cooks help edit *Taste of Home* magazine.
On the following pages, you'll "meet"
six of our field editors who share their favorite meals.

By Ruth Andrewson
Leavenworth, Washington

I HAVE a large notebook filled with delicious down-to-earth recipes I keep close at hand so I can have a "from scratch" meal ready in short order when guests drop in. I call this collection of favorite recipes my "treasure book". Its pages reflect a love of cooking that began with my childhood on a farm and has lasted through raising a family and owning a small restaurant.

One page in particular is well-worn—it contains a simple but special chicken dinner that has roots back in Michigan's Upper Peninsula, where husband Severt and I lived before moving here to Washington's "apple country" about 15 years ago.

When one of our small Midwestern town's only restaurants closed its doors, we added a restaurant to our motel to give overnight guests and folks from the area a place to eat. Soon we gained a reputation for homemade rolls, pies and entrees not normally served at other places.

Like many of my tried-and-true dishes, I modified a basic recipe from one of the church or specialty cookbooks I collect and came up with Honey-Glazed Chicken. Adding curry powder spiced up the quick-and-easy basting sauce that richly glazes this tasty entree. Patrons loved the down-home country flavor!

Spiced Carrot Strips have a delicate buttery flavor with just a hint of cinnamon. The sauteed Paprika Potatoes proved so successful that we served them often...and still do to family and friends. They're especially nice because they leave the oven free for other things.

And for the perfect ending to this meal, I prepared delectable Fruit 'n' Nut Cherry Pie. Because it's not too heavy or rich, this pie remains a much-requested recipe.

I hope you find these delicious new jewels irresistible...and hope you add them to your own "treasure book" of family favorites!

♥☎♥☎♥☎♥☎♥☎♥☎♥

Honey-Glazed Chicken

My family raves over this beautifully browned chicken. The rich honey glaze gives each luscious piece a spicy tang. This dish is simple enough to prepare for a family dinner and delightful enough to serve to guests.

    1/2 cup all-purpose flour
      1 teaspoon salt
    1/2 teaspoon cayenne pepper
      1 broiler-fryer chicken (about 3
        pounds), cut up
    1/2 cup butter or margarine,
        melted, *divided*
    1/4 cup packed brown sugar
    1/4 cup honey
    1/4 cup lemon juice
      1 tablespoon soy sauce
  1-1/2 teaspoons curry powder

In a bowl or bag, combine flour, salt and cayenne pepper; add chicken pieces and dredge or shake to coat. Pour 4 tablespoons butter into a 13-in. x 9-in. x 2-in. baking pan; place chicken in pan, turning pieces once to coat. Bake, uncovered, at 350° for 30 minutes. Combine brown sugar, honey, lemon juice, soy sauce, curry powder and remaining butter; pour over chicken. Bake 45 minutes more or until the chicken is tender, basting several times with pan drippings. **Yield:** 4-6 servings.

♥☎♥☎♥☎♥☎♥☎♥☎♥

Spiced Carrot Strips

These lightly sweet strips get unique flavor from cinnamon, which enhances the fresh carrot taste. Give this special yet simple side dish a try!

      5 large carrots, julienned
      2 tablespoons butter or
        margarine, melted
      1 tablespoon sugar
      1 teaspoon salt
    1/4 teaspoon ground cinnamon

Place carrots in a saucepan; cover with water. Cook until tender, about 8-10 minutes. Drain. Combine butter, sugar, salt and cinnamon; pour over carrots and toss to coat. Serve immediately. **Yield:** 4-6 servings.

♥☎♥☎♥☎♥☎♥☎♥☎♥

Paprika Potatoes

These tasty potatoes are golden and crusty on the outside and tender on the inside. I've served them with many kinds of meat. When a meal needs a comforting, homey touch, I whip up a batch...much to everyone's delight.

      4 large potatoes, peeled,
        cooked and quartered
      3 tablespoons butter or
        margarine
    1/2 teaspoon paprika

In a large skillet, slowly saute potatoes in butter until golden brown, about 10-15 minutes. Sprinkle with paprika. **Yield:** 4-6 servings.

♥☎♥☎♥☎♥☎♥☎♥☎♥

Fruit 'n' Nut Cherry Pie

It's a pleasure to serve this festive ruby-colored pie, which tastes as good as it looks! The filling is an irresistible combination of fruits and nuts. Topped with a bit of whipped cream, a lovely slice of this pie is a refreshing end to an enjoyable meal.

      1 can (21 ounces) cherry pie
        filling
      1 can (20 ounces) crushed
        pineapple, undrained
    3/4 cup sugar
      1 tablespoon cornstarch
      1 teaspoon red food coloring,
        optional
      4 medium firm bananas, sliced
    1/2 cup chopped pecans or
        walnuts
      2 pastry shells (9 inches),
        baked
  Whipped cream

In a saucepan, combine pie filling, pineapple, sugar, cornstarch and food coloring if desired; mix well. Bring to a boil over medium heat, stirring constantly. Cook and stir for 2 minutes. Cool. Fold in the bananas and nuts. Pour into pie shells. Chill for 2-3 hours. Garnish with whipped cream. Store in the refrigerator. **Yield:** 12-16 servings.

By Ruth Andrewson
Leavenworth, Washington

I HAVE a large notebook filled with delicious down-to-earth recipes I keep close at hand so I can have a "from scratch" meal ready in short order when guests drop in. I call this collection of favorite recipes my "treasure book". Its pages reflect a love of cooking that began with my childhood on a farm and has lasted through raising a family and owning a small restaurant.

One page in particular is well-worn—it contains a simple but special chicken dinner that has roots back in Michigan's Upper Peninsula, where husband Severt and I lived before moving here to Washington's "apple country" about 15 years ago.

When one of our small Midwestern town's only restaurants closed its doors, we added a restaurant to our motel to give overnight guests and folks from the area a place to eat. Soon we gained a reputation for homemade rolls, pies and entrees not normally served at other places.

Like many of my tried-and-true dishes, I modified a basic recipe from one of the church or specialty cookbooks I collect and came up with Honey-Glazed Chicken. Adding curry powder spiced up the quick-and-easy basting sauce that richly glazes this tasty entree. Patrons loved the down-home country flavor!

Spiced Carrot Strips have a delicate buttery flavor with just a hint of cinnamon. The sauteed Paprika Potatoes proved so successful that we served them often…and still do to family and friends. They're especially nice because they leave the oven free for other things.

And for the perfect ending to this meal, I prepared delectable Fruit 'n' Nut Cherry Pie. Because it's not too heavy or rich, this pie remains a much-requested recipe.

I hope you find these delicious new jewels irresistible…and hope you add them to your own "treasure book" of family favorites!

♥☕♥☕♥☕♥☕♥☕♥☕♥

Honey-Glazed Chicken

My family raves over this beautifully browned chicken. The rich honey glaze gives each luscious piece a spicy tang. This dish is simple enough to prepare for a family dinner and delightful enough to serve to guests.

  1/2 **cup all-purpose flour**
    1 **teaspoon salt**
  1/2 **teaspoon cayenne pepper**
    1 **broiler-fryer chicken (about 3 pounds), cut up**
  1/2 **cup butter** *or* **margarine, melted,** *divided*
  1/4 **cup packed brown sugar**
  1/4 **cup honey**
  1/4 **cup lemon juice**
    1 **tablespoon soy sauce**
1-1/2 **teaspoons curry powder**

In a bowl or bag, combine flour, salt and cayenne pepper; add chicken pieces and dredge or shake to coat. Pour 4 tablespoons butter into a 13-in. x 9-in. x 2-in. baking pan; place chicken in pan, turning pieces once to coat. Bake, uncovered, at 350° for 30 minutes. Combine brown sugar, honey, lemon juice, soy sauce, curry powder and remaining butter; pour over chicken. Bake 45 minutes more or until the chicken is tender, basting several times with pan drippings. **Yield:** 4-6 servings.

♥☕♥☕♥☕♥☕♥☕♥☕♥

Spiced Carrot Strips

These lightly sweet strips get unique flavor from cinnamon, which enhances the fresh carrot taste. Give this special yet simple side dish a try!

  5 **large carrots, julienned**
  2 **tablespoons butter** *or* **margarine, melted**
  1 **tablespoon sugar**

  1 **teaspoon salt**
1/4 **teaspoon ground cinnamon**

Place carrots in a saucepan; cover with water. Cook until tender, about 8-10 minutes. Drain. Combine butter, sugar, salt and cinnamon; pour over carrots and toss to coat. Serve immediately. **Yield:** 4-6 servings.

♥☕♥☕♥☕♥☕♥☕♥☕♥

Paprika Potatoes

These tasty potatoes are golden and crusty on the outside and tender on the inside. I've served them with many kinds of meat. When a meal needs a comforting, homey touch, I whip up a batch…much to everyone's delight.

  4 **large potatoes, peeled, cooked and quartered**
  3 **tablespoons butter** *or* **margarine**
1/2 **teaspoon paprika**

In a large skillet, slowly saute potatoes in butter until golden brown, about 10-15 minutes. Sprinkle with paprika. **Yield:** 4-6 servings.

♥☕♥☕♥☕♥☕♥☕♥☕♥

Fruit 'n' Nut Cherry Pie

It's a pleasure to serve this festive ruby-colored pie, which tastes as good as it looks! The filling is an irresistible combination of fruits and nuts. Topped with a bit of whipped cream, a lovely slice of this pie is a refreshing end to an enjoyable meal.

  1 **can (21 ounces) cherry pie filling**
  1 **can (20 ounces) crushed pineapple, undrained**
3/4 **cup sugar**
  1 **tablespoon cornstarch**
  1 **teaspoon red food coloring, optional**
  4 **medium firm bananas, sliced**
1/2 **cup chopped pecans** *or* **walnuts**
  2 **pastry shells (9 inches), baked**
Whipped cream

In a saucepan, combine pie filling, pineapple, sugar, cornstarch and food coloring if desired; mix well. Bring to a boil over medium heat, stirring constantly. Cook and stir for 2 minutes. Cool. Fold in the bananas and nuts. Pour into pie shells. Chill for 2-3 hours. Garnish with whipped cream. Store in the refrigerator. **Yield:** 12-16 servings.

OUR EDITORS' FAVORITE MEALS

1,000 great country cooks help edit *Taste of Home* magazine.
On the following pages, you'll "meet"
six of our field editors who share their favorite meals.

CONTENTS

TO ORDER ADDITIONAL COPIES of *The Taste of Home Recipe Book, Second Edition,* send your name and address, along with $12.99 each (plus $2.50 shipping/insured delivery) to Country Store, Suite 3613, 5925 Country Lane, Greendale WI 53129. Specify item number 20286. For credit card orders, call toll-free 1-800/558-1013. The first edition of *The Taste of Home Recipe Book* is also available. Specify item number 19550 when ordering.

By Eunice Stoen, Decorah, Iowa

EVERYDAY MEALS can be hurried here on the dairy and grain farm husband Wilbur and I operate with our son, Bill. But now and then, I enjoy preparing a special feast.

My farm background, Norwegian heritage and love of sharing recipes all come through in this mouth-watering menu. Ham is my meat of choice—we used to raise hogs, and I'm a big promoter of Iowa farm products.

Not only is my Baked Ham with Cumberland Sauce easy to prepare, but it looks so impressive served on your largest platter. Simply slice it at the table and then pass the fruity sauce, which adds a nice tangy touch.

My Asparagus with Sesame Butter recipe retains the color and shape of the spears, accentuating the fresh flavor and adding some crunch. And a deliciously simple side dish like Norwegian Parsley Potatoes goes well with the ham and honors my heritage.

I also like to serve warm rolls, a relish tray and a make-ahead seven-layer salad or coleslaw. Hawaiian Dessert is a perfect refreshing end to this meal. It makes two large pans, so there's one to serve and another to freeze or— better yet—to share with your neighbor.

Preparing as much of my meal as possible on the day before allows me to enjoy our guests and the food, too. I dish up and sit where I can reach bowls and platters to pass for "seconds".

Our guests often say that I make putting on a meal like this look easy. I gratefully respond that my secret to success is planning and preparing ahead of time…and, of course, using never-fail recipes like these!

♥☎♥☎♥☎♥☎♥☎♥

Baked Ham with Cumberland Sauce

The centerpiece of a beautiful family dinner, this golden ham with tangy jewel-toned sauce is impressive to serve.

> 1/2 fully cooked ham with bone
>   (4 to 5 pounds)
> 1/2 cup packed brown sugar
> 1 teaspoon dry mustard
> Whole cloves
> **CUMBERLAND SAUCE:**
>   1 cup red currant *or* apple jelly
> 1/4 cup orange juice
> 1/4 cup lemon juice
> 1/4 cup red wine *or* apple juice
> 2 tablespoons honey
> 1 tablespoon cornstarch

Remove skin from ham; score the surface with shallow diagonal cuts, making diamond shapes. Mix brown sugar and mustard; rub into fat of ham. Insert a whole clove in the center of each diamond. Place ham in a large roaster with a baking rack. Bake, uncovered, at 325° for 20-22 minutes *per pound* or until ham is heated through and a thermometer reads 140°. For sauce, combine all of the ingredients in a medium saucepan. Cook over medium heat until thickened, stirring often. Serve over the sliced ham. (Sauce recipe can be doubled if desired.) **Yield:** 8-10 servings (1-3/4 cups sauce).

♥☎♥☎♥☎♥☎♥☎♥

Asparagus with Sesame Butter

Fresh asparagus is a delightful treat any time of year. This light butter sauce lets the asparagus flavor come through, and the sprinkling of sesame seeds adds a delicate crunch. This is a simple yet delicious dish you'll prepare often.

> 2 pounds fresh asparagus
> 1 cup boiling water
> 1/2 teaspoon salt
> 1 tablespoon cornstarch
> 1/4 cup cold water
> 1/4 cup butter *or* margarine
> 3 tablespoons sesame seeds,
>   toasted

Place asparagus spears in a large skillet; add boiling water and salt. Cook for 5-7 minutes or until tender. Remove the asparagus and keep warm. Drain cooking liquid, reserving 1/2 cup in a small saucepan. Combine cornstarch and cold water; stir into liquid. Cook and stir over medium heat until thickened and bubbly; cook and stir 1 minute more.

Stir in butter until melted. Spoon over asparagus; sprinkle with sesame seeds and serve immediately. **Yield:** 6-8 servings.

♥☎♥☎♥☎♥☎♥☎♥

Norwegian Parsley Potatoes

I love to use parsley in many dishes, and it suits the fresh taste of small red potatoes well. Even though they're easy to prepare, they look fancy and go great with baked ham.

> 2 pounds small red new
>   potatoes
> 1/2 cup butter *or* margarine
> 1/4 cup chopped fresh parsley
> 1/4 teaspoon dried marjoram

Cook potatoes in boiling salted water for 15 minutes or until tender. Cool slightly. With a sharp knife, remove one narrow strip of skin around the middle of each potato. In a large skillet, melt butter; add parsley and marjoram. Add the potatoes and stir gently until coated and heated through. **Yield:** 6-8 servings.

♥☎♥☎♥☎♥☎♥☎♥

Hawaiian Dessert

A chilled fluffy dessert like this one is a satisfying way to finish off a big meal. I got the recipe from a woman I happened to meet in a department store one day. Leftovers taste just as good the next day, and this dessert can also be frozen.

> 1 package (18-1/4 ounces)
>   yellow cake mix
> 3 packages (3.4 ounces *each*)
>   instant vanilla pudding mix
> 4 cups cold milk
> 1-1/2 teaspoons coconut extract
> 1 package (8 ounces) cream
>   cheese, softened
> 1 can (20 ounces) crushed
>   pineapple, well drained
> 2 cups heavy cream, whipped
>   and sweetened
> 2 cups flaked coconut, toasted

Mix cake batter according to package directions. Pour into two greased 13-in. x 9-in. x 2-in. baking pans. Bake at 350° for 15 minutes or until the cakes test done. Cool completely. In a large mixing bowl, combine pudding mixes, milk and coconut extract; beat for 2 minutes. Add the cream cheese and beat well. Stir in pineapple. Spread over the cooled cakes. Top with whipped cream; sprinkle with coconut. Chill for at least 2 hours. **Yield:** 24 servings. **Editor's Note:** Prepared dessert can be covered and frozen for up to 1 month.

By Janet Mooberry, Peoria, Illinois

EVERYONE who samples this "Berry Special Luncheon" loves the result! To start things off, I ladle up some sparkly, refreshing Springtime Punch.

To complement the fruity Cool Raspberry Soup, I pass around a basket brimming with easy yet elegant Cinnamon Twists. Spinach Chicken Salad evolved from a recipe given to me by a friend. And Sky-High Strawberry Pie is my own creation. I've never had anyone turn down a slice!

Have a *berry* good time trying my luscious luncheon!

♥🕿♥🕿♥🕿♥🕿♥🕿♥🕿♥

Springtime Punch

Fruit juices give this punch a sunny color while ginger ale adds zesty fizz.

- 2 cups sugar
- 2-1/2 cups water
- 1 cup fresh lemon juice (3 to 4 lemons)
- 1 cup fresh orange juice (2 to 3 oranges)
- 1 can (6 ounces) frozen pineapple juice concentrate, thawed
- 2 quarts ginger ale, chilled

In a saucepan, bring sugar and water to a boil. Boil for 10 minutes; remove from the heat. Stir in the lemon, orange and pineapple juices. Refrigerate. Just before serving, combine with ginger ale in a large punch bowl. **Yield:** 16-20 servings (3 quarts).

♥🕿♥🕿♥🕿♥🕿♥🕿♥🕿♥

Cool Raspberry Soup

An exquisite combination of spices and a rich berry flavor make this beautiful soup so refreshing.

- 1 bag (20 ounces) frozen raspberries, thawed

- 1-1/4 cups water
- 1/4 cup white wine, optional
- 1 cup cran-raspberry juice
- 1/2 cup sugar
- 1-1/2 teaspoons ground cinnamon
- 3 whole cloves
- 1 tablespoon lemon juice
- 1 carton (8 ounces) raspberry-flavored yogurt
- 1/2 cup sour cream

In a blender, puree raspberries, water and wine if desired. Transfer to a large saucepan; add the cran-raspberry juice, sugar, cinnamon and cloves. Bring just to a boil over medium heat. Remove from the heat; strain and allow to cool. Whisk in lemon juice and yogurt. Refrigerate. To serve, pour into small bowls and top with a dollop of sour cream. **Yield:** 4-6 servings.

♥🕿♥🕿♥🕿♥🕿♥🕿♥🕿♥

Sky-High Strawberry Pie

This pie is my specialty. It's fairly simple to make but so dramatic to serve.

- 3 quarts fresh strawberries, *divided*
- 1-1/2 cups sugar
- 6 tablespoons cornstarch
- 2/3 cup water
- Red food coloring, optional
- 1 deep-dish pastry shell (10 inches), baked
- 1 cup heavy cream
- 1-1/2 tablespoons instant vanilla pudding mix

In a large bowl, mash enough berries to equal 3 cups. In a saucepan, combine the sugar and cornstarch. Stir in the mashed berries and water; mix well. Bring to a boil over medium heat, stirring constantly. Cook and stir for 2 minutes. Remove from the heat; add food coloring if desired. Pour into a large bowl. Chill for 20 minutes, stirring occasionally, until mixture is just slightly warm. Fold in the remaining berries. Pile into pie shell. Chill for 2-3 hours. In a small mixing bowl, whip cream until soft peaks form. Sprinkle pudding mix over cream and whip until stiff. Pipe around edge of pie or dollop on individual slices. **Yield:** 8-10 servings.

♥🕿♥🕿♥🕿♥🕿♥🕿♥🕿♥

Cinnamon Twists

The brown sugar and cinnamon give these twists a delicate spicy flavor.

- 1 package (1/4 ounce) active dry yeast
- 3/4 cup warm water (110° to 115°), *divided*
- 4 to 4-1/2 cups all-purpose flour
- 1/4 cup sugar
- 1-1/2 teaspoons salt
- 1/2 cup warm milk (110° to 115°)
- 1/4 cup butter *or* margarine, softened

- 1 egg
- FILLING:
- 1/4 cup butter *or* margarine, melted
- 1/2 cup packed brown sugar
- 4 teaspoons ground cinnamon

In a large mixing bowl, dissolve yeast in 1/4 cup warm water. Add 2 cups of flour, sugar, salt, milk, butter, egg and remaining water; beat on medium speed for 2 minutes. Stir in enough remaining flour to form a soft dough. Turn onto a floured board; knead until smooth and elastic, about 6-8 minutes. Place in a greased bowl, turning once to grease top. Cover and let rise in a warm place until doubled, about 1 hour. Punch down. Roll into a 16-in. x 12-in. rectangle. Brush with butter. Combine brown sugar and cinnamon; sprinkle over butter. Let dough rest for 6 minutes. Cut lengthwise into three 16-in. x 4-in. strips. Cut each strip into sixteen 4-in. x 1-in. pieces. Twist and place on greased baking sheets. Cover and let rise until doubled, about 30 minutes. Bake at 350° for 15 minutes or until golden. **Yield:** 4 dozen.

♥🕿♥🕿♥🕿♥🕿♥🕿♥🕿♥

Spinach Chicken Salad

This crunchy salad showcases an interesting mixture of chicken, pasta, spinach and other vegetables.

- 5 cups cubed cooked chicken (about 3 whole breasts)
- 2 cups green grape halves
- 1 cup snow peas
- 2 cups packed torn spinach
- 2-1/2 cups sliced celery
- 7 ounces corkscrew pasta *or* elbow macaroni, cooked and drained
- 1 jar (6 ounces) marinated artichoke hearts, drained and quartered
- 1/2 large cucumber, sliced
- 3 green onions with tops, sliced
- Large spinach leaves, optional
- Orange slices, optional
- DRESSING:
- 1/2 cup vegetable oil
- 1/4 cup sugar
- 2 tablespoons white wine vinegar
- 1 teaspoon salt
- 1/2 teaspoon dried minced onion
- 1 teaspoon lemon juice
- 2 tablespoons minced fresh parsley

In a large bowl, combine chicken, grapes, peas, spinach, celery, pasta, artichoke hearts, cucumber and green onions. Cover and refrigerate. Combine all dressing ingredients in a jar or small bowl; mix well and refrigerate. Just before serving, pour dressing over salad and toss. If desired, serve on a spinach leaf and garnish with oranges. **Yield:** 8-10 servings.

By Anne Heinonen, Howell, Michigan

FRIENDS with smaller families say that cooking for my "crew" must be like having company every day! But to me, planning and preparing meals for husband Fred and our 12 children—ranging in age from 17 to infant—is a joy.

I'm always looking for new recipes we all like. Fortunately, Fred is not just a "meat and potatoes" man. He likes to try different foods and is very willing to critique any dishes I try. The kids also like it when I serve something new, and they're quick to tell me if it's a "hit" or "miss"!

A hit with everyone in the family is my Savory Spaghetti Sauce. I serve it family-style, putting out a big bowl of pasta, a dish of steaming sauce and freshly grated Parmesan cheese to sprinkle on top.

Fred and I are both of Finnish descent, and my Finnish Flat Bread (ricska) is a satisfying staple we grew up eating. The combination of white and wheat flours adds old-world appeal, and the buttermilk makes it extra tasty.

Mandarin Almond Salad is our family's favorite, hands down! I clipped the recipe from a magazine years ago and vary it with different garden greens. The combination of vanilla, chocolate and nuts makes Chocolate Walnut Squares better than any other dessert I prepare.

I hope you receive lots of compliments when you try my favorite meal in your home!

Savory Spaghetti Sauce

This fresh-tasting spaghetti sauce is a real crowd-pleaser that I rely on often.

It tastes especially good in the summer made with fresh garden herbs.

> 1 pound ground beef
> 1 large onion, chopped
> 2 cans (15 ounces *each*) tomato sauce
> 1 garlic clove, minced
> 1 bay leaf
> 1 tablespoon minced fresh basil *or* 1 teaspoon dried basil
> 2 teaspoons minced fresh oregano *or* 3/4 teaspoon dried oregano
> 2 teaspoons sugar
> 1/2 to 1 teaspoon salt
> 1/2 teaspoon pepper
> Hot cooked spaghetti
> Fresh oregano, optional

In a Dutch oven, cook ground beef and onion until meat is browned and onion is tender; drain. Add the next eight ingredients; bring to a boil. Reduce heat; cover and simmer for 1 hour, stirring occasionally. Remove the bay leaf. Serve over spaghetti. Garnish with oregano if desired. **Yield** 4-6 servings (about 1 quart).

Finnish Flat Bread

My husband and I have eaten this simple-to-make bread for years. It's nice to have homemade bread with spaghetti.

> 1-1/2 cups all-purpose flour
> 3/4 cup whole wheat flour
> 2 tablespoons sugar
> 1-1/2 teaspoons baking powder
> 1 teaspoon salt
> 1/2 teaspoon baking soda
> 1/4 cup shortening
> 1 cup buttermilk

In a bowl, combine flours, sugar, baking powder, salt and baking soda. Cut in shortening until the mixture resembles coarse crumbs. Add milk and mix just until dough is moistened. Knead on floured board for 3-5 minutes. Pat onto an ungreased 12-in. pizza pan. Bake at 350° for 30 minutes or until golden. Cool for 10 minutes before removing to a wire rack. Cut into pieces. **Yield:** 6-8 servings.

Mandarin Almond Salad

Here's a refreshing salad that's always a hit at our house. Crisp greens, bright oranges and red onion add pretty color to your meal, and the sweet caramelized almonds provide a unique crunch.

> 4 tablespoons sugar, *divided*
> 1/2 cup slivered almonds
> 1/4 cup vegetable oil
> 2 tablespoons vinegar

> 1 tablespoon minced fresh parsley
> 1/2 teaspoon salt
> 1/8 teaspoon pepper
> 1/8 teaspoon hot pepper sauce
> 1 bunch red leaf lettuce, torn
> 1 can (11 ounces) mandarin oranges, drained
> 1 small red onion, sliced

In a small skillet, melt 3 tablespoons sugar over low heat. Add almonds; stir until coated. Cool; break into small pieces and set aside. In a jar with a tight-fitting lid, combine oil, vinegar, parsley, salt, pepper, hot pepper sauce and remaining sugar; shake well. Just before serving, combine lettuce, oranges, onion and almonds in a large salad bowl. Shake dressing; pour over salad and toss. **Yield:** 4-6 servings.

Chocolate Walnut Squares

Rich and satisfying, these bars create a symphony of flavors with every bite. The nutty crust, exquisite chocolate layer and creamy frosting make this dessert one of my personal favorites. It's fun to take these treats to a potluck.

> 1 cup butter *or* margarine, softened
> 2 cups sugar
> 4 eggs, lightly beaten
> 1 tablespoon vanilla extract*
> 2 cups all-purpose flour
> 1/2 teaspoon salt
> 2 cups chopped walnuts
> 2 squares (1 ounce *each*) unsweetened chocolate, melted
> **FROSTING:**
> 5 tablespoons all-purpose flour
> 1 cup milk
> 1 cup butter *or* margarine, softened
> 1 cup confectioners' sugar
> 2 teaspoons vanilla extract

In a mixing bowl, cream butter and sugar. Beat in eggs and vanilla. Add flour and salt; mix well. Fold in the walnuts. Spread half of the batter into a greased 13-in. x 9-in. x 2-in. baking pan. Add chocolate to the remaining batter; mix well. Carefully spread over batter in pan. Bake at 350° for 30-35 minutes or until cake tests done. Cool completely. For frosting, mix the flour and milk in a saucepan. Cook and stir over medium heat until a thick paste forms, about 10 minutes. Cool completely. In a mixing bowl, cream butter and confectioners' sugar. Add vanilla and mix well. Gradually add the milk mixture; beat for 5 minutes. Frost cake. Store in the refrigerator. **Yield:** 20-24 servings. *Editor's Note: The amount of vanilla is correct.

By Rita Reifenstein
Evans City, Pennsylvania

ON FALL SATURDAYS, husband Rick and I attend Penn State University home football games with my dad, Martin Marburger. For me, planning good food for our "tailgate parties" at the stadium is part of the fun!

On game days, we leave bright and early in Dad's motor home for the 4-hour drive to the stadium. There we find a spot in the grassy parking lots and enjoy a picnic alongside our vehicle with thousands of other "tailgating" fans.

Our enthusiastic group can vary from four to 16, and I love trying out new recipes on them. But my Glazed Corned Beef Sandwiches score so high that I serve them often during the season. I prepare the beef brisket a day or two ahead, simmering it with peppercorns and spices until it's wonderfully tender. The glaze is rubbed into the meat while it's still warm and can best absorb the zesty flavor.

Two colorful side dishes I like to serve with these hearty sandwiches were inspired by my garden's bounty. Sweet corn—fresh-cut from the cob or frozen—gives my Corn Salad its sunny appeal. Refreshing Stuffed Cherry Tomatoes are fun-to-munch treats during our pregame banter.

No tailgate meal would be complete without a sweet ending like Apple Cobbler. This treasured family dessert was a staple when I was growing up. Before she died, Mom passed on the treasured recipe to my sister-in-law. We were thrilled that Mom's recipe was not lost.

I hope you decide to try my recipes for a picnic or supper or any time you need tasty food that travels well. You and your guests will surely be pleased!

Glazed Corned Beef Sandwiches

Fans of good food will cheer when you bring out these full-flavored hearty sandwiches! Made of tender corned beef and a special sweet and spicy seasoning, they're always a hit.

- 1 corned beef brisket (3 to 4 pounds)
- 12 peppercorns
- 4 bay leaves
- 3 garlic cloves, minced
- 2 cinnamon sticks (3 inches), broken
- 1 tablespoon crushed red pepper flakes

Sandwich buns
GLAZE:
- 1/2 cup packed brown sugar
- 1/2 teaspoon ground cloves
- 1/2 teaspoon ground ginger
- 1/2 teaspoon dry mustard
- 1/4 teaspoon celery salt
- 1/4 teaspoon caraway seed

Place corned beef with its seasoning packet in a Dutch oven; cover with water. Add seasonings and bring to a boil. Reduce heat; cover and simmer for 4 to 4-1/2 hours or until meat is tender. Drain, discarding juices; blot the brisket dry. In a small bowl, combine the glaze ingredients. Rub onto top of warm meat. Grill or broil for 5-10 minutes on each side until glazed. Slice meat and serve warm or chilled on buns. **Yield:** 12-16 servings.

Corn Salad

This sensational salad is a delight to serve because you can put your garden bounty to good use and make it ahead.

✓ This tasty dish uses less sugar, salt and fat. Recipe includes *Diabetic Exchanges*.

- 2 cups fresh *or* frozen sweet corn
- 3/4 cup chopped tomato
- 1/2 cup chopped green pepper
- 1/2 cup chopped celery
- 1/4 cup chopped onion
- 1/4 cup prepared ranch salad dressing

In a large salad bowl, combine vegetables; stir in dressing. Cover and refrigerate until serving. **Yield:** 8 servings.
Diabetic Exchanges: One 1/2-cup serving (prepared with fat-free dressing) equals 1 starch; also, 64 calories, 93 mg sodium, 0 cholesterol, 15 gm carbohydrate, 2 gm protein, 1 gm fat.

Stuffed Cherry Tomatoes

Try this simple recipe for a crowd-pleasing appetizer. They may be small, but these tomatoes have big garden-fresh flavor enhanced by the cool, zesty filling.

- 2 packages (one 8 ounces, one 3 ounces) cream cheese, softened
- 2 tablespoons mayonnaise
- 1 package (.4 ounce) ranch salad dressing mix
- 3 dozen cherry tomatoes

Alfalfa sprouts, optional

In a mixing bowl, blend cream cheese, mayonnaise and salad dressing mix until smooth. Slice a thin slice off tops of tomatoes and carefully remove insides; invert on paper towel to drain. Fill with cream cheese mixture. Serve on a bed of alfalfa sprouts if desired. **Yield:** 12-16 servings.

Apple Cobbler

A treasured family recipe, this cobbler is a delicious old-fashioned dessert. It travels well and slices nicely, so it's perfect for picnics or tailgate parties.

- 3 cups all-purpose flour
- 1 cup sugar, *divided*
- 1-1/2 teaspoons baking powder
- 1/2 teaspoon salt
- 1/2 cup butter *or* margarine
- 2 eggs
- 1 tablespoon vanilla extract
- 3 to 4 tablespoons milk
- 8 cups thinly sliced peeled baking apples
- 2 tablespoons quick-cooking tapioca
- 1/2 teaspoon ground cinnamon

TOPPING:
- 1 tablespoon milk
- 3/4 teaspoon sugar
- 1/4 teaspoon ground cinnamon

In a bowl, combine flour, 1/4 cup sugar, baking powder and salt. Cut in butter until crumbly. In another bowl, lightly beat eggs and vanilla; add to crumb mixture. With a fork, gently mix in milk to moisten. Stir until dough forms a ball. Press half of the dough into the bottom of a greased 13-in. x 9-in. x 2-in. baking pan. Chill the remaining dough. Toss apples with tapioca, cinnamon and remaining sugar; place over dough in pan. On a lightly floured surface, roll chilled dough to fit top of pan. Place over apples. Brush with milk. Combine sugar and cinnamon; sprinkle on top. Bake at 350° for 45-50 minutes or until apples are tender and crust is golden. **Yield:** 12-16 servings.

By Marge Clark, West Lebanon, Indiana

CHRISTMAS EVE is always a time of excitement in everyone's homes. Each year on our farm, husband Dick and I look forward to opening our house to our four grown sons and their families, including five grandchildren.

So when I plan Christmas Eve dinner, I try to include foods that will be enjoyed by young and old alike. And anything that can be prepared a day or more in advance is surely a welcome choice.

Our family loves ham and potatoes, so I dress them up for the holiday. Apricot Baked Ham gets a tangy-sweet taste from the fruity glaze, which also adds a beautiful "finish" to the meat.

I prepare my Stuffed Baked Potatoes up to a week before our dinner, wrap them well and freeze them to thaw (still wrapped) the morning of Christmas Eve. Everyone loves their smooth texture and rich flavor.

Ruby Red Raspberry Salad is lovely, and we think the combination of raspberry, cherry, cranberry and pineapple flavors is fabulous. I also serve homemade rolls with strawberry jam, a green salad and herbed breadsticks.

Our special dinner ends with moist Cranberry Sauce Cake. You and your family will love it, both because of its beautiful texture and ease of preparation. I hope this tasty traditional meal will live on for many, many years in your kitchen. I know it will in mine!

♥☎♥☎♥☎♥☎♥☎♥☎♥

Apricot Baked Ham

Ham is a super choice for a holiday meal because once you put it in the oven, it practically takes care of itself until dinnertime. The sugary crust makes the ham beautiful to serve.

>   1/2 fully cooked ham with bone
>   (5 to 7 pounds)
>   20 whole cloves
>   1/2 cup apricot preserves
>   3 tablespoons dry mustard
>   1/2 cup packed light brown sugar

Score the surface of the ham with shallow diamond-shaped cuts. Insert cloves in cuts. Combine preserves and mustard; spread over ham. Pat brown sugar over apricot mixture. Place ham on a rack in a roasting pan. Bake at 325° for 20 minutes *per pound* or until ham is heated through and thermometer reads 140°. **Yield:** 10-14 servings.

♥☎♥☎♥☎♥☎♥☎♥☎♥

Stuffed Baked Potatoes

These special potatoes are a hit with my whole family, from the smallest grandchild on up. I prepare them up to a week in advance, wrap them well and freeze.

>   3 large baking potatoes
>   (1 pound *each*)
>   1-1/2 teaspoons vegetable oil,
>   optional
>   1/2 cup sliced green onions
>   1/2 cup butter *or* margarine,
>   *divided*
>   1/2 cup light cream
>   1/2 cup sour cream
>   1 teaspoon salt
>   1/2 teaspoon white pepper
>   1 cup (4 ounces) shredded
>   cheddar cheese
> **Paprika**

Rub potatoes with oil if desired; pierce with a fork. Bake at 400° for 1 hour and 20 minutes or until tender. Allow potatoes to cool to the touch. Cut potatoes in half lengthwise; carefully scoop out pulp, leaving a thin shell. Place pulp in a large bowl. Saute onions in 1/4 cup butter until tender. Add to potato pulp along with the light cream, sour cream, salt and pepper. Beat until smooth. Fold in cheese. Stuff potato shells and place in a 13-in. x 9-in. x 2-in. baking pan. Melt remaining butter; drizzle over the potatoes. Sprinkle with paprika. Bake at 350° for 20-30 minutes or until heated through. **Yield:** 6 servings. **Editor's Note:** Potatoes may be stuffed ahead of time and refrigerated or frozen. Allow additional time for reheating.

♥☎♥☎♥☎♥☎♥☎♥☎♥

Ruby Red Raspberry Salad

A refreshing and attractive side dish, this salad adds a festive touch to your holiday table.

>   1 package (3 ounces) raspberry-
>   flavored gelatin
>   2 cups boiling water, *divided*
>   1 package (10 ounces) frozen
>   raspberries in syrup
>   1-1/2 cups sour cream
>   1 package (3 ounces) cherry-
>   flavored gelatin
>   1 can (20 ounces) crushed
>   pineapple, drained
>   1 can (16 ounces) whole-berry
>   cranberry sauce
> **Lettuce leaves**
> **Mayonnaise *or* salad dressing,**
>   **optional**
> **Mint leaves, optional**

Dissolve raspberry gelatin in 1 cup boiling water. Add raspberries and stir until berries are thawed and separated. Pour into a 13-in. x 9-in. x 2-in. pan; chill until set. Carefully spread with sour cream; chill. Dissolve cherry gelatin in remaining boiling water. Add pineapple and cranberry sauce and mix well. Allow to thicken slightly. Carefully spoon over the sour cream mixture; chill. Cut into squares and serve on lettuce leaves. If desired, top each with a dollop of mayonnaise and garnish with a mint leaf. **Yield:** 12-16 servings.

♥☎♥☎♥☎♥☎♥☎♥☎♥

Cranberry Sauce Cake

This cake is so easy to make because it mixes in one bowl. Slice it at the table so everyone can see how beautiful it is.

>   3 cups all-purpose flour
>   1-1/2 cups sugar
>   1 cup mayonnaise
>   1 can (16 ounces) whole-berry
>   cranberry sauce
>   1/3 cup orange juice
>   1 tablespoon grated orange peel
>   1 teaspoon baking soda
>   1 teaspoon salt
>   1 teaspoon orange extract
>   1 cup chopped walnuts
> **ICING:**
>   1 cup confectioners' sugar
>   1 to 2 tablespoons orange juice

In a mixing bowl, combine flour, sugar, mayonnaise, cranberry sauce, orange juice and peel, baking soda, salt and extract; mix well. Fold in the walnuts. Cut waxed or parchment paper to fit the bottom of a 10-in. tube pan. Spray the pan and paper with nonstick cooking spray. Pour batter into paper-lined pan. Bake at 350° for 60-70 minutes or until the cake tests done. Cool 10 minutes in pan before removing to a wire rack. Combine icing ingredients; drizzle over the warm cake. **Yield:** 12-16 servings. **Editor's Note:** It is not recommended that you use light or low-fat mayonnaise products in this recipe.

'MY MOM'S BEST MEAL'

In this chapter, six cooks share one of their mom's most treasured meals. They're likely to become your family's favorites, too!

Mom Made Simple Meals Special

By Ruth Ann Stelfox, Raymond, Alberta

WHENEVER I prepare this mouth-watering meal for my own family these days, the wonderful aroma never fails to remind me of my childhood and our family gathered around the big kitchen table with Dad at the head.

He especially loved the Sweet-and-Sour Spareribs with their thick, tangy sauce. Mom liked them because the sauce was no hassle to make! She made Creamy Pineapple Salad often, but we kids didn't mind. Whenever we saw this salad appear on the table, we couldn't wait to eat.

Confetti Rice is a classic dish that's stood the test of time. Much to our disappointment—and Mom's amazement—there never seemed to be any left over…no matter how much she made! After these delicious dishes were served up, we knew Mom's Raisin Custard Pie was sure to follow. Cutting the pie into seven equal pieces was tricky, but Dad never complained.

Mom's meals weren't fancy, but they *were* delicious. She felt it was important for us to eat together, and that fostered a special family closeness we've tried to carry over to our own homes today. Now you can make your own sweet memories with this meal.

Sweet-and-Sour Spareribs

Nothing takes me back in time to Mom's kitchen like the aroma of these robust ribs slowly baking in the oven. And now they're a finger-licking favorite in my own family.

> **5 to 6 pounds pork spareribs *or* pork loin back ribs**
> **1/2 cup packed brown sugar**
> **1/2 cup sugar**
> **2 tablespoons cornstarch**
> **1 cup ketchup**
> **2/3 cup vinegar**
> **1/2 cup cold water**

Place ribs on a rack in a large shallow roasting pan. Bake, uncovered, at 350° for 1-1/2 hours. Meanwhile, combine sugars and cornstarch in a medium saucepan. Stir in ketchup, vinegar and water; bring to a boil. Cook and stir until thickened and clear. Remove ribs and rack from pan. Discard fat. Place ribs back in roasting pan; pour about 1 1/2 cups of the sauce over ribs. Bake 30 minutes longer. Cut ribs into serving-size pieces; brush with remaining sauce. **Yield:** 6-8 servings.

Creamy Pineapple Salad

With its cool, creamy texture, this slightly sweet salad pairs nicely with the zesty, hearty ribs. As an added plus, it can be prepared the night before, so it's a no-fuss recipe that's also delicious.

> **1 can (20 ounces) crushed pineapple**
> **1 package (3 ounces) lemon-flavored gelatin**
> **1 cup heavy cream**
> **1/4 cup sugar**
> **1 cup cottage cheese**

Drain pineapple, reserving the juice in a small saucepan. Set pineapple aside. Add enough water to juice to make 1-1/3 cups; bring to a boil. Place gelatin in a bowl; add boiling liquid and stir to dissolve. Cool until slightly thickened. In a mixing bowl, whip cream; gradually beat in sugar. Fold into the gelatin mixture. Stir in pineapple and cottage cheese; blend well. Pour into a 1-1/2-qt. serving bowl; chill at least 3 hours or overnight. **Yield:** 8-10 servings.

Confetti Rice

I still enjoy the superb combination of bacon and rice in this dish. The peas add color and a bit of crunch. It's so easy to make and so good.

> **1/2 pound sliced bacon, diced**
> **1 cup long grain rice, cooked**
> **1 cup diced carrots, parboiled**
> **1 cup diced celery, parboiled**
> **1/2 cup fresh *or* frozen peas**
> **Soy sauce, optional**

In a large skillet, cook bacon until crisp. Remove to paper towels; drain all but 3 tablespoons of the drippings. Cook rice, carrots, celery and peas in drippings until heated through, about 5-7 minutes. Stir in bacon. Serve with soy sauce if desired. **Yield:** 6-8 servings.

Raisin Custard Pie

A comforting, old-fashioned dessert, this custard pie is one of my mom's best. The fluffy meringue makes it look so special, and the raisins are a nice surprise.

> **1/2 cup sugar**
> **3 tablespoons cornstarch**
> **3 egg yolks**
> **2 cups milk**
> **2 teaspoons lemon juice**
> **1/2 cup raisins**
> **1 pastry shell (9 inches), baked**
> **MERINGUE:**
> **3 egg whites**
> **1/4 cup sugar**

In a medium saucepan, combine sugar and cornstarch. Whisk in the egg yolks and milk until thoroughly combined. Cook over medium heat, stirring constantly, until mixture comes to a boil; boil for 1 minute. Remove from the heat. Add lemon juice and raisins. Pour into pie shell. For meringue, beat egg whites in a small bowl until foamy. Gradually add sugar, about 1 tablespoon at a time, beating until stiff and glossy. Spread over warm pie, making sure meringue covers all of the filling. Bake at 350° for 10-15 minutes or until light golden brown. Serve warm or cold. Store leftovers in the refrigerator. **Yield:** 8 servings. **Variation:** Cool filling in crust completely, then refrigerate. Just before serving, top with whipped cream instead of meringue.

Old-Fashioned Dinner on the Farm

By Vera Reid, Laramie, Wyoming

MY MOM is a great cook, and she worked hard to prepare delicious meals for Dad, my two sisters and me.

I especially remember her crispy Buttermilk Fried Chicken, served with wonderful old-fashioned gravy. As the plate was passed, we girls knew not to touch until Dad and Mom had each selected their favorites. We could hardly resist snatching a piece as the plate passed us by, but there was always plenty of chicken to go around.

I can still see Mom pulling the fluffy Buttermilk Biscuits biscuits out of the oven. They always seemed to disappear too quickly. With crisp radishes and crumbled bacon, Mom made Wilted Lettuce Salad look and taste so tempting. It was the only salad we wanted her to make.

We couldn't wait until dessert—her Hot Fudge Cake was a rich, satisfying end to a perfect meal. Mom served it with a scoop of ice cream or cream poured over.

Living on a farm is not easy, but growing up there with all the cool green grass, the endless blue sky and Mom's home cooking, we knew we were safe and loved. That's something I wish every child was able to experience. This memorable meal helps capture the flavor of farm life.

Buttermilk Fried Chicken With Gravy

We raised our own meat and vegetables when I was a girl. This golden chicken reminds me of home...there's nothing quite like a crispy piece smothered in creamy gravy.

- 1 broiler-fryer chicken (2-1/2 to 3 pounds), cut up
- 1 cup buttermilk
- 1 cup all-purpose flour
- 1-1/2 teaspoons salt
- 1/2 teaspoon pepper
- Cooking oil for frying

GRAVY:
- 3 tablespoons all-purpose flour
- 1 cup milk
- 1-1/2 to 2 cups water
- Salt and pepper to taste

Place chicken in a large flat dish. Pour buttermilk over; cover and refrigerate for 1 hour. Combine flour, salt and pepper in a double-strength paper bag. Drain chicken pieces; toss, one at a time, in flour mixture. Shake off excess; place on waxed paper for 15 minutes to dry. Heat 1/8 to 1/4 in. of oil in a large skillet; fry chicken until browned on all sides. Cover and simmer, turning occasionally, for 40-45 minutes, or until juices run clear and chicken is tender. Uncover and cook 5 minutes longer. Remove chicken and keep warm. Drain all but 1/4 cup drippings in skillet; stir in flour until bubbly. Add milk and 1-1/2 cups water; cook and stir until thickened and bubbly. Cook 1 minute more. Add remaining water if needed. Season with salt and pepper. Serve with chicken. **Yield:** 4-6 servings.

Mom's Buttermilk Biscuits

These biscuits are so tasty served warm, slathered with butter or used to mop up every last drop of homemade gravy off your plate.

- 2 cups all-purpose flour
- 2 teaspoons baking powder
- 1/2 teaspoon baking soda
- 1/2 teaspoon salt
- 1/4 cup shortening
- 3/4 cup buttermilk

In a bowl, combine the flour, baking powder, baking soda and salt; cut in shortening until the mixture resembles coarse crumbs. Stir in buttermilk; knead dough gently. Roll out to 1/2-in. thickness. Cut with a 2-1/2-in. biscuit cutter and place on a lightly greased baking sheet. Bake at 450° for 10-15 minutes or until golden brown. **Yield:** 10 biscuits.

Wilted Lettuce Salad

Fresh, colorful and lightly coated with a delectable dressing, this salad is perfect for a special meal or Sunday dinner. I'm sure you'll make it often.

- 1 bunch leaf lettuce, torn
- 6 to 8 radishes, thinly sliced
- 4 to 6 green onions with tops, thinly sliced

DRESSING:
- 4 to 5 bacon strips
- 2 tablespoons red wine vinegar
- 1 tablespoon lemon juice
- 1 teaspoon sugar
- 1/2 teaspoon pepper

Toss lettuce, radishes and onions in a large salad bowl; set aside. In a skillet, cook bacon until crisp. Remove to paper towels to drain. To the hot drippings, add vinegar, lemon juice, sugar and pepper; stir well. Immediately pour dressing over salad; toss gently. Crumble the bacon and sprinkle on top. **Yield:** 6-8 servings.

Hot Fudge Cake

Here's a wonderful way to top off a great meal—a rich, chocolaty cake that's not overly sweet. I'd always have room for a serving of Hot Fudge Cake at Mom's dinner table.

- 1 cup all-purpose flour
- 3/4 cup sugar
- 6 tablespoons baking cocoa, *divided*
- 2 teaspoons baking powder
- 1/4 teaspoon salt
- 1/2 cup milk
- 2 tablespoons vegetable oil
- 1 teaspoon vanilla extract
- 1 cup packed brown sugar
- 1-3/4 cups hot water
- Whipped cream *or* ice cream, optional

In a medium bowl, combine flour, sugar, 2 tablespoons cocoa, baking powder and salt. Stir in the milk, oil and vanilla until smooth. Spread in an ungreased 9-in. square baking pan. Combine brown sugar and remaining cocoa; sprinkle over batter. Pour hot water over all; do not stir. Bake at 350° for 35-40 minutes. Serve warm. Top with whipped cream or ice cream if desired. **Yield:** 9 servings.

Mom's Kitchen Was Really Cookin'!

By Sally Holbrook, Pasadena, California

I HAVE many fond memories of my years growing up in a household where the kitchen was the center of activity.

Ours was a large, sunny kitchen with a work table in the center. It was a wonderful place where my mother and grandmother would spend hours lovingly preparing delicious meals, from simple fare to delectable party dishes, filling the house with appealing aromas.

My parents and grandparents often entertained friends on the patio overlooking the bay. A long wooden table was spread with a blue and white cloth.

Hungry guests enjoyed a hearty casserole Mom called Sausage Pie, featuring produce found in her own garden. With Buttery French Bread, Mom would dress up plain bread with some simple seasonings and real butter.

As a special treat, Mom would give salad greens an added punch by preparing zippy Creamy Garlic Dressing. And for a fantastic finale, Mom's Peach Pie would overflow with fresh peach flavor, making it a delightful treat.

Now, when my brother, sisters and I get together with friends and family in our own homes, we still use all these wonderful recipes from Mom's delicious menu!

Sausage Pie

This tasty casserole is a great use of garden vegetables, and the sausage adds comforting flavor. I'm sure you'll enjoy it as much as we do.

- 16 small fresh pork sausage links (about 1 pound)
- 1/2 medium green pepper, chopped
- 1/2 medium sweet red pepper, chopped
- 1 tablespoon cooking oil
- 3 cups cooked long grain rice
- 4 to 5 medium tomatoes, peeled and chopped
- 1 package (10 ounces) frozen corn, thawed
- 1 cup (4 ounces) shredded cheddar cheese
- 1 tablespoon Worcestershire sauce
- 1 teaspoon salt
- 2 tablespoons chopped fresh parsley
- 1 teaspoon dried basil
- 1 cup soft bread crumbs
- 2 tablespoons butter *or* margarine, melted

Place sausages on a rack in a baking pan; bake at 350° for 15 minutes or until lightly browned. Cut into 1-in. pieces; set aside. In a skillet, saute peppers in oil for 3 minutes. Place in a 3-qt. casserole; add the sausages and the next eight ingredients. Combine bread crumbs and butter; sprinkle on top of casserole. Bake, uncovered, at 350° for 30-40 minutes or until heated through. **Yield:** 6-8 servings.

Buttery French Bread

The combination of paprika, celery seed and butter makes for a full-flavored bread. It also looks lovely when it bakes to a golden brown.

- 1/2 cup butter *or* margarine, softened
- 1/4 teaspoon paprika
- 1/4 teaspoon celery seed
- 1 loaf French bread (about 20 inches), sliced

In a small bowl, combine butter, paprika and celery seed; spread between bread slices and over top. Wrap bread tightly in foil. Bake at 375° for 15 minutes. Open the foil and bake 5 minutes longer. **Yield:** 6-8 servings.

> **LOOKING TO SAVE TIME** when entertaining? Try this the night before: Prepare the Creamy Garlic Dressing (recipe below) and wash, cut and dry all salad ingredients. Then refrigerate until mealtime. You'll love the extra time spent with guests.

Creamy Garlic Dressing

The wonderful garlic taste in this dressing comes through as the creamy mixture coats the lettuce beautifully.

- 1 cup vegetable oil
- 1/2 cup sour cream
- 1/4 cup heavy cream
- 1/4 cup cider vinegar
- 1 teaspoon salt
- 1 large garlic clove, minced

Salad greens

In a small bowl, combine oil, sour cream, heavy cream, vinegar, salt and garlic; stir until smooth. Chill. Serve over salad greens. Refrigerate leftovers. **Yield:** 1-2/3 cups.

Mom's Peach Pie

The streusel topping makes this pie a little different than the ordinary and adds homemade flair. Each sweet slice is packed with old-fashioned appeal.

- 1 egg white
- 1 unbaked pastry shell (9 inches)
- 3/4 cup all-purpose flour
- 1/2 cup packed brown sugar
- 1/3 cup sugar
- 1/4 cup chilled butter *or* margarine, cut into 6 pieces
- 6 cups sliced peeled fresh peaches

Beat egg white until foamy; brush over the bottom and sides of the pastry. In a small bowl, combine flour and sugars; cut in butter until mixture resembles fine crumbs. Sprinkle two-thirds into the bottom of the pastry; top with peaches. Sprinkle with remaining crumb mixture. Bake at 375° for 40-45 minutes or until filling is bubbly and peaches are tender. **Yield:** 6-8 servings.

Busy Mom Made Timeless Meals

By Bernice Morris, Marshfield, Missouri

THINKING back to my childhood, I wonder how my mom ever found time to cook three meals a day! Not only did she help Dad milk cows, she planted a large garden each spring to keep the grocery bills down. Still, she always managed to set a table laden with delicious food for the family and hired hands at noon.

Every meal Mom prepared was wonderful. But I'd have to rank the meal featured here as one of my all-time favorites. Packed with hearty ingredients and flavorful seasonings, Pork Chops with Scalloped Potatoes was a welcome sight at the table.

In her Pineapple Beets recipe, Mom easily dressed up ordinary beets by adding pineapple and a sweet sauce. Golden-brown Make-Ahead Butterhorns really completed the meal.

For dessert, Mom would slice hearty helpings of Banana Cream Pie and top them with rich whipped cream from our Guernsey cows. Fortified with a marvelous meal like this, we could tackle afternoon chores with smiles on our faces!

Pork Chops with Scalloped Potatoes

This all-in-one main dish has fantastic flavor that appeals to everyone.

- 3 tablespoons butter *or* margarine
- 3 tablespoons all-purpose flour
- 1-1/2 teaspoons salt
- 1/4 teaspoon pepper
- 1 can (14-1/2 ounces) chicken broth
- 6 rib *or* loin pork chops (3/4 inch thick)
- 2 tablespoons cooking oil
- Additional salt and pepper, optional
- 6 cups thinly sliced peeled potatoes (about 4 pounds)
- 1 medium onion, sliced
- Paprika and chopped fresh parsley, optional

In a saucepan, melt butter; stir in flour, salt and pepper. Add broth; cook and stir constantly until mixture boils. Cook for 1 minute; remove from the heat and set aside. In a skillet, brown pork chops in oil; season to taste with additional salt and pepper if desired. In a greased 13-in. x 9-in. x 2-in. baking dish, layer potatoes and onion. Pour the broth mixture over. Place pork chops on top. Cover and bake at 350° for 1 hour; uncover and bake 30 minutes longer or until potatoes are tender. If desired, sprinkle with paprika and parsley. **Yield:** 6 servings.

Pineapple Beets

This side dish has a slightly sweet taste that has even people who don't usually like beets taking second helpings

- 2 tablespoons brown sugar

- 1 tablespoon cornstarch
- 1/4 teaspoon salt
- 1 can (8 ounces) pineapple tidbits, undrained
- 1 can (16 ounces) sliced beets, drained
- 1 tablespoon butter *or* margarine
- 1 tablespoon lemon juice

In a saucepan, combine brown sugar, cornstarch and salt; add pineapple and bring to a boil, stirring constantly until thick, about 2 minutes. Add the beets, butter and lemon juice; cook over medium heat for 5 minutes, stirring occasionally. **Yield:** 4 servings.

Make-Ahead Butterhorns

Mom loved to make these fresh-from-the-oven rolls. They're beautiful and impressive to serve.

- 2 packages (1/4 ounce *each*) active dry yeast
- 1/3 cup warm water (110° to 115°)
- 9 cups all-purpose flour, *divided*
- 2 cups warm milk (110° to 115°)
- 1 cup shortening
- 1 cup sugar
- 6 eggs
- 2 teaspoons salt
- 3 to 4 tablespoons butter *or* margarine, melted

In a large mixing bowl, dissolve yeast in water. Add 4 cups flour, milk, shortening, sugar, eggs and salt; beat for 2 minutes or until smooth. Add enough remaining flour to form a soft dough. Turn onto a floured board; knead lightly. Place in a greased bowl, turning once to grease top. Cover and let rise in a warm place until doubled, about 2-3 hours. Punch dough down; divide into four equal parts. Roll each into a 9-

in. circle; brush with butter. Cut each circle into eight pie-shaped wedges; roll up each wedge from wide edge to tip of dough and pinch to seal. Place rolls with tip down on baking sheets; freeze. When frozen, place in freezer bags and keep frozen until needed. To bake, place on greased baking sheets; thaw 5 hours or until doubled in size. Bake at 375° for 12-15 minutes or until lightly browned. Remove from baking sheets and serve immediately or cool on wire racks. **Yield:** 32 rolls.

Banana Cream Pie

Made from farm-fresh dairy products, this pie was a sensational creamy treat anytime Mom served it.

- 3/4 cup sugar
- 1/3 cup all-purpose flour
- 1/4 teaspoon salt
- 2 cups milk
- 3 egg yolks, lightly beaten
- 2 tablespoons butter *or* margarine
- 1 teaspoon vanilla extract
- 1 pastry shell (9 inches), baked
- 3 medium firm bananas
- Whipped cream and additional sliced bananas

In a saucepan, combine sugar, flour and salt; stir in milk and mix well. Cook over medium heat, stirring constantly, until the mixture thickens and comes to a boil; boil for 2 minutes. Remove from the heat. Stir a small amount into egg yolks; return all to saucepan. Cook for 2 minutes, stirring constantly; remove from the heat. Add butter and vanilla; cool slightly. Slice the bananas into pastry shell; pour filling over. Cool. Before serving, garnish with whipped cream and bananas. Refrigerate any leftovers. **Yield:** 6-8 servings.

Mom's Reputation for Roasts Unrivaled

By Linda Gaido, New Brighton, Pennsylvania

FOR YEARS, Mom has had a reputation in the family for making the very best roast beef. And that honor still stands today. Mom is one of those people born to be a good cook. She rarely measures anything, and everything she makes tastes wonderful.

When my two older sisters and I were growing up, the house smelled heavenly on those chilly fall days when the roast beef was cooking. People always ask what her secret ingredients are. And they're surprised to hear that the rich flavor comes from coffee!

To make Country Green Beans, Mom added garlic, chopped ham and onion. These additions blend so well with the beans and really complement the beef.

The melt-in your mouth Oven-Roasted Potatoes really round out this meat-and-potatoes meal. They're also convenient because they can share the oven with Baked Apple Slices. Mom enjoyed serving this updated version of baked apples over vanilla ice cream.

Mom and I are now thrilled to share the recipes for this warm satisfying meal. Give these dishes a try when cooler weather has you craving hearty old-fashioned foods!

Mom's Roast Beef

This well-seasoned roast is Mom's specialty. Everyone loves slices of this fork-tender roast beef and its savory gravy. Hard as I try, I can never make it taste just like Mom's!

1 tablespoon cooking oil
1 eye of round beef roast (about 2-1/2 pounds)
1 medium onion, chopped
1 cup brewed coffee
1 cup water, *divided*
1 beef bouillon cube
2 teaspoons dried basil
1 teaspoon dried rosemary, crushed
1 garlic clove, minced
1 teaspoon salt
1/2 teaspoon pepper
1/4 cup all-purpose flour

Heat oil in a Dutch oven; brown roast on all sides. Add onion; cook until transparent. Add coffee, 3/4 cup water, bouillon, basil, rosemary, garlic, salt and pepper. Cover and simmer for 2-1/2 hours or until the meat is tender. Combine the flour and remaining water until smooth; stir into pan juices. Cook and stir until thickened and bubbly. Remove roast and slice. Pass the gravy. **Yield:** 8 servings.

GOOD GRAVY. When making a big family dinner, make your gravy as usual and then put it in a slow cooker. It's easy to refill the gravy boat with hot gravy throughout the meal.

Country Green Beans

This deliciously different way to dress up green beans is sure to become a much-requested recipe at your house.

1 pound fresh green beans, trimmed
1/4 cup chopped onion
1/4 cup chopped fully cooked ham
1/4 cup butter *or* margarine
1/4 cup water
1 garlic clove, minced
1/2 teaspoon salt
1/4 teaspoon pepper

In a saucepan, combine all ingredients. Cover and simmer for 15-20 minutes or until beans are tender. **Yield:** 4 servings.

Oven-Roasted Potatoes

For a side dish with real country appeal, why not try these golden potato wedges? You'll watch them disappear right before your eyes.

4 baking potatoes (about 2 pounds)
2 tablespoons butter *or* margarine, melted
2 teaspoons paprika
1 teaspoon salt
1/2 teaspoon pepper

Peel potatoes and cut into large chunks; place in a shallow 2-qt. baking pan. Pour butter over and toss until well coated. Sprinkle with paprika, salt and pepper. Bake, uncovered, at 350° for 45-60 minutes or until tender. **Yield:** 4 servings.

Baked Apple Slices

For satisfying harvest flavor, nothing beats oven-fresh apple slices. This old-fashioned treat is a new twist on traditional baked apples.

3 large baking apples, peeled and sliced
3/4 cup sugar
1 tablespoon ground cinnamon
1/4 teaspoon ground nutmeg
1/4 teaspoon ground ginger
1/4 cup apple cider
1/2 cup butter *or* margarine
1/2 cup walnuts *or* raisins
Vanilla ice cream

Place apples in a greased 1-qt. baking dish. Combine sugar, cinnamon, nutmeg, ginger and apple cider; pour over apples. Dot with butter. Sprinkle with nuts or raisins. Bake, uncovered, at 350° for 45-60 minutes or until apples are tender. Serve warm over ice cream. **Yield:** 4 servings.

Down-Home Dinner with Midwestern Flair

By Linda Nilsen, Anoka, Minnesota

MY MOTHER was a busy teacher when my younger brother and I were children. She was always on the go, but that didn't stop her from making luscious meals for our family.

We lived in California, but Mom was from a Swedish Minnesota farm family. When she got homesick for the farm, she'd make hearty meals with down-home flair. We always looked forward to those meals more than any others she prepared!

I especially remember Mom's Best Meat Loaf. The zesty seasoning gives the flavor a spark. And the wonderful aroma while baking was unbeatable. I often capture that mouth-watering fragrance in my own kitchen today.

Creamed Peas and Potatoes make a hearty side dish that also adds appealing color to the table. My mom and her cousin came up with the recipe for Favorite French Dressing many years ago. You'll find it really perks up ordinary salad greens.

To top off her meal, Mom prepared a special dessert from an old recipe handed down in the family. Swedish Creme is thick, rich, beautiful and delicious. I guarantee this menu will be favored by your family no matter where you live.

Mom's Best Meat Loaf

This is no ordinary meat loaf—the recipe is so good it's been passed down in our family for three generations. Mom loved to serve this to friends and family.

- 1-1/2 pounds lean ground beef
- 1 cup milk
- 1 egg, lightly beaten
- 3/4 cup soft bread crumbs
- 1 medium onion, chopped
- 1 tablespoon chopped green pepper
- 1 tablespoon ketchup
- 1-1/2 teaspoons salt
- 1 teaspoon prepared horseradish
- 1 teaspoon sugar
- 1 teaspoon ground allspice
- 1 teaspoon dill weed
- Additional ketchup

In a large bowl, combine the first 12 ingredients; mix well. Press into an ungreased 8-1/2-in. x 4-1/2-in. x 2-1/2-in. loaf pan. Bake at 350° for 1 hour. Drizzle top of loaf with ketchup; bake 15 minutes more or until no pink remains. **Yield:** 6-8 servings.

Creamed Peas and Potatoes

Nothing beats this comforting side dish to go with Mom's meat loaf. Everyone will enjoy the peas and potatoes combined with a creamy white sauce.

- 4 medium red potatoes, cubed
- 1 package (10 ounces) frozen peas
- 1 teaspoon sugar
- 2 tablespoons butter *or* margarine
- 2 tablespoons all-purpose flour
- 1/2 teaspoon salt
- 1/4 teaspoon white pepper
- 1-1/2 cups milk
- 2 tablespoons minced fresh dill

Place potatoes in a saucepan; cover with water and cook until tender. Cook peas according to package directions, adding the sugar. Meanwhile, melt butter in a saucepan; add flour, salt and pepper to form a paste. Gradually stir in milk. Bring to a boil; boil for 1 minute. Add dill; cook until thickened and bubbly. Drain potatoes and peas; place in a serving bowl. Pour sauce over and stir to coat. Serve immediately. **Yield:** 6-8 servings.

Favorite French Dressing

You'll find this dressing holds together nicely once mixed. And after one bite, friends and family alike will ask for the recipe.

- 1 cup vinegar
- 3/4 cup sugar
- 1/4 cup grated onion
- 1-1/2 teaspoons salt
- 1-1/2 teaspoons dry mustard
- 1-1/2 teaspoons paprika
- 1 bottle (12 ounces) chili sauce
- 1 cup vegetable oil

In a bowl or jar with tight-fitting lid, mix vinegar, sugar and onion. Combine salt, mustard, paprika and 2 tablespoons chili sauce to form a paste. Add remaining chili sauce and mix well. Pour into vinegar mixture; add oil and mix or shake well. Store in the refrigerator. **Yield:** 3-1/2 cups.

Swedish Creme

This thick creamy dessert is a great finale to one of Mom's hearty meals. It has just a hint of almond flavor and looks spectacular.

- 2 cups heavy cream
- 1 cup plus 2 teaspoons sugar, *divided*
- 1 envelope unflavored gelatin
- 1 teaspoon clear imitation vanilla extract
- 1 teaspoon almond extract
- 2 cups (16 ounces) sour cream
- 1 cup fresh *or* frozen red raspberries, crushed

In a saucepan, combine cream and 1 cup sugar. Cook and stir constantly over low heat until candy thermometer reads 160° or steam rises from pan (do not boil). Stir in gelatin until dissolved; add extracts. Cool 10 minutes. Whisk in sour cream. Pour into eight dessert glasses or small bowls; chill at least 1 hour. Before serving, combine raspberries and remaining sugar; spoon over each serving. **Yield:** 8 servings.

MEALS ON A BUDGET

With these frugal yet flavorful meals, you don't have to sacrifice taste or quality to feed your family for just pennies a person.

FEED YOUR FAMILY... FOR $1.25 PER PLATE!

THE FESTIVE MEAL featured here comes from two great cooks who estimate the cost of just $1.25 a setting using ingredients purchased at their local grocery stores. So you can make it often without breaking the bank.

Anita Gibson of Clinton, Illinois shares her colorful and crunchy Mixed Vegetable Salad. It's a cool, refreshing side dish you'll likely prepare with many main meals.

Slightly Spicy Taco Bake is a specialty of Marlene Logan's in Colorado Springs, Colorado. Her hearty dish is perfect for feeding a hungry family or serving to company.

Anita and Marlene guarantee that *your* family will enjoy these palate-pleasing recipes!

♥🐘♥🐘♥🐘♥🐘♥🐘♥

Mixed Vegetable Salad

- **1 package (10 ounces) frozen mixed vegetables**
- **1 can (15 ounces) kidney beans, rinsed and drained**
- **1/2 cup chopped celery**
- **1/2 cup chopped onion**
- **1/2 cup chopped green pepper**
- **3/4 cup sugar**
- **1/2 cup vinegar**
- **1 tablespoon cornstarch**

Cook the mixed vegetables on the stove or in the microwave until crisp-tender. Drain; place in a large bowl. Add kidney beans, celery, onion and green pepper. In a saucepan over medium heat, bring sugar, vinegar and cornstarch to a boil, stirring constantly, until thickened. Cool slightly. Pour over vegetables and toss. Refrigerate until ready to serve. **Yield:** 8 servings.

♥🐘♥🐘♥🐘♥🐘♥🐘♥

Taco Bake

- **1 pound ground beef**
- **1 small onion, chopped**
- **3/4 cup water**
- **1 package (1-1/4 ounces) taco seasoning**
- **1 can (15 ounces) tomato sauce**
- **1 package (8 ounces) shell macaroni, cooked and drained**
- **1 can (4 ounces) chopped green chilies**
- **2 cups (8 ounces) shredded cheddar cheese, *divided***

In a skillet, brown ground beef and onion over medium heat; drain. Add the water, taco seasoning and tomato sauce; mix. Bring to a boil; reduce heat and simmer for 20 minutes. Stir in macaroni, chilies and 1-1/2 cups of cheese. Pour into a greased 1-1/2-qt. baking dish. Sprinkle with the remaining cheese. Bake at 350° for 30 minutes or until heated through. **Yield:** 6 servings.

CASSEROLES have always been a penny-wise way to eat. And this Chicken Rice Casserole—from Marcia Hostetter of Canton, New York—can be doubly thrifty because only 1 cup of the Homemade Seasoned Rice Mix is used in the casserole.

You can use the remainder of the rice as a gift (as in the photo above) or as a side dish with meat another day.

Soft Breadsticks come from Hazel Fritchie of Palestine, Illinois, who's been making them for 30 years. You and your family can enjoy this robust meal for just $1.09 a setting.

♥☎♥☎♥☎♥☎♥☎♥☎♥

Chicken Rice Casserole

2-1/2 cups cubed cooked chicken
1-1/2 cups frozen mixed vegetables
  1 cup Homemade Seasoned Rice Mix (recipe at right)
1/2 cup chopped onion
  1 can (4 ounces) mushroom stems and pieces, drained
  2 cups water
  1 can (10-3/4 ounces) condensed cream of chicken soup, undiluted
1/4 teaspoon onion salt
1/4 teaspoon dried thyme
1/4 cup crushed potato chips

In a greased 2-qt. casserole, combine chicken, vegetables, rice mix, onion and mushrooms. Combine water, soup, onion salt and thyme, mix well. Pour over the rice mixture; stir. Cover and bake at 375° for 55-65 minutes or until the rice is tender, stirring occasionally. Sprinkle with potato chips. **Yield:** 6 servings.

♥☎♥☎♥☎♥☎♥☎♥☎♥

Homemade Seasoned Rice Mix

3 cups uncooked long grain rice
6 teaspoons instant chicken bouillon granules
1/4 cup dried parsley flakes
2 teaspoons onion powder
1/2 teaspoon garlic powder
1/4 teaspoon dried thyme

Combine all ingredients in a storage container with a tight-fitting lid. **Yield:** 3-1/2 cups. **Editor's Note:** To prepare rice as a side dish, combine 2 cups water and 1 tablespoon butter in a saucepan; bring to a boil. Stir in 1 cup mix. Reduce heat; cover and simmer for 15-20 minutes. **Yield:** 6 servings.

♥☎♥☎♥☎♥☎♥☎♥☎♥

Soft Breadsticks

✓ This tasty dish uses less sugar, salt and fat. Recipe includes *Diabetic Exchanges.*

  1 package (1/4 ounce) active dry yeast
  1 cup warm water (110° to 115°)
  3 tablespoons sugar
  1 teaspoon salt
1/4 cup vegetable oil
  3 cups all-purpose flour, divided
Cornmeal
  1 egg white
  1 tablespoon water
Coarse salt, optional

In a mixing bowl, dissolve yeast in water. Add sugar, salt and oil; stir until dissolved. Add 2 cups of flour; beat until smooth. Add enough remaining flour to form a soft dough. Turn onto a floured board; knead until smooth and elastic, about 6-8 minutes. Place in a greased bowl, turning once to grease top. Cover and let rise in a warm place until doubled, about 1 hour. Punch dough down and divide into 12 portions. Using your hands, roll each portion into a 10-in. x 1/2-in. strip. Place 1 in. apart on a greased baking sheet sprinkled with cornmeal. Let rise, uncovered, until doubled, about 45-60 minutes. Beat egg white and water; brush over breadsticks. Sprinkle with coarse salt if desired. Place baking sheet on middle rack of oven; place a large shallow pan filled with boiling water on lowest rack. Bake at 400° for 10 minutes. Brush again with egg white. Bake 5 minutes more or until golden brown. **Yield:** 1 dozen. **Diabetic Exchanges:** One breadstick (prepared without coarse salt) equals 2 starch, 1 fat; also, 178 calories, 194 mg sodium, 0 cholesterol, 29 gm carbohydrate, 4 gm protein, 5 gm fat.

THIS FRUGAL yet flavorful meal comes from two great cooks who estimate the cost of just $1.35 a setting (including purchased breadsticks!).

Meatless Spaghetti is a delicious main dish from Barbara Njaa of Nikishka, Alaska. "This sauce is so chunky and good you'll think it's loaded with meat. But it actually features a whole bushel of fantastic produce!"

Tomato Parmesan Salad—from Michelle Bently of Niceville, Florida —adds just the right amount of color and crunch to this Italian-style supper.

♥☎♥☎♥☎♥☎♥☎♥☎♥

Meatless Spaghetti

✓ This tasty dish uses less sugar, salt and fat. Recipe includes *Diabetic Exchanges.*

- 6 garlic cloves, minced
- 1 cup chopped celery
- 1 medium *or* large onion, chopped
- 2 tablespoons cooking oil
- 6 small zucchini, chopped (about 2 pounds)
- 1 green pepper, chopped
- 1 can (6 ounces) pitted ripe olives, drained and sliced
- 4 beef bouillon cubes
- 1 cup hot water
- 1 jar (6 ounces) sliced mushrooms, drained
- 1 can (28 ounces) diced tomatoes, undrained
- 2 cans (15 ounces *each*) tomato sauce
- 1 can (6 ounces) tomato paste
- 1 tablespoon brown sugar, optional
- 2 teaspoons dried basil
- 2 teaspoons dried oregano
- 2 teaspoons dried parsley flakes
- 1 teaspoon salt, optional
- 1/2 teaspoon pepper
- 2 pounds spaghetti, cooked and drained

In a large saucepan or a Dutch oven, saute garlic, celery and onion in oil until tender. Add zucchini, green pepper and olives; saute for 2-3 minutes. Dissolve bouillon in water; add to vegetables. Add the next 10 ingredients and bring to a boil. Reduce heat; cover and simmer for 1 hour, stirring occasionally. Serve over spaghetti. **Yield:** 14 servings. **Diabetic**

Exchanges: One 1-cup serving of sauce (prepared with low-sodium bouillon and without brown sugar or salt) equals 3 vegetable, 1 fat; also, 102 calories, 624 mg sodium, 0 cholesterol, 14 gm carbohydrate, 4 gm protein, 5 gm fat.

♥☎♥☎♥☎♥☎♥☎♥☎♥

Tomato Parmesan Salad

- 1-1/3 cups vegetable *or* olive oil
- 1 cup red wine vinegar
- 2 garlic cloves, minced
- Salt and pepper to taste
- 2 bunches romaine lettuce, torn
- 1 head iceberg lettuce, torn
- 2 small red onions, thinly sliced
- 2 large tomatoes, diced
- 1 jar (4 ounces) diced pimientos, drained
- 2/3 cup shredded Parmesan cheese

In a small bowl or jar with a tight-fitting lid, combine oil, vinegar, garlic, salt and pepper; set aside. In a large salad bowl, combine all remaining ingredients. Chill until ready to serve. Just before serving, whisk or shake dressing; pour over salad and toss. **Yield:** 14 servings.

WOULD YOU like to host a special spring luncheon for family and friends without breaking your budget? Try this colorful, not costly, meal shared by two country cooks who estimate the cost of $1.30 per setting.

Diane Hixon of Niceville, Florida contributed her special Crunchy Chicken Salad recipe. You'll love the fabulous fresh flavor. (And the purchased breadsticks are included in the cost!)

Whether you serve it as a salad or dessert, Rhubarb Berry Delight—from Joan Sieck of Rensselaer, New York —will be an instant success with your friends and family.

♥☎♥☎♥☎♥☎♥☎♥☎♥

Crunchy Chicken Salad

✓ This tasty dish uses less sugar, salt and fat. Recipe includes *Diabetic Exchanges*.

        4 cups shredded cooked
          chicken
        2 cups shredded lettuce
        1 cup julienned carrots
        1 cup julienned cucumber
    2/3 cup green onion strips (2-inch
          pieces)

        1 cup fresh bean sprouts
    DRESSING:
        2 tablespoons peanut *or*
          vegetable oil
        2 tablespoons lemon juice
        2 tablespoons sesame seeds,
          toasted
    1-1/2 teaspoons soy sauce
        1/2 teaspoon salt, optional
        1/4 teaspoon pepper
        1/4 teaspoon dry mustard
    Hot pepper sauce to taste

In a large salad bowl, toss the chicken, lettuce, carrots, cucumber, green onion and bean sprouts. Refrigerate. In a small bowl, combine dressing ingredients. Refrigerate. Just before serving, pour dressing over salad and toss gently. Serve with breadsticks. **Yield:** 10 servings. **Diabetic Exchanges:** One 1-cup serving of salad (without added salt) equals 2 lean meat, 1 vegetable, 1/2 fat; also, 156 calories, 201 mg sodium, 42 mg cholesterol, 5 gm carbohydrate, 19 gm protein, 6 gm fat.

♥☎♥☎♥☎♥☎♥☎♥

Rhubarb Berry Delight

        4 cups diced rhubarb

        2 cups fresh *or* frozen
          strawberries
    1-1/2 cups sugar, *divided*
        1 package (6 ounces)
          raspberry-flavored gelatin
        2 cups boiling water
        1 cup milk
        1 envelope unflavored gelatin
        1/4 cup cold water
    1-1/2 teaspoons vanilla extract
        2 cups (16 ounces) sour cream

In a saucepan, cook rhubarb, strawberries and 1 cup sugar until fruit is tender. In a large bowl, dissolve the raspberry gelatin in boiling water. Stir in fruit; set aside. In another pan, heat the milk and remaining sugar over low until sugar is dissolved. Meanwhile, soften unflavored gelatin in cold water. Add to hot milk mixture and stir until gelatin dissolves. Remove from the heat; add vanilla. Cool to lukewarm; blend in sour cream. Set aside at room temperature. Pour a third of the fruit mixture into a 3-qt. bowl; chill until almost set. Spoon a third of the sour cream mixture over fruit; chill until almost set. Repeat layers twice, chilling between layers if necessary. Refrigerate until firm, at least 3 hours. **Yield:** 12 servings.

FEED YOUR FAMILY...
FOR 94¢ PER PLATE!

LOOKING for a low-budget menu that's perfect for brunch or a special Sunday breakfast? Marsha Ransom of South Haven, Michigan dishes up generous helpings of this meal...for just 94¢ a setting.

Eggs are always a filling, flavorful dish. And Hearty Egg Scramble is extra-special because it's loaded with ham and potatoes.

You can capture the wonderful taste of fresh fruit anytime of year with Ambrosia Fruit. With its combination of canned pineapple, apples and coconut, it's the perfect recipe.

Marsha adds that this breakfast wouldn't be complete without pretty and pleasing Jellied Biscuits. "They're a pleasure to serve because they look so lovely with the colorful jelly on them."

Why not try these dishes today for a rise-and-shine morning meal that your family is sure to savor?

♥☎♥☎♥☎♥☎♥☎♥☎♥

Hearty Egg Scramble

1/3 cup chopped onion
1/4 cup chopped green pepper
1/4 cup butter *or* margarine
**2 medium potatoes,
    peeled, cooked and cubed**
**1-1/2 cups julienned fully cooked
    ham**
6 eggs
2 tablespoons water
Dash pepper

In a large skillet, cook onion and green pepper in butter until crisp-tender. Add potatoes and ham; cook and stir for 5 minutes. In a bowl, beat eggs, water and pepper; pour over ham mixture. Cook over low heat, stirring occasionally, until eggs are set. **Yield:** 6 servings.

♥☎♥☎♥☎♥☎♥☎♥☎♥

Ambrosia Fruit

**1 can (20 ounces) pineapple
    tidbits**
1/4 cup packed brown sugar
1/2 teaspoon grated orange peel
2 medium oranges
**2 medium unpeeled apples,
    diced**
1 tablespoon shredded coconut

Drain pineapple, reserving 1/4 cup juice

in a saucepan; set pineapple aside. Add the brown sugar and orange peel to the juice; heat until sugar dissolves. Peel and section oranges into a large bowl, reserving any juice; add the apples and pineapple. Add pineapple juice mixture and stir gently. Chill. Just before serving, sprinkle with coconut. **Yield:** 6 servings.

♥☎♥☎♥☎♥☎♥☎♥☎♥

Jellied Biscuits

2 cups all-purpose flour
4 teaspoons baking powder
2 teaspoons sugar
1/2 teaspoon salt
1/2 teaspoon cream of tartar
1/2 cup shortening
3/4 cup milk
1/3 cup jelly

In a bowl, combine flour, baking powder, sugar, salt and cream of tartar. Cut in shortening until the mixture resembles coarse crumbs. Add milk; stir quickly with a fork just until mixed. Drop by rounded tablespoonfuls onto a greased baking sheet. Make a deep thumbprint in tops; fill each with 1 teaspoon of jelly. Bake at 450° for 10-12 minutes or until biscuits are browned. **Yield:** about 1 dozen.

EVEN at today's prices, you can feed your family for just pennies a person. Judith Anglen shows how easy it is to put together a low-budget menu sure to please everyone.

"One of our favorite meals around here is also really affordable," assures this Riverton, Wyoming cook. "I buy chicken thighs when they're on sale and freeze them for use in this meal later. Everyone enjoys the truly country-style combination of chicken, rice and mushrooms."

"Colorful Marinated Garden Salad is tangy and crunchy and complements the main dish nicely. The spread featured here makes a fabulous company meal. Friends and family are always happy to see this meal on the table."

And you'll be happy to hear that this impressive meal (including purchased bake-shop dinner rolls) costs only $1.31 a setting. Leave it to a country cook like Judith to tastefully prove you really don't have to forgo flavor when eating inexpensively!

♥☎♥☎♥☎♥☎♥☎♥☎♥

Chicken and Rice Dinner

- 1/2 cup all-purpose flour
- 1 teaspoon salt
- 1/2 teaspoon pepper
- 10 chicken thighs (about 3 pounds)
- 3 tablespoons cooking oil
- 1 cup uncooked long grain rice
- 1/4 cup chopped onion
- 2 garlic cloves, minced
- 1 can (4 ounces) mushroom stems and pieces, undrained
- 2 chicken bouillon cubes
- 2 cups boiling water

Minced fresh parsley, optional

Combine flour, salt and pepper; coat chicken pieces. In a large skillet over medium heat, brown the chicken in oil. Place rice in an ungreased 13-in. x 9-in. x 2-in. baking dish. Sprinkle with onion and garlic; top with mushrooms. Dissolve bouillon in boiling water; pour over all. Place chicken pieces on top. Cover and bake at 350° for 1 hour or un-

til chicken juices run clear and rice is tender. Sprinkle with parsley if desired. **Yield:** 5 servings.

♥☎♥☎♥☎♥☎♥☎♥☎♥

Marinated Garden Salad

✓ This tasty dish uses less sugar, salt and fat. Recipe includes *Diabetic Exchanges*.

- 1/2 cup sliced celery
- 1/2 cup sliced cucumber
- 1/2 cup sliced carrots
- 1/2 cup sliced radishes
- 1/2 cup bottled Italian salad dressing
- 5 cups torn salad greens

In a large bowl, combine the celery, cucumber, carrots and radishes. Add the dressing and refrigerate for 1 hour. Just before serving, add greens and toss. **Yield:** 5 servings. **Diabetic Exchanges:** One serving (prepared with light salad dressing) equals 1 vegetable, 1/2 fat; also, 44 calories, 216 mg sodium, 2 mg cholesterol, 5 gm carbohydrate, 1 gm protein, 3 gm fat.

MEALS IN MINUTES

Here cooks contribute timeless dishes that together make for meals you can take from start to serving in half an hour or less!

ITALIAN-STYLE SUPPER IN A SNAP

WHEN you need a satisfying supper in a hurry, nothing compares to the ease of preparation of skillet specialties.

So it's no surprise that Marcia Hostetter of Canton, New York reaches for her Quick Chicken Cacciatore recipe often. "It's a colorful, zesty main meal that I like to serve with a crisp lettuce and tomato salad topped with my family's favorite dressing."

Myrtle Albrecht's brood in Cameron Park, California loves the fabulous flavor of fresh-from-the-oven bread. But when time doesn't allow, Myrtle simply dresses up refrigerated breadsticks and serves Mini Blue Cheese Rolls.

"I've made this recipe for 30 years and find the rolls also make quick appetizers to hold the family until dinner," Myrtle reveals.

Proving that a quick meal doesn't have to go without dessert, Jeanette Fuehring of Concordia, Missouri adds her recipe for No-Cook Coconut Pie. It's a no-hassle favorite that's impressive enough to serve family as well as company.

♥☎♥☎♥☎♥☎♥☎♥☎♥

Quick Chicken Cacciatore

- 1 medium green pepper, cut into strips
- 1 medium onion, sliced into rings
- 8 ounces fresh mushrooms, sliced
- 1 tablespoon olive oil
- 4 chicken breast halves, boned and skinned
- 1 can (15 ounces) tomato sauce
- 1 can (4 ounces) chopped green chilies
- 1/4 to 1/2 teaspoon dried basil
- 1/4 to 1/2 teaspoon dried oregano
- 1/8 to 1/4 teaspoon garlic powder

Dash cayenne pepper
Cooked spaghetti *or* rice, optional

In a large skillet, saute green pepper, onion and mushrooms in olive oil for 4-5 minutes or until crisp-tender. Place the chicken breasts over the vegetables. In a bowl, combine tomato sauce, chilies and seasonings. Pour over the chicken; cover and simmer for 20 minutes or until chicken is tender and no longer pink. Serve over spaghetti or rice if desired. **Yield:** 4 servings.

♥☎♥☎♥☎♥☎♥☎♥☎♥

Mini Blue Cheese Rolls

- 1/4 cup butter *or* margarine
- 1/2 cup (4 ounces) blue cheese
- 1 tube (11 ounces) refrigerated breadsticks

In a saucepan, melt the butter and blue cheese over low heat. Unroll dough and cut each breadstick into six pieces; place in a foil-lined 11-in. x 7-in. x 2-in. baking pan. Pour cheese mixture over dough. Bake at 400° for 20 minutes or until butter is absorbed and rolls are lightly browned. Carefully lift foil out of pan; place on a serving dish. Serve hot. **Yield:** 4-6 servings.

♥☎♥☎♥☎♥☎♥☎♥☎♥

No-Cook Coconut Pie

- 2 packages (3.4 ounces *each*) instant vanilla pudding mix
- 2-3/4 cups cold milk
- 1 teaspoon coconut extract
- 1 carton (8 ounces) frozen whipped topping, thawed
- 1/2 cup flaked coconut
- 1 graham cracker crust (9 inches)

Toasted coconut

In a large mixing bowl, beat pudding mixes, milk and coconut extract on low speed until combined. Beat on high for 2 minutes. Fold in whipped topping and coconut. Pour into the crust. Sprinkle with toasted coconut. Chill until serving time. Refrigerate leftovers. **Yield:** 6-8 servings.

SAUCY STEAK IS SURE TO SATISFY

WHEN the hustle and bustle of the holidays keeps you out of the kitchen more than you'd like, why not present your family with this fast and flavorful home-cooked meal? They'll shower you with mmm-many thanks!

"Salisbury Steak can be made in about 25 minutes," shares Carol Callahan of Rome, Georgia. "And to save even more time, I often prepare these patties ahead and reheat them with the gravy in the microwave. It seems I always have the ingredients for this recipe on hand."

Quick Carrots is a versatile colorful side dish from Florence Jacoby. "The carrots and green onions are a flavorful combination that your family will enjoy as much as mine," assures this Granite Falls, Minnesota cook.

Banana Pudding Dessert comes from Hazel Merrill of Greenville, South Carolina. "This creamy dessert with mild banana taste is a true 'comfort food'," Hazel says. "As an added plus, it looks and tastes like you fussed all day!"

❤🍲❤🍲❤🍲❤🍲❤🍲❤

Salisbury Steak

✓ This tasty dish uses less sugar, salt and fat. Recipe includes *Diabetic Exchanges*.

- 1 pound lean ground beef
- 1 egg white, lightly beaten
- 1/3 cup chopped onion
- 1/4 cup saltine crumbs
- 2 tablespoons milk
- 1 tablespoon prepared horseradish
- 1/4 teaspoon salt, optional
- 1/8 teaspoon pepper
- 1 jar (12 ounces) beef gravy
- 1-1/4 to 1-1/2 cups sliced fresh mushrooms
- 2 tablespoons water

Hot cooked noodles, optional

In a bowl, combine the beef, egg white, onion, crumbs, milk, horseradish, salt if desired and pepper. Shape into four oval patties. Fry in a skillet over medium heat for 10-12 minutes or until cooked through, turning once. Remove patties and keep warm. Add gravy, mushrooms and water to skillet; heat for 3-5 minutes. Serve over patties and noodles if desired. **Yield:** 4 servings. **Diabetic Exchanges:** One serving (prepared with low-fat gravy and skim milk and without salt or noodles) equals 3 meat, 1/2

starch, 1/2 vegetable, also, 248 calories, 205 mg sodium, 66 mg cholesterol, 9 gm carbohydrate, 25 gm protein, 12 gm fat.

KEEP THE COLOR. For a lovely looking vegetable dish, add a bit of vinegar to the water when cooking. This trick helps all vegetables hold their fresh, bright color.

❤🍲❤🍲❤🍲❤🍲❤🍲❤

Quick Carrots

- 2 cups fresh *or* frozen sliced carrots
- 1 tablespoon butter *or* margarine
- 2 tablespoons sliced green onions
- 1 tablespoon water
- 1/4 teaspoon salt

Chopped fresh parsley

In a saucepan, combine first five ingredients. Cover and simmer for 8-10 minutes or until the carrots are crisp-tender. Sprinkle with parsley. **Yield:** 4 servings.

❤🍲❤🍲❤🍲❤🍲❤🍲❤

Banana Pudding Dessert

- 1 package (3.4 ounces) instant vanilla pudding mix
- 1-1/4 cups cold water
- 1 can (14 ounces) sweetened condensed milk
- 2 cups whipped topping
- 24 to 32 vanilla wafers
- 3 large firm bananas, sliced

In a large bowl, combine pudding mix, water and milk; beat on low speed for 2 minutes. Chill for 5 minutes. Fold in the whipped topping. In individual dessert dishes, layer wafers, pudding, bananas and more pudding. Top each with a wafer. Chill until serving. **Yield:** 6-8 servings.

BECKON YOUR CLAN WITH BURGERS

THE appealing lunch or supper menu featured here is made up of family-tested-and-approved recipes from three time-conscious cooks. It'll surely fill the bill when you find yourself short on time.

"Pronto Pizza Burgers are my family's all-time favorite quick main dish," admits Karen Kruse of Gahanna, Ohio. "Just one bite and they can't resist these zesty satisfying sandwiches. Folks love their true pizza taste. They're a fun treat for kids of all ages."

Salad with Vinaigrette Dressing is shared by Fayne Lutz of Taos, New Mexico. "The unique dressing really gives the lettuce and vegetables some zip. And it's a nice change of pace from bottled dressings. I also like to serve this for special dinners," Fayne adds.

Lemon Custard Cake, from Sue Gronholz of Columbus, Wisconsin, is treasured for two reasons. "This recipe from my grandma has been in the family for generations, and now I pass it on to you. I'm sure you'll receive lots of requests for this recipe."

Sue continues, "Plus, being quick and easy, it's nice to whip up when unexpected company drops in. This old-fashioned dessert is cool and creamy!"

Pronto Pizza Burgers

    1 **pound lean ground beef**
  1/3 **cup grated Parmesan cheese**
    1 **tablespoon chopped onion**
    1 **tablespoon tomato paste**
    1 **teaspoon dried oregano**
  1/2 **teaspoon salt**
  1/4 **teaspoon pepper**
    4 **English muffins, split**
    8 **tomato slices**
    8 **mozzarella cheese slices**
Additional oregano, optional

In a bowl, mix beef, Parmesan cheese, onion, tomato paste, oregano, salt and pepper just until combined. Toast the muffins in broiler until lightly browned. Divide meat mixture among muffins. Broil 4 in. from the heat for 8-10 minutes or until meat is cooked. Top with tomato and cheese slices. Return to broiler until cheese is melted. If desired, sprinkle with oregano. Serve immediately. **Yield:** 4 servings.

Salad with Vinaigrette Dressing

  3/4 **cup vegetable oil**
  1/4 **cup white wine vinegar**
    1 **teaspoon salt**
    1 **teaspoon dry mustard**
  1/2 **teaspoon sugar**
  1/2 **teaspoon garlic powder**
  3 **to 4 drops hot pepper sauce**
Salad greens
Bell peppers, mushrooms, tomatoes
   and/or **other vegetables of**
   your choice

In a jar with a tight-fitting lid, combine the first seven ingredients and shake well. Toss salad greens and vegetables in a large bowl or arrange on individual salad plates. Serve with dressing. **Yield:** 1 cup dressing.

Lemon Custard Cake

    1 **prepared angel food cake (10**
      inches)
    1 **package (3.4 ounces) instant**
      lemon pudding mix
1-1/2 **cups cold milk**
    1 **cup (8 ounces) sour cream**
    1 **can (21 ounces) cherry** *or*
      strawberry pie filling

Tear the angel food cake into bite-size pieces. Place in a 13-in. x 9-in. x 2-in. pan. In a mixing bowl, combine the pudding mix, milk and sour cream. Beat until thickened, about 2 minutes. Spread over cake. Spoon pie filling on top. Chill until serving time. **Yield:** 12-16 servings.

SERVE UP FRESH FISH IN A FLASH

WHEN cooler days signal the start of the busy pre-holiday season, you'll give thanks for unwrapping this fast-to-fix meal featuring flaky fish!

"I frequently rely on seafood recipes for quick meals," reports Marilyn Paradis of Woodburn, Oregon. "Sole in Herbed Butter is a much-asked-for meal in my family. But I don't mind making it often…it's easy to prepare and ready in just a few minutes."

Red Potato Medley is a dish Cathy Buetow Schroeder shares at family gatherings in Taylor, Texas. Now she's glad to share her recipe with you! "The fresh flavors of potatoes, onion and parsley blend well, and it's so pretty on the table."

Is your family in the mood for pumpkin pie, but you don't have time to prepare it? Linda Clapp of Stow, Ohio guarantees they'll be delighted when you dish up Pumpkin Whip.

"Even though this dessert is quick to fix, it has a creamy pumpkin taste and golden harvest look. It's perfect for both everyday dinners and special-occasion suppers."

Sole in Herbed Butter

✓ This tasty dish uses less sugar, salt and fat. Recipe includes *Diabetic Exchanges*.

    4 tablespoons butter *or*
      margarine, softened
    1 teaspoon dill weed
1/2 teaspoon onion powder
1/2 teaspoon garlic powder
1/2 teaspoon salt, optional
1/4 teaspoon white pepper
    2 pounds sole fillets
Fresh dill and lemon wedges,
    optional

In a bowl, mix butter, dill, onion powder, garlic powder, salt if desired and pepper. Transfer to a skillet; heat on medium until melted. Add the sole and saute for several minutes on each side or until it flakes easily with a fork. Garnish with dill and lemon if desired. **Yield:** 6 servings. **Diabetic Exchanges:** One serving (prepared with light margarine and without added salt) equals 4-1/2 lean meat, 1/2 fat; also, 256 calories, 303 mg sodium, 72 mg cholesterol, trace carbohydrate, 35 gm protein, 12 gm fat.

Red Potato Medley

    2 tablespoons butter *or*
      margarine
    3 cups cubed red potatoes
      (about 2-1/2 pounds)
1-1/2 cups diagonally sliced
      carrots
  3/4 cup chopped onion
  1/4 cup minced fresh parsley
    1 garlic clove, minced
  1/4 teaspoon salt
  1/4 teaspoon pepper

In a large skillet over medium heat, melt butter. Add potatoes and carrots; toss to coat. Add remaining ingredients and mix well. Reduce heat to medium-low. Cover and cook for 15-20 minutes or until vegetables are tender, stirring every 5 minutes. **Yield:** 6 servings.

Pumpkin Whip

    1 package (3.4 ounces) instant
      butterscotch pudding mix
1-1/2 cups cold milk
    1 cup canned pumpkin
    1 teaspoon pumpkin pie spice
1-1/2 cups whipped topping
Gingersnaps, optional

In a mixing bowl, beat pudding and milk until well blended, about 1-2 minutes. Blend in pumpkin and pie spice. Fold in whipped topping. Spoon into dessert dishes. Chill. Garnish with gingersnaps if desired. **Yield:** 6 servings.

SIZZLING SKILLET SUPPER IS SPEEDY

AS any country cook knows, fresh air builds hearty appetites. So after a day outdoors, fast-to-fix, nutritious meals that keep time spent in the kitchen to a minimum are treasured possessions! And thanks to three cooks, just such a meal is right at your fingertips.

Lemon Chicken is shared by Lori Schlecht of Wimbeldon, North Dakota. "I originally tried this recipe because I love rice and chicken," Lori reports. "I made a few changes to suit my tastes and was pleased with how it looks and the short time needed to prepare it.

"Your family will love the combination of tender chicken and crunchy carrots and broccoli."

Herb Bread comes from Debbie Carlson of San Diego, California. "This bread is especially nice for a no-fuss meal," remarks Debbie. "Plus it's my mom's recipe…so every time I make it, wonderful memories come back to me!"

Quick Fruit Salad is a beautiful, refreshing side dish or dessert from Sue Call of Beech Grove, Indiana. "With canned peaches and fresh bananas, strawberries and grapes, it's a great way to round out meals year-round!"

Lemon Chicken

✓ This tasty dish uses less sugar, salt and fat. Recipe includes *Diabetic Exchanges*.

- 1 **pound boneless skinless chicken breasts, cut into strips**
- 1 **medium onion, chopped**
- 1 **large carrot, thinly sliced**
- 1 **garlic clove, minced**
- 2 **tablespoons butter *or* margarine**
- 1 **tablespoon cornstarch**
- 1 **can (14-1/2 ounces) chicken broth**
- 2 to 3 **tablespoons fresh lemon juice**
- 1 **teaspoon grated lemon peel**
- 1/2 **teaspoon salt, optional**
- 1-1/2 **cups uncooked instant rice**
- 1 **cup frozen chopped broccoli, thawed**
- 1/4 **cup minced fresh parsley**

In a skillet, cook chicken, onion, carrot and garlic in butter until chicken is lightly browned, about 5 minutes. In a bowl, combine the cornstarch and broth; stir in lemon juice, peel, salt and rice. Add to skillet and bring to a boil. Reduce heat; add broccoli and parsley. Cover and simmer 5-10 minutes or until rice is tender. **Yield:** 4 servings. **Diabetic Exchanges:** One serving (prepared without added salt) equals 3 lean meat, 2 starch, 1 vegetable; also, 367 calories, 132 mg sodium, 73 mg cholesterol, 39 gm carbohydrate, 31 gm protein, 9 gm fat.

Herb Bread

- 6 **tablespoons butter *or* margarine, softened**
- 1 to 2 **garlic cloves, minced**
- 2 **teaspoons dried parsley flakes**
- 1/2 **teaspoon dried oregano**
- 1/2 **teaspoon dill weed**
- 1 **teaspoon grated Parmesan cheese**
- 1 **loaf sourdough *or* French bread, sliced**

In a bowl, combine the first six ingredients. Spread on one side of each bread slice; wrap loaf in foil. Bake at 350° for 20-25 minutes or until heated through. **Yield:** 6-8 servings.

Quick Fruit Salad

- 1 **can (21 ounces) peach pie filling**
- 3 **firm bananas, sliced**
- 2 **cups strawberries, halved**
- 1 **cup seedless grapes**

Combine all ingredients in a bowl. Refrigerate until serving. **Yield:** 6-8 servings.

MEXICAN MEAL FEATURES PRODUCE

WHEN it's summertime, there's nothing like sitting down to a hearty meal that spotlights some of the season's freshest produce—like green peppers! So why not give this mouth-watering menu a try soon?

In her Taco-Filled Peppers, Nancy McDonald of Burns, Wyoming dresses up plain green peppers for a filling main meal. "With the refreshing vegetables, hearty beef and beans and zippy seasoning, this is a tasty dish that's also easy to make. I serve them often during the summer and fall...much to my family's delight!"

With her Spanish Rice recipe, Anne Yaeger of Washington, D.C. proves that from-scratch rice can be easy to prepare and very flavorful. "You'll find it's so much better than any boxed variety of Spanish rice found in grocery stores," assures Anne.

"Cool and creamy Caramel Pie complements the slightly spicy peppers," reports Ozela Haynes of Emerson, Arkansas. "I got the recipe for this sweet, fluffy dessert from my niece. Whenever this pie is served, it goes fast! You'll find yourself making this pleasing pie even when you do have extra time."

Taco-Filled Peppers

- 1 pound ground beef
- 1 package (1-1/4 ounces) taco seasoning mix
- 1 can (0 ounces) kidney beans, rinsed and drained
- 1 cup salsa
- 4 medium green peppers
- 1 medium tomato, chopped
- 1/2 cup shredded cheddar cheese
- 1/2 cup sour cream

In a large skillet, brown the ground beef; drain. Stir in the taco seasoning, beans and salsa. Bring to a boil; reduce heat and simmer for 5 minutes. Cut peppers in half lengthwise; remove and discard seeds and stems. Immerse peppers in boiling water for 3 minutes; drain. Spoon about 1/2 cup meat mixture into each pepper half. Place in an ungreased 13-in. x 9-in. x 2-in. baking dish. Cover and bake at 350° for 15-20 minutes or until the peppers are crisp-tender and filling is heated through. Top each with tomato, cheese and a dollop of sour cream. **Yield:** 4 servings.

THE UPPER CRUST. To avoid that gritty feel of your homemade graham cracker crust, stir the sugar into the melted butter until dissolved, then add the cracker crumbs.

Spanish Rice

- 1/4 cup butter *or* margarine
- 2 cups uncooked instant rice
- 1 can (14-1/2 ounces) tomatoes with liquid, cut up
- 1 cup boiling water
- 2 beef bouillon cubes
- 1 medium onion, chopped
- 1 garlic clove, minced
- 1 bay leaf
- 1 teaspoon sugar
- 1 teaspoon salt
- 1/4 teaspoon pepper

In a saucepan over medium heat, melt butter. Add rice and stir until browned. Add remaining ingredients and bring to a boil. Reduce heat; cover and simmer 10-15 minutes or until the liquid is absorbed and rice is tender. Remove bay leaf before serving. **Yield:** 4-6 servings.

Caramel Pie

- 4 ounces cream cheese, softened
- 1/2 cup sweetened condensed milk
- 1 carton (8 ounces) frozen whipped topping, thawed
- 1 graham cracker crust (9 inches)
- 1/2 cup caramel ice cream topping
- 3/4 cup coconut, toasted
- 1/4 cup chopped pecans, toasted

In a mixing bowl, blend cream cheese and milk; fold in the whipped topping. Spread half into pie crust. Drizzle with half of the caramel topping. Combine coconut and pecans; sprinkle half over the caramel. Repeat layers. Chill or freeze until serving. **Yield:** 6-8 servings. **Editor's Note:** This is also a convenient recipe for serving a crowd. The recipe can be doubled as well as made ahead of time and stored in the freezer.

COOKING FOR ONE OR TWO

After sampling these marvelous main meals, side dishes and desserts, you'll agree good things really do come in small packages!

Orange-Glazed Chicken

(PICTURED ON THIS PAGE)

"The sweet tangy glaze dresses up chicken," says Diane Madonna of Brunswick, Ohio. *"It's a terrific main meal that will have you treating yourself like an honored guest!"*

✓ This tasty dish uses less sugar, salt and fat. Recipe includes *Diabetic Exchanges*.

  1 tablespoon all-purpose flour
1/2 teaspoon salt, optional
1/4 teaspoon pepper
  1 boneless skinless chicken breast half
  2 teaspoons vegetable oil
1/2 teaspoon orange marmalade
Dash ground nutmeg
1/2 cup orange juice

Combine flour, salt if desired and pepper; coat chicken breast. In a skillet, heat oil on medium; brown chicken. Spread marmalade on top of chicken; sprinkle with nutmeg. Add orange juice and simmer for 10-15 minutes or until the chicken juices run clear. **Yield:** 1 serving. **Diabetic Exchanges:** One serving (without added salt) equals 4 lean meat, 1 fat, 1 fruit, 1/2 starch; also, 370 calories, 71 mg sodium, 83 mg cholesterol, 23 gm carbohydrate, 31 gm protein, 17 gm fat.

Herbed Rice

(PICTURED ON THIS PAGE)

"I recently put together a special cookbook for folks who cook for themselves," informs John Davis of Mobile, Alabama. *"One of my favorite recipes in the book is this nicely seasoned rice."*

✓ This tasty dish uses less sugar, salt and fat. Recipe includes *Diabetic Exchanges*.

1/4 cup uncooked long grain rice
  1 green onion with top, cut into 1-inch pieces
  1 tablespoon butter *or* margarine
1/8 teaspoon *each* dried tarragon, thyme, basil, parsley flakes and pepper

1/2 cup chicken broth
Salt to taste, optional

In a small saucepan, cook rice and onion in butter until onion is tender. Add the seasonings; cook for 1 minute. Add broth and salt if desired; bring to a boil. Cover and simmer for 15 minutes or until liquid is absorbed and rice is tender. **Yield:** 1 serving. **Diabetic Exchanges:** One serving (prepared with margarine and low-sodium broth and without added salt) equals 2-1/2 starch, 2 fat; also, 284 calories, 129 mg sodium, 0 cholesterol, 39 gm carbohydrate, 5 gm protein, 12 gm fat.

French Peas

(PICTURED ON THIS PAGE)

"I'm always on the lookout for side dishes that I can make with nearly any main meal," says John Davis of Mobile, Alabama. *"This medley of peas, onions, and mushrooms is sure to satisfy everyone who tries it."*

✓ This tasty dish uses less sugar, salt and fat. Recipe includes *Diabetic Exchanges*.

  1 teaspoon butter *or* margarine
  2 teaspoons water
  2 medium fresh mushrooms, thinly sliced
1/2 cup frozen peas
  2 thin onion slices
Pinch salt, optional

Melt butter in a small saucepan; add all remaining ingredients. Cover and cook until the peas are tender, stirring occasionally. **Yield:** 1 serving. **Diabetic Exchanges:** One serving (prepared with margarine and without added salt) equals 1 starch, 1 fat; also, 104 calories, 104 mg sodium, 0 cholesterol, 13 gm carbohydrate, 4 gm protein, 1 gm fat.

TIMELESS TEMPTING TASTE TRIO. Fast and flavorful Orange-Glazed Chicken, Herbed Rice and French Peas (recipes on this page) make a very special supper for one any time of year.

Dan's Peppery London Broil

(PICTURED ON THIS PAGE)

At their home in San Jose, California, Dan Wright enjoys making meals for his wife, Cookie. "I became bored making the usual London broil," he says. "So I got a little creative and sparked up the flavor with red pepper flakes, garlic and Worcestershire sauce."

>   1 beef flank steak (about 3/4 pound)
>   1 garlic clove, minced
>   1/2 teaspoon seasoned salt
>   1/8 teaspoon crushed red pepper flakes
>   1/4 cup Worcestershire sauce

With a meat fork, poke holes in both sides of meat. Make a paste with garlic, seasoned salt and red pepper flakes; rub over both sides of meat. Place the steak in a resealable gallon-size plastic bag. Add Worcestershire sauce and close bag. Refrigerate for at least 4 hours, turning once. Remove meat; discard marinade. Broil or grill over hot coals until meat reaches desired doneness, 4-5 minutes per side. To serve, slice thinly across the grain. **Yield:** 2 servings.

Italian Herb Salad Dressing

(PICTURED ON THIS PAGE)

"We prefer this savory homemade Italian dressing to any other variety," Dan reports.

>   3/4 cup olive oil
>   1/2 cup red wine vinegar
>   1 tablespoon grated Parmesan *or* Romano cheese
>   1 garlic clove, minced
>   1/2 teaspoon salt
>   1/2 teaspoon sugar
>   1/2 teaspoon dried oregano
> Pinch pepper

In a jar with a tight-fitting lid, combine all ingredients; shake well. Refrigerate. Shake well again before serving over greens. **Yield:** 1-1/4 cups.

Mini White Breads

(PICTURED ON THIS PAGE)

"You'll find these mini breads are the

SMALL SERVINGS...BIG FLAVOR. Three delicious dishes—Dan's Peppery London Broil, Italian Herb Salad Dressing and Mini White Breads (recipes on this page)—make a terrific meal for two.

perfect size for just the two of you," assures Nila Towler of Baird, Texas. *"With their wonderful flavor and texture, they're sure to disappear quickly!"*

✓ This tasty dish uses less sugar, salt and fat. Recipe includes *Diabetic Exchanges*.

>   1 package (1/4 ounce) active dry yeast
>   1 tablespoon sugar
>   1/3 cup warm water (110° to 115°)
> 2-1/4 to 2-1/2 cups all-purpose flour
>   1 teaspoon salt
> 1/2 cup milk
>   2 teaspoons butter *or* margarine, melted
> Additional melted butter *or* margarine

Combine the yeast, sugar and water in a large mixing bowl. Add 1-1/2 cups of flour, salt, milk and butter. Mix for 3 minutes on medium speed. Add enough remaining flour to form a soft dough. Turn onto a floured board; knead until smooth and elastic, 6-8 minutes. Place in a greased bowl, turning once to grease top. Cover and let rise in a warm place until doubled, about 45 minutes. Punch dough down. Divide in half; shape into two loaves and place in greased 5-3/4-in. x 3-1/8-in. x 2-1/4-in. pans. Cover and let rise until doubled, about 30 minutes. Bake at 375° for 30 minutes or until golden brown. Remove from pans; cool on wire racks. Brush tops with melted butter. **Yield:** 2 mini loaves. **Diabetic Exchanges:** One 1/2-inch slice (using margarine) equals 1 starch; also, 69 calories, 135 mg sodium, 0 cholesterol, 14 gm carbohydrate, 2 gm protein, 1 gm fat.

Tomato Strip Salad

(PICTURED ON THIS PAGE)

"My mother used to make this fresh, colorful salad and set it on the table in a yellow bowl," reflects Mary Jo Amos of Noel, Missouri. *"Now I make it often for myself when running between school, work and meetings."*

✓ This tasty dish uses less sugar, salt and fat. Recipe includes *Diabetic Exchanges*.

- 1 tomato, peeled, seeded and cut into strips
- 1/4 cup fresh *or* frozen peas, parboiled
- 2 tablespoons fresh green chili strips
- 1/2 teaspoon lemon juice
- 1/2 teaspoon minced fresh cilantro *or* parsley

Lettuce leaves

In a bowl, toss tomato strips, peas, chili strips, lemon juice and cilantro or parsley. Cover and chill. Serve on a bed of lettuce. **Yield:** 1 serving. **Diabetic Exchanges:** 1 vegetable, 1/2 starch; also, 61 calories, 48 mg sodium, 0 cholesterol, 12 gm carbohydrate, 3 gm protein, 1 gm fat.

One-Serving Cheese Puff

(PICTURED ON THIS PAGE)

"This simple-to-prepare cheese puff is perfect for breakfast, lunch or dinner," assures Sharon McClatchey of Muskogee, Oklahoma.

- 1-1/2 slices white *or* whole wheat bread, buttered
- 1 egg
- 1/2 cup milk
- 1/4 cup shredded process American cheese
- 1/8 teaspoon onion salt
- 1/8 teaspoon salt

Hot pepper sauce to taste

Cut bread into strips; place with buttered sides down along the sides and on the bottom of 10-oz. custard cup. In a bowl, lightly beat the egg; add milk, cheese, onion salt, salt and hot pepper sauce. Pour into custard cup. Place on a baking sheet. Bake at 350° for 35-40 minutes or until puffy and golden brown. Serve immediately. **Yield:** 1 serving.

Zesty Ham Sandwich

"I read that in parts of Italy, pizza started out as a bread with oil, herbs, produce and meat," reports Mara McAuley from her home in Hinsdale, New York. *"That inspired me to make a modern version of that ancient classic!"*

- 1 submarine roll (6 to 7 inches)
- 2 to 3 thin slices fully cooked ham
- 3 to 4 slices mozzarella cheese
- 1 small tomato, thinly sliced
- 4 sprigs fresh parsley, chopped
- 4 fresh basil leaves, chopped *or* 1/2 teaspoon dried basil
- 1 tablespoon prepared Italian *or* Caesar salad dressing

Split roll enough to open (don't cut all the way through); place open-faced on a baking sheet. Layer remaining ingredients in order listed over roll. Bake at 350° for 10 minutes or until the cheese is melted and sandwich is warm. Fold top of roll over and serve immediately. **Yield:** 1 serving.

Cool Lime Salad

Elnora Johnson of Union City, Tennessee prepares this refreshing salad often, especially in the summer. "I've been making this for about 6 years," says Elnora. *"Since my husband is diabetic, one-portion recipes work out very well for us."*

- 1/2 cup undrained canned crushed pineapple
- 2 tablespoons lime-flavored gelatin mix
- 1/4 cup cottage cheese
- 1/4 cup whipped topping

In a small saucepan, bring pineapple to a boil. Remove from the heat and stir in the gelatin until dissolved. Cool to room temperature. Stir in cottage cheese and whipped topping. Chill until set. **Yield:** 1 serving.

DELIGHTFUL DUET of One-Serving Cheese Puff and Tomato Strip Salad (recipes on this page) is a symphony of fabulous flavor to your taste buds. Why not make this marvelous meal tonight?

Pasta with Tomatoes

(PICTURED ON THIS PAGE)

"I found this recipe in the newspaper years ago and have used it frequently ever since," asserts Earlene Ertelt of Woodburn, Oregon. "Husband Charles and I are busy on our farm and with other activities, so quick and easy dishes like this are important to me."

> 2 large tomatoes, chopped
> 2 tablespoons snipped fresh basil *or* 2 teaspoons dried basil
> 1 garlic clove, minced
> 1/2 teaspoon salt
> 1/4 teaspoon pepper
> 4 ounces bow tie pasta *or* spaghetti, cooked and drained
> Fresh basil and grated Parmesan cheese, optional

Combine the tomatoes, basil, garlic, salt and pepper. Set aside at room temperature for several hours. Serve over hot pasta. If desired, garnish with basil and sprinkle with Parmesan cheese. **Yield:** 2 servings.

Basil Buttered Beans

(PICTURED ON THIS PAGE)

Laura Porter of Sheridan, Oregon comments, "This small portioned fresh tasting side dish goes great with any meat entree. You'll love the subtle seasoned butter flavor."

> 2 cups fresh green beans, cut into 2-inch pieces
> 2 tablespoons chopped onion
> 2 tablespoons chopped celery
> 1/4 cup water
> 2 tablespoons butter *or* margarine, melted
> 1-1/2 teaspoons minced fresh basil *or* 1/2 teaspoon dried basil
> 1/4 teaspoon salt
> 1/8 teaspoon pepper

In a saucepan, combine beans, onion, celery and water. Cover and cook for 5 minutes or until beans are tender. Drain. Add the butter, basil, salt and pepper; stir to coat. Serve immediately. **Yield:** 2 servings.

Tuna Salad for Two

"We have long, hot summers here in the desert Southwest," explains Sharon Balzer of Phoenix, Arizona. "So I try to get creative with salads and come up with cool dinners for my husband, Roger, and me. We think this one is simply scrumptious!"

> 2 cups torn lettuce
> 1 package (5 ounces) corkscrew macaroni, cooked and drained
> 1 can (6-1/8 ounces) tuna, drained and flaked
> 1 medium tomato, cut into wedges
> 1 celery rib, sliced
> 1 carrot, peeled and sliced
> 1 small cucumber, sliced
> 1/4 cup green pepper strips
> 1 cup broccoli florets
> 1/2 cup julienned Provolone *or* mozzarella cheese
> DRESSING:
> 1/4 cup olive oil
> 1 tablespoon lemon juice
> 1 small garlic clove, minced
> 1-1/2 teaspoons white wine vinegar
> 3/4 teaspoon Italian seasoning
> 1/4 teaspoon salt
> 1/8 teaspoon pepper

On two salad plates, arrange the first 10 ingredients in order listed. In a jar with tight-fitting lid, combine dressing ingredients; shake well. Pour over salads and serve immediately. **Yield:** 2 servings.

PERFECT PAIR. Pasta with Tomatoes and Basil Buttered Beans (recipes on this page) feature fresh produce and ease of preparation—a winning combination any busy cook will surely enjoy!

SINGLE SERVING SUGGESTIONS

COOKING for one can be as satisfying as cooking for a group. Check out these strategies from readers:

● It's very simple to make one cup of coffee brewed without all the fuss of using the coffeepot. Just put a level tablespoon of coffee in a tea strainer, place in a cup and add boiling water. —C.M. Wegner Minneapolis, Minnesota

● For a perfect soft-boiled egg, I carefully prick an egg at each end with a pin, then gently place it in boiling water for 4 minutes. For me, this is the perfect meal.
—Sister Barbara Ann Dearborn, Michigan

● I make a puree with tomatoes and other garden vegetables. I pour it into ice cube trays and freeze, then pop the cubes out into a plastic bag to store in the freezer. I use one or two as a base for soups or stews when cooking for myself.
—Mrs. Alex Vajda, Lakewood, Ohio

WHEN THE GANG'S ALL HERE

Experienced cooks offer a host of tried-and-true recipes for when you're cooking for a crowd.

Sausage Mozzarella Supper

"I've used this casserole for many church meals, and it's always a hit," states Clara Honeyager of Mukwonago, Wisconsin. *"Everyone loves the combination of sausage, mushrooms, cheese and noodles."*

- 20 pounds link *or* bulk Italian sausage, sliced or crumbled
- 3 gallons spaghetti sauce
- 16 cups sliced fresh mushrooms
- 1-1/2 quarts tomato juice
- 3 large onions, chopped
- 3 tablespoons Italian seasoning
- 2 tablespoons salt
- 1 tablespoon pepper
- 12 pounds corkscrew noodles, cooked and drained
- 5 pounds mozzarella cheese, sliced
- 8 pounds mozzarella cheese, shredded

Brown sausage; drain fat. Mix with the spaghetti sauce, mushrooms, tomato juice, onions, Italian seasoning, salt and pepper. Grease eight 6-qt. baking pans. Layer half of the noodles, sliced cheese and meat sauce in pans. Repeat layers. Sprinkle shredded cheese equally over each pan. Cover and bake at 350° for 1 hour. Uncover and bake 15 minutes longer or until cheese is melted. **Yield:** 150-175 servings.

Ample Brown Betty

"Not only is this country-style dessert tasty, it's also a great way to use leftover bread," informs Evelyn Kennell of Roanoke, Illinois. *"No one can resist this sweet treat."*

- 2 loaves (20 ounces *each*) white bread with crusts, cut into 1-inch cubes (about 32 cups)
- 2 cups butter *or* margarine, melted
- 40 cups (about 12 pounds) sliced peeled apples

- 3 cups packed brown sugar, *divided*
- 2 cups sugar
- 2 teaspoons ground nutmeg
- 2 teaspoons ground cinnamon
- 4 cups water
- 3 tablespoons lemon juice

Toss bread cubes with butter; divide half of the cubes among four greased 13-in. x 9-in. x 2-in. baking pans. Arrange apples over bread, using 10 cups per pan. Mix 2 cups of brown sugar, sugar, nutmeg and cinnamon; divide into fourths and sprinkle over the apples. Mix water and lemon juice; pour a fourth into each pan. Top with remaining bread cubes. Sprinkle remaining brown sugar equally over pans. Cover and bake at 375° for 30 minutes. Uncover and bake 25-30 minutes longer. **Yield:** 50-60 servings.

Macaroni Salad for 100

"Whenever I make this traditional salad, hungry guests leave few leftovers!" reports Judy Dupree of Thief River Falls, Minnesota.

- 5 to 6 pounds macaroni, cooked and drained
- 5 to 6 pounds fully cooked ham, cubed
- 3 pounds shredded cheddar cheese
- 2 bags (20 ounces *each*) frozen peas, thawed
- 2 bunches celery, chopped (about 12 cups)
- 2 large onions, chopped (2 to 2-1/2 cups)
- 2 cans (5-3/4 ounces *each*) pitted ripe olives, drained and sliced

DRESSING:
- 2 quarts mayonnaise
- 1 bottle (8 ounces) Western *or* French salad dressing
- 1/4 cup vinegar
- 1/4 cup sugar
- 1 cup light cream
- 1-1/2 teaspoons onion salt
- 1-1/2 teaspoons garlic salt
- 1 teaspoon salt
- 1 teaspoon pepper

Combine first seven ingredients. Combine all dressing ingredients; pour over

the macaroni mixture and toss. Refrigerate. **Yield:** 100 servings.

Crowd Chicken Casserole

"Here's a no-fuss feast that will bring you rave reviews," says Marna Dunn of Bullhead City, Arizona. *"It's a creamy, comforting casserole that appeals to everyone."*

- 10 cups diced cooked chicken
- 10 cups chopped celery
- 2 bunches green onions with tops, sliced
- 2 cans (4 ounces *each*) chopped green chilies
- 1 can (5-3/4 ounces) pitted ripe olives, drained and sliced
- 2 cups slivered almonds
- 5 cups (20 ounces) shredded cheddar cheese, *divided*
- 2 cups mayonnaise
- 2 cups (16 ounces) sour cream
- 5 cups crushed potato chips

Combine the first six ingredients. Add 2 cups cheese. Mix mayonnaise and sour cream; add to chicken mixture and toss. Spoon into two greased 13-in. x 9-in. x 2-in. baking dishes. Sprinkle with chips. Top with remaining cheese. Bake, uncovered, at 350° for 20-25 minutes or until hot. **Yield:** 24 servings.

Hawaiian Baked Beans

"I made these festive, one-of-a-kind baked beans for my daughter's wedding reception," informs Charlene Laper of Lakeview, Michigan. *"The guests really enjoyed the sweet-and-sour flavor."*

- 4 jars (48 ounces *each*) great northern beans, rinsed and drained
- 4 cups chopped onion
- 1 bag (2 pounds) dark brown sugar
- 2 pounds fully cooked ham, cubed
- 1 bottle (28 ounces) ketchup
- 1 can (20 ounces) crushed pineapple, drained

1/2 cup prepared mustard
1/3 cup vinegar

Combine all ingredients; mix well. Divide among four greased 13-in. x 9-in. x 2-in. baking pans. Cover tightly; bake at 350° for 1-1/2 hours. Uncover and bake 20-30 minutes more. **Yield:** 80-100 servings.

Honey Mustard Dressing

"It's nice to offer people a simple green salad at gatherings," asserts Judy Roehrman of Phoenix, Arizona. "And this tangy dressing adds just the right amount of zip."

> 2 quarts mayonnaise
> 4 cups (32 ounces) sour cream
> 12 ounces honey
> 12 ounces Dijon mustard
> 6 tablespoons mustard seed
Salad greens

Combine the mayonnaise, sour cream, honey, mustard and mustard seed until smooth. Serve over salad greens. **Yield:** 100 servings (about 4 quarts).

Party Punch

"Here's a traditional fruity punch I've come to rely on when serving crowds," declares Donna Long of Searcy, Arkansas. "It's a refreshing beverage with tropical flair."

> 3 cups warm water
> 2 cups sugar
> 3 ripe bananas, sliced
> 1 can (46 ounces) pineapple juice
> 1-1/2 cups orange juice
> 1/4 cup lemon juice
> 3 quarts ginger ale, chilled

In a blender or food processor, blend the water, sugar and bananas until smooth. Pour into a large container. Add pineapple juice, orange juice and lemon juice; mix well. Freeze, stirring occasionally, until slushy. Add ginger ale when ready to serve. **Yield:** about 24 servings.

Barbecued Beef Sandwiches

"These 'Big Sky Country' barbecued sandwiches are one of my specialties. They really capture the flavor of hearty foods we serve here in Billings, Montana," remarks Lorraine Elvbakken.

> 2 beef briskets, trimmed (about 12 pounds)
> 6 cups barbecue sauce

2 cups water
40 to 50 hamburger buns

Place briskets in a large roasting pan. Combine barbecue sauce and water; pour over meat. Cover tightly and bake at 325° for 4 to 4-1/2 hours or until fork-tender. Remove meat from juices; cool. Skim fat from juices. Thinly slice meat; return to pan and heat in juices. Serve on buns. **Yield:** 40-50 servings.

Meat Loaf for 120

Joanne Shew Chuk of St. Benedict, Saskatchewan shares this terrific recipe for meat loaf. "A friend of mine gave me the recipe, which was a favorite at 4-H camp."

> 40 pounds ground beef
> 16 eggs, lightly beaten
> 8 cups old-fashioned oats
> 5 cups tomato juice
> 3 large onions, chopped
> 1/3 cup salt
> 2 tablespoons pepper
SAUCE:
> 3 cups water
> 1-1/2 cups ketchup
> 6 tablespoons vinegar
> 2 tablespoons prepared mustard
> 2 tablespoons brown sugar

Combine beef, eggs, oats, tomato juice, onions, salt and pepper. Form into 16 loaves. Place in 9-in. x 5-in. x 3-in. loaf pans. Combine sauce ingredients; pour 3 tablespoons over each loaf. Bake at 350° for 1-1/2 to 2 hours or until no pink remains, basting once with remaining sauce. **Yield:** 120 servings.

Spicy Chicken Wings

"These finger-licking-good wings always disappear quickly," shares Gay Avery of Massena, New York. "The tangy sauce clings very well to the chicken."

> 8 bags (4 pounds *each*) frozen chicken wings
> 8 cups soy sauce
> 1/2 cup to 2 cups hot pepper sauce
> 2 cups water
> 2 cups vegetable oil
> 3/4 cup cornstarch
> 8 teaspoons ground ginger
> 4 teaspoons minced garlic

Place the frozen wings on baking sheets that have been sprayed with nonstick cooking spray. Bake at 375° for 50-60 minutes. Meanwhile, combine the remaining ingredients in a saucepan; bring to a boil, stirring occasionally. Boil for 2

minutes or until thickened. Drain wings; transfer to large roasting pans. Cover with sauce. Bake, uncovered, for 60-70 minutes, stirring occasionally. **Yield:** about 240 appetizers.

Turkey Salad for 50

"With its relatively short list of ingredients and ease of preparation, this is one salad I frequently volunteer to bring to functions," comments Helen Lord-Burr of Oshkosh, Wisconsin.

> 18 cups diced cooked turkey (about one 14-pound turkey)
> 8 cups thinly sliced celery
> 8 cups seedless grapes
> 18 hard-cooked eggs, diced
> 2 cups slivered almonds, toasted
DRESSING:
> 1 quart salad dressing *or* mayonnaise
> 1 pint (16 ounces) heavy cream, whipped
> 1/4 cup lemon juice
> 1/4 cup sugar
> 1 teaspoon salt
> 1/2 teaspoon pepper

In one large bowl or several smaller bowls, combine turkey, celery, grapes, eggs and almonds. Combine dressing ingredients; mix until smooth. Pour over salad and stir gently. Chill until serving. **Yield:** 50 servings.

Big Batch Cookies

"It takes some time to prepare all these delicious cookies, but after one taste, you'll agree it was worth it!" admits Diana Dube of Rockland, Maine.

> 1 pound (2 cups) butter *or* margarine, softened
> 1-1/2 cups sugar
> 1-1/2 cups packed brown sugar
> 4 eggs, lightly beaten
> 1 tablespoon vanilla extract
> 5 cups all-purpose flour
> 1 tablespoon baking soda
> 1 teaspoon salt
> 1 pound (3-3/4 cups) chopped walnuts
> 2 bags (10 ounces *each*) peanut butter-flavored chips

In a large mixing bowl, cream butter and sugars. Add eggs and vanilla; mix well. Combine flour, baking soda and salt; add to creamed mixture and mix well. Fold in the nuts and chips. Drop by rounded teaspoonfuls onto ungreased baking sheets. Bake at 350° for 10-12 minutes or until lightly browned. **Yield:** 12 dozen.

LOVE THOSE SNACKS!

When your family gets hungry at mid-afternoon or midnight, reach for these hearty appetizers and refreshing beverages.

Homemade Orange Refresher

(PICTURED ON THIS PAGE)

"Family and friends will thank you for serving this cool, tangy orange drink on warm evenings," assures Iola Egle of McCook, Nebraska.

> 1 can (6 ounces) frozen orange juice concentrate, thawed
> 1/3 cup sugar
> 1/3 cup nonfat dry milk powder
> 2 teaspoons vanilla extract
> 3/4 cup cold water
> 10 to 12 ice cubes
> **Orange slices and mint, optional**
> **Sugar and orange juice, optional**

Combine the first five ingredients in a blender container and process at high speed. Add ice cubes, a few at a time, blending until slushy. Garnish with orange slices and mint if desired. Serve immediately. **Yield:** 4 servings. **Editor's Note:** For a fancy glass edge, invert glass and dip into orange juice and then sugar; let dry 1 hour before filling glass.

Mini Hamburgers

(PICTURED ON THIS PAGE)

Reports Judy Lewis of Sterling Heights, Michigan, "I guarantee these will be the first snack cleared from your table."

> 1/2 cup chopped onion
> 1 tablespoon butter *or* margarine
> 1 pound lean ground beef *or* ground round
> 1 egg, beaten
> 1/4 teaspoon seasoned salt
> 1/4 teaspoon ground sage
> 1/4 teaspoon salt
> 1/8 teaspoon pepper
> 40 mini rolls, split

> 8 ounces process American cheese slices, cut into 1-1/2-inch squares, optional
> 40 dill pickle slices, optional

In a skillet, saute onion in butter. Transfer to a bowl; add meat, egg and seasonings. Spread over bottom halves of the rolls; replace tops. Place on baking sheets; cover with foil. Bake at 350° for 20 minutes. If desired, place a cheese square and pickle on each hamburger; replace tops and foil and return to the oven for 5 minutes. **Yield:** 40 appetizers.

Tater-Dipped Veggies

(PICTURED ON THIS PAGE)

"With this great recipe, you get the crispiness of deep-fried vegetables without the mess and fuss," shares Earleen Lillegard of Prescott, Arizona.

> 1 cup instant potato flakes
> 1/3 cup grated Parmesan cheese
> 1/2 teaspoon celery salt
> 1/4 teaspoon garlic powder
> 1/4 cup butter *or* margarine, melted and cooled
> 2 eggs
> 4 to 5 cups raw bite-size vegetables (mushrooms, peppers, broccoli, cauliflower, zucchini *and/or* parboiled carrots)
> **Prepared ranch salad dressing *or* dip, optional**

In a small bowl, combine potato flakes, Parmesan cheese, celery salt, garlic powder and butter. In another bowl, beat eggs. Dip vegetables, one at a time, into egg, then into potato mixture, coating well. Place on an ungreased baking sheet. Bake at 400° for 20-25 minutes. Serve with dressing or dip if desired. **Yield:** 6-8 servings.

SUPER SNACK APPEAL. Homemade Orange Refresher, Mini Hamburgers and Tater-Dipped Veggies (all recipes on this page) are pleasingly perfect foods any time of day or year!

Parmesan-Garlic Popcorn

(PICTURED ON THIS PAGE)

"This is my husband's favorite late-night snack," reveals Sharon Skildum of Maple Grove, Minnesota. "He can gobble the entire bowlful."

2-1/2 quarts popped popcorn, buttered
1/4 cup grated Parmesan cheese
1 teaspoon garlic powder
1 teaspoon dried parsley flakes
1/2 teaspoon dill weed

Place popcorn in a large bowl. In a small bowl, combine Parmesan cheese, garlic powder, parsley and dill; sprinkle over popcorn and toss lightly. Serve immediately. **Yield:** 2-1/2 quarts.

Caramel Corn

(PICTURED ON THIS PAGE)

"For years, I've taken this snack to our church retreat," says Nancy Breen of Canastota, New York. "I take it in two containers—one for each night—so it doesn't all disappear the first night. Other church members tell us that if we can't attend, we should just send the caramel corn."

12 quarts plain popped popcorn
1 pound peanuts
2 cups butter *or* margarine
2 pounds brown sugar
1/2 cup dark corn syrup
1/2 cup molasses

Place popcorn in two large bowls. Mix 1/2 pound nuts into each bowl. In a 5-qt. saucepan, combine remaining ingredients. Bring to a boil over medium heat; boil and stir for 5 minutes. Pour half of syrup over each bowl of popcorn and stir to coat. Turn coated popcorn into a large roasting pan. Bake at 250° for 1 hour. Remove from the oven and break apart while warm. Cool. Store in airtight containers. **Yield:** 12 quarts.

Candied Popcorn

(PICTURED ON THIS PAGE)

"I got this family-favorite recipe in the 1950's," remarks Victoria Walzer of Lakeport, California. "It makes a big chewy batch that you can't stop eating until it's gone!"

6 quarts plain popped popcorn

GET YOUR EVENINGS POPPING with surefire treats like (clockwise from bottom) Parmesan-Garlic Popcorn, Caramel Corn and Candied Popcorn (all recipes on this page).

3/4 cup light corn syrup
1/4 cup butter *or* margarine
2 tablespoons water
4 cups (1 pound) confectioners' sugar
1 cup miniature marshmallows

Place popcorn in a large roasting pan. In a 3-qt. saucepan, combine remaining ingredients; cook and stir over low heat just until mixture comes to a boil. Pour over popcorn and toss to coat. Cool. Store in an airtight container. **Yield:** 6 quarts.

Cheese Popcorn

"This great snack reminds me of my high school days," comments Denise Baumert of Jameson, Missouri. "My sisters and girlfriends and I would stay up late, listen to music, talk and munch this crunchy treat."

4 quarts plain popped popcorn
1/4 cup butter *or* margarine, melted
1/2 teaspoon garlic salt
1/2 teaspoon onion salt
2 cups (8 ounces) shredded cheddar cheese

Place popcorn in two 13-in. x 9-in. x 2-in. baking pans. Drizzle with melted butter. Combine garlic salt and onion salt; sprinkle over popcorn. Top with cheese. Bake at 300° for 5-10 minutes. Serve immediately. **Yield:** 4 quarts.

Sweet and Spicy Popcorn

"This crisp snack has a fun and different flavor," shares Flo Burnett of Gage, Oklahoma. "I took some to my neighbor's one evening when we were visiting and it didn't last long!"

1 tablespoon sugar
1 teaspoon chili powder
1/2 teaspoon ground cinnamon
1/4 teaspoon salt
Dash cayenne pepper
6 cups plain popped popcorn

Place sugar, chili powder, cinnamon, salt and cayenne pepper in a zip-type plastic bag or other 2-qt. airtight container. Mix. Add popcorn. Spray popcorn with nonstick cooking spray. Close bag and shake. Repeat one or two times until popcorn is coated. **Yield:** 6 cups.

Snack Crackers

(PICTURED ON THIS PAGE)

Says Sue Manel of Milladore, Wisconsin, "Our daughter loves to make this crunchy snack. Her four older brothers finish off a batch in no time."

- **3/4 cup vegetable oil**
- **1-1/2 teaspoons dill weed**
- **1 envelope (1 ounce) dry ranch salad dressing mix**
- **2 packages (10 ounces *each*) oyster crackers**

Combine oil, dill and salad dressing mix. Place the crackers in a large bowl; pour dressing mixture over and toss gently. Allow to stand at least 1 hour before serving. **Yield:** 12 cups.

Tomato Cheese Melt

(PICTURED ON THIS PAGE)

"I love this as a late-night snack, but it also goes great with a bowl of soup at lunch," assures Suzanne Winters of Middletown, Delaware. "The cayenne pepper gives it just a bit of zip. It tastes and looks great."

- **1 onion bagel *or* English muffin, split**
- **1/4 cup shredded cheddar cheese**
- **1/8 teaspoon cayenne pepper**
- **2 tomato slices**
- **1 tablespoon shredded Parmesan cheese**

On each bagel or muffin half, sprinkle half of the cheddar cheese and cayenne pepper. Top with a tomato slice. Sprinkle half of the Parmesan cheese over each tomato. Broil 6 in. from the heat for 4-5 minutes or until cheese is bubbly. **Yield:** 2 servings.

Quick Guacamole

(PICTURED ON PAGE 81)

"This delicious dip is extremely easy to make and always hits the spot when we have a craving for something to munch on," assures Linda Fox of Soldotna, Alaska.

- **1 ripe avocado**
- **1/2 cup small curd cottage cheese**
- **1/3 cup hot picante sauce *or* salsa**
- **1/2 teaspoon minced seeded jalapeno pepper, optional**

Tortilla chips *or* raw vegetables

In a bowl, mash the avocado. Stir in cottage cheese and picante sauce. Add jalapeno if desired. Serve with chips or vegetables. **Yield:** about 1-1/2 cups.

Sausage Cheese Bites

"These little bites are a tasty snack to serve for a get-together," reports Nancy Reichert of Thomasville, Georgia. "They also make a nice breakfast treat with a thermos of hot coffee if you're on your way early in the morning."

- **1 pound mild pork sausage**
- **4 cups buttermilk biscuit mix**
- **2 cups (8 ounces) shredded cheddar cheese**
- **1 cup water**

In a skillet, cook and crumble sausage. Drain. In a large bowl, combine biscuit mix and cheese. Add the sausage and stir until well blended. Stir in water just until mixed. Shape into 1-1/2-in. balls. Place on greased baking sheets. Bake at 375° for about 15 minutes or until golden. Baked bites may be frozen; reheat at 375° for 6-8 minutes. **Yield:** 4 dozen.

Sugar-Free Holiday Nog

"Coming up with holiday beverages that everyone is able to enjoy can be a real challenge," explains Nancy Schickling of Bedford, Virginia. "This nog is so refreshing you'll be tempted to make it throughout the year."

✓ This tasty dish uses less sugar, salt and fat.
Recipe includes *Diabetic Exchanges*.

- **1 package (.9 ounce) sugar-free instant vanilla pudding mix**
- **7 cups skim milk, *divided***
- **1 to 2 teaspoons vanilla extract *or* rum flavoring**
- **2 to 4 packets sugar substitute**
- **1 cup evaporated skim milk**

Combine pudding mix, 2 cups of milk, vanilla and sugar substitute in a bowl; mix according to pudding directions. Pour into a half-gallon container with a tight-fitting lid. Add 3 cups milk; shake well. Add evaporated milk and shake. Add remaining milk; shake well. Chill. **Yield:** 8 servings. **Diabetic Exchanges:** One serving equals 1 skim milk, 1/4 starch; also, 107 calories, 187 mg sodium, 1 mg cholesterol, 15 gm carbohydrate, 10 gm protein, 1 gm fat.

QUICK-AND-EASY TREATS like Snack Crackers, Tomato Cheese Melt (recipes on this page) and Seven-Minute Pudding (recipe on page 105) appeal to the kid in all of us.

Savory Rye Snacks

(PICTURED ON THIS PAGE)

"I make the flavorful spread ahead of time and refrigerate it," reports Connie Simon, Reed City, Michigan. *"Then all I have to do to have a quick snack is put it on the rye bread and bake."*

- 1 cup sliced green onions
- 1 cup mayonnaise
- 1 cup (4 ounces) shredded Monterey Jack cheese
- 1 cup (4 ounces) shredded cheddar cheese
- 1 can (4 ounces) mushroom stems and pieces, drained
- 1/2 cup chopped ripe olives
- 1/2 cup chopped stuffed green olives
- 1 loaf (1 pound) cocktail rye bread

In a bowl, combine the first seven ingredients. Spread on bread slices and place on ungreased baking sheets. Bake at 350° for 8-10 minutes or until bubbly. **Yield:** about 4 dozen.

Cheese Crisps

(PICTURED ON THIS PAGE)

"The surprising crunch of these fun snacks makes them great for parties or anytime of day," assures Janelle Lee of Sulphur, Louisiana, who shares this simple recipe.

- 1 cup butter *or* margarine, softened
- 2 cups all-purpose flour
- 1/2 teaspoon salt
- 1/4 teaspoon cayenne pepper
- 2 cups (8 ounces) shredded sharp cheddar cheese
- 3 cups crisp rice cereal

In a mixing bowl, cream the butter until fluffy. Slowly mix in the flour, salt and cayenne pepper. Stir in cheese and cereal. Shape into 1-1/2-in. balls and place on ungreased baking sheets. Bake at 350° for 15-17 minutes or until lightly browned. Serve warm or cold. **Yield:** 3 dozen.

Broccoli Dip

"With its creamy cheese and broccoli flavor, I always choose this nicely seasoned dip for parties," comments Bertha Johnson of Indianapolis, Indiana.

- 1 small onion, chopped
- 3/4 cup finely chopped celery

BRING A CONTENTED CLOSE to your hectic days with scrumptious snacks like Apricot Bars (recipe on page 94), Savory Rye Snacks and Cheese Crisps (recipes on this page).

- 1 tablespoon butter *or* margarine
- 1 package (10 ounces) frozen chopped broccoli, cooked and drained
- 1 carton (8 ounces) garlic process cheese spread
- 1 can (10-3/4 ounces) condensed cream of mushroom soup, undiluted
- Dash *each* hot pepper sauce, cayenne pepper, paprika and Worcestershire sauce
- Corn chips *or* raw vegetables

In saucepan, saute onion and celery in butter until tender. Chop broccoli in small pieces. Add to onion mixture with cheese spread, soup and seasonings. Cook and stir over low heat until cheese is melted. Serve warm with corn chips or vegetables. **Yield:** 12-16 servings (4 cups).

Italian Stuffed Mushrooms

"Throughout the year, I use this delicious recipe I got from my brother. These appetizers look lovely and really curb the hunger of guests waiting for a meal," writes Virginia Slater of West Sunbury, Pennsylvania.

- 4 bacon strips, diced
- 24 to 30 large fresh mushrooms
- 1/4 pound ground fully cooked ham
- 2 tablespoons minced fresh parsley
- 1/4 cup grated Parmesan cheese
- 1 cup onion and garlic salad croutons, crushed
- 1 cup (4 ounces) shredded mozzarella cheese
- 1 medium tomato, finely chopped
- 1-1/2 teaspoons minced fresh oregano *or* 1/2 teaspoon dried oregano

In a skillet, cook the bacon until crisp. Meanwhile, remove mushroom stems from caps; set caps aside. Mince half the stems and discard the rest. Add minced stems to bacon and drippings, saute for 2-3 minutes. Remove from the heat and stir in remaining ingredients. Firmly stuff into mushroom caps. Place in a greased jelly roll pan. Bake at 425° for 12-15 minutes or until the mushrooms are tender. **Yield:** 2-1/2 to 3 dozen.

POTLUCK PLEASERS

Bring special flair to your buffet table with this appealing
assortment of snacks, side dishes, main meals, desserts and more.

Fourth of July Bean Casserole

(PICTURED ON THIS PAGE)

Donna Fancher of Indianapolis, Indiana comments, "The outstanding barbecue taste of these beans makes them a favorite all year long. It's a popular dish with everyone—even kids."

- 1/2 pound sliced bacon, diced
- 1/2 pound ground beef
- 1 cup chopped onion
- 1 can (28 ounces) pork and beans
- 1 can (17 ounces) lima beans, rinsed and drained
- 1 can (15 to 16 ounces) kidney beans, rinsed and drained
- 1/2 cup barbecue sauce
- 1/2 cup ketchup
- 1/2 cup sugar
- 1/2 cup packed brown sugar
- 2 tablespoons prepared mustard
- 2 tablespoons molasses
- 1 teaspoon salt
- 1/2 teaspoon chili powder

In a large skillet, cook bacon, beef and onion until meat is browned and onion is tender; drain. Transfer to a greased 2-1/2-qt. baking dish; add all of the beans and mix well. In a small bowl, combine the remaining ingredients; stir into beef and bean mixture. Cover and bake at 350° for 45 minutes. Uncover; bake 15 minutes longer. **Yield:** 12 servings.

Onion Cheese Ball

(PICTURED ON THIS PAGE)

"This hearty cheese ball is as wonderful to eat as it is beautiful to serve. A delicious combination of cheeses makes it a real crowd-pleaser, and it's so quick and easy to make—perfect for open houses, wedding receptions and holiday gatherings," shares Anna Mayer of Fort Branch, Indiana.

- 2 cups (8 ounces) shredded cheddar cheese, room temperature
- 3 to 4 ounces Roquefort cheese, room temperature

- 4 packages (3 ounces *each*) cream cheese, softened
- 3 tablespoons dried minced onion
- 1 tablespoon Worcestershire sauce
- 1 cup minced fresh parsley

Crackers

In a mixing bowl, beat cheeses, onion and Worcestershire sauce until well mixed. Shape into a ball and roll in parsley. Chill. Serve with crackers. **Yield:** 1 cheese ball (4 inches).

Picnic Coleslaw

(PICTURED ON THIS PAGE)

Karen Page of St. Louis, Missouri declares, "I usually prepare this distinctive, colorful coleslaw for picnics, block parties and potlucks. No matter where I take this tasty dish, people are always asking for the recipe, so I have copies written out in advance. The bacon adds rich flavor to the fresh crisp carrots and cabbage. Plus, it travels well."

- 6 cups shredded cabbage
- 2 cups shredded carrots
- 8 bacon strips, cooked and crumbled
- 12 green onions with tops, thinly sliced
- 1/2 cup cider vinegar
- 1/3 cup vegetable oil
- 1/3 cup sugar
- 1 teaspoon salt

In a bowl, combine cabbage, carrots, bacon and onions. In a jar with tight-fitting lid, mix vinegar, oil, sugar and salt; shake well. Just before serving, pour dressing over cabbage mixture and toss. **Yield:** 12-16 servings.

ADD SOME FIREWORKS to your next picnic or potluck. Just serve this colorful display of Fourth of July Bean Casserole, Onion Cheese Ball and Picnic Coleslaw (all recipes on this page).

Chicken Spinach Bake

(PICTURED ON THIS PAGE)

Sue Braunschweig, Delafield, Wisconsin, writes, "A good friend shared this recipe with me years ago, and I've used it often. With the creamy sauce and lovely look of this dish, even people who aren't very fond of spinach seem to enjoy it served this way."

- 3 packages (10 ounces *each*) frozen chopped spinach, thawed
- 3 eggs
- 1/2 teaspoon onion salt
- 1/2 teaspoon ground nutmeg
- 3/4 cup grated Parmesan cheese, *divided*
- 3/4 cup Italian-seasoned bread crumbs
- 16 boneless skinless chicken breast halves

Salt and pepper to taste
- 5 tablespoons butter *or* margarine, melted

CHEESE SAUCE:
- 6 tablespoons butter *or* margarine, *divided*
- 1/4 cup all-purpose flour
- 1/2 teaspoon salt
- 2 cups milk
- 2 cups (8 ounces) shredded cheddar cheese
- 1 cup sliced fresh mushrooms

Drain and squeeze out excess moisture from spinach. Beat eggs, onion salt and nutmeg. Add spinach and 1/4 cup Parmesan cheese; mix well. Combine the bread crumbs and remaining Parmesan. Sprinkle chicken with salt and pepper; coat with crumb mixture. Place in two greased 13-in. x 9-in. x 2-in. baking pans. Spread 2 tablespoons of spinach mixture onto each breast. Sprinkle with remaining crumb mixture; drizzle with butter. Bake at 350° for 35-40 minutes or until chicken juices run clear. For sauce, melt 4 tablespoons butter; blend in flour and salt. Stir to form a smooth paste. Add milk; cook and stir until thickened and bubbly. Add cheese and stir until melted. Saute mushrooms in remaining butter. Stir into the cheese mixture. Carefully pour sauce over chicken, or pour into a serving bowl and pass. **Yield:** 16 servings.

Barbecued Bean Salad

(PICTURED ON THIS PAGE)

"This tangy hearty salad is a refreshing dish to serve with any main meal," re-

ports Linda Ault of Newberry, Indiana. *"Mild spices blend nicely with the beans and garden ingredients. Be prepared to bring home an empty bowl."*

- 1 package (16 ounces) dry pinto beans, rinsed
- 1 medium onion, chopped
- 1 medium green pepper, diced
- 1 medium sweet red pepper, diced
- 1 can (17 ounces) whole kernel corn, drained

DRESSING:
- 1/4 cup ketchup
- 1/4 cup cider vinegar
- 1/4 cup olive oil
- 3 tablespoons brown sugar
- 1 tablespoon Worcestershire sauce
- 1 tablespoon chili powder
- 5 teaspoons Dijon mustard
- 1 teaspoon ground cumin
- 1 teaspoon salt
- 1/4 teaspoon pepper

In a large kettle, cover beans with water; bring to a boil. Boil for 2 minutes. Remove from the heat and let stand 1 hour. Drain and rinse beans; return to the kettle. Cover with water again and bring to a boil. Reduce heat; cover and simmer for 1-1/2 hours or until beans are tender. Drain and rinse beans; place in a large bowl and cool to room temperature. Add the onion, peppers and corn; toss. In a saucepan, combine all dressing ingredients; simmer

NEED WINNING RECIPES FOR PARTIES? You're in luck—potluck, that is—with Chicken Spinach Bake, Barbecued Bean Salad and Tangy Tomato Slices (all recipes on this page).

for 10 minutes. Pour over vegetables and mix well. Cover and chill. **Yield:** 16-20 servings.

Tangy Tomato Slices

(PICTURED ON THIS PAGE)

"Fresh garden tomatoes are a treat at a picnic or family gathering. The zesty flavor of this dish is a crowd-pleaser, and it's a colorful addition to the buffet. I'm grateful to the friend who gave me the recipe," says Lois Fetting of Nelson, Wisconsin.

- 1 cup vegetable oil
- 1/3 cup vinegar
- 1/4 cup minced fresh parsley
- 3 tablespoons minced fresh basil *or* 1 tablespoon dried basil
- 1 tablespoon sugar
- 1 teaspoon salt
- 1/2 teaspoon pepper
- 1/2 teaspoon dry mustard
- 1/2 teaspoon garlic powder
- 1 medium sweet onion, thinly sliced
- 6 large tomatoes, thinly sliced

In a small bowl or a jar with a tight-fitting lid, mix the first nine ingredients. Layer onion and tomatoes in a shallow glass dish. Pour the marinade over; cover and refrigerate for several hours. **Yield:** 12 servings.

Caramel Apple Cake

(PICTURED ON THIS PAGE)

Marilyn Paradis of Woodburn, Oregon relates, "When I go to potlucks, family gatherings or on hunting and fishing trips with my husband and son, this cake is one of my favorite desserts to bring. It stays moist as long as it lasts, which isn't long!"

 1-1/2 cups vegetable oil
 1-1/2 cups sugar
   1/2 cup packed brown sugar
     3 eggs
     3 cups all-purpose flour
     2 teaspoons ground cinnamon
   1/2 teaspoon ground nutmeg
     1 teaspoon baking soda
   1/2 teaspoon salt
 3-1/2 cups diced peeled apples
     1 cup chopped walnuts
     2 teaspoons vanilla extract
CARAMEL ICING:
   1/2 cup packed brown sugar
   1/3 cup light cream
   1/4 cup butter *or* margarine
Dash salt
     1 cup confectioners' sugar
Chopped walnuts, optional

In a mixing bowl, combine oil and sugars. Add eggs, one at a time, beating well after each addition. Combine dry ingredients; add to batter and stir well. Fold in the apples, walnuts and vanilla. Pour into a greased and floured 10-in. tube pan. Bake at 325° for 1-1/2 hours or until cake tests done. Cool in pan 10 minutes; remove to a wire rack to cool completely. In the top of a double boiler over simmering water, heat brown sugar, cream, butter and salt until sugar is dissolved. Cool to room temperature. Beat in the confectioners' sugar until smooth; drizzle over cake. Sprinkle with nuts if desired. **Yield:** 12-16 servings.

Cranberry Conserve

(PICTURED ON THIS PAGE)

"I still remember my grandmother from Germany making this lovely, delicious conserve for the holidays. She'd often give a jar to family members and friends as a gift. It tastes great served as a relish alongside meat or even spread on biscuits," writes Mildred Marsh Banker of Austin, Texas.

     4 cups fresh *or* frozen
       cranberries, halved
     1 tablespoon grated orange
       peel

     2 oranges, peeled, sliced and
       quartered
     1 cup raisins
 1-1/4 cups water
     1 cup chopped pecans
 2-1/2 cups sugar

In a large saucepan, combine cranberries, orange peel, oranges, raisins and water. Cover and simmer over medium heat until cranberries are soft. Add pecans and sugar; stir well. Simmer, uncovered, 10-15 minutes, stirring often. Cool. Spoon into covered containers. Refrigerate. Serve as a relish with poultry or pork, or spread on biscuits or rolls. **Yield:** 3 pints.

Turkey with Sausage Stuffing

(PICTURED ON THIS PAGE)

Aura Lee Johnson of Vermilion, Ohio shares, "Here's a super way to savor roast turkey and stuffing without having to cook the entire bird. The stuffing is hearty, and the meat is always juicy and tender."

     1 whole bone-in turkey breast
       (5 to 7 pounds)
   1/4 cup butter *or* margarine,
       melted
     2 packages (12 ounces *each*)
       bulk pork sausage
     2 cups sliced celery
     2 medium onions, chopped
     4 cups dry bread cubes
     2 cups pecan halves
     1 cup raisins
   2/3 cup chicken broth
     2 eggs, beaten
     1 teaspoon salt
   1/2 teaspoon rubbed sage
   1/4 teaspoon pepper

Rinse turkey breast and pat dry. Place with breast side up in a shallow baking dish. Brush with butter. Bake, uncovered, at 325° for 2 to 2-1/2 hours or until the internal temperature reaches 170°. Cover loosely with foil to prevent excess browning if necessary. Meanwhile, in a skillet, cook sausage, celery and onions until the sausage is browned and vegetables are tender; drain. Remove from the heat; add all remaining ingredients and mix well. Spoon into a greased 3-qt. casserole. Cover and bake at 325° for 1 hour. Serve with sliced turkey. **Yield:** 15-20 servings.

A HARVEST OF HELPINGS. Don't wait for the holidays to serve Caramel Apple Cake, Cranberry Conserve and Turkey with Sausage Stuffing (recipes on this page). They make meals special.

Sweet Peanut Treats

(PICTURED ON THIS PAGE)

"We sold tempting bars almost like these at the refreshment stand at a Minnesota state park where I worked in the '70's, and they were a favorite of employees and visitors alike. Now I make this recipe when I want to serve a special treat," says Phyllis Smith of Olympia, Washington.

- 2 cups (12 ounces) semisweet chocolate chips
- 2 cups (12 ounces) butterscotch chips
- 1 jar (18 ounces) creamy peanut butter
- 1 cup butter *or* margarine
- 1 can (5 ounces) evaporated milk
- 1/4 cup vanilla cook and serve pudding mix
- 1 bag (2 pounds) confectioners' sugar
- 1 pound salted peanuts

In the top of a double boiler over simmering water, melt chocolate chips, butterscotch chips and peanut butter; stir until smooth. Spread half into a greased 15-in. x 10-in. x 1-in. baking pan. Chill until firm. Meanwhile, in a saucepan, bring butter, milk and pudding mix to a boil. Cook and stir for 2 minutes. Remove from the heat; add confectioners' sugar and beat until smooth. Spread over chocolate mixture in pan. Stir the peanuts into remaining chocolate mixture; mix well. Carefully spread over pudding layer. Refrigerate. Cut into 1-in. squares. **Yield:** 10 dozen.

SWEET SENSATION. Sweet Peanut Treats (recipe on this page) are tempting snacks.

Tropical Carrot Cake

Victoria Teeter-Casey of Enterprise, Oregon shares this moist classic cake, which gets its tropical flair from pineapple. "My great-aunt gave me this recipe, and I always make it for our annual family reunion."

- 3 eggs
- 3/4 cup vegetable oil
- 3/4 cup buttermilk
- 2 cups all-purpose flour
- 2 cups sugar
- 2 teaspoons baking soda
- 2 teaspoons ground cinnamon
- 1/2 teaspoon salt
- 2 teaspoons vanilla extract
- 2 cups finely shredded carrots
- 1 cup raisins
- 1 can (8 ounces) crushed pineapple, undrained
- 1 cup chopped walnuts
- 1 cup flaked coconut

FROSTING:
- 1 package (8 ounces) cream cheese, softened
- 4 to 4-1/2 cups confectioners' sugar
- 1 to 2 tablespoons heavy cream
- 1 teaspoon vanilla extract

In a large mixing bowl, beat eggs, oil and buttermilk. Combine flour, sugar, baking soda, cinnamon and salt; add to egg mixture and mix well. Stir in vanilla, carrots, raisins, pineapple, walnuts and coconut; mix well. Pour into a greased 13-in. x 9-in. x 2-in. baking pan. Bake at 350° for 45-50 minutes or until cake tests done. Cool. For frosting, beat all ingredients in a mixing bowl until smooth. Frost cake. **Yield:** 12-16 servings.

Date Nut Log

"My mother served this dessert one year after a big holiday meal, and we all thought it was delicious," recalls Carla Hodenfield, Mandan, North Dakota.

- 40 graham cracker squares, finely crushed, *divided*
- 24 large marshmallows, snipped
- 8 ounces dates, chopped
- 2 cups chopped walnuts
- 1-1/4 cups heavy cream

Whipped cream, optional

In a bowl, combine 2 cups of graham cracker crumbs, marshmallows, dates and walnuts. Stir in cream; mix thoroughly. Shape into a 14-in. x 3-in. log. Roll in remaining crumbs. Wrap tightly in plastic wrap or foil. Refrigerate at least 6 hours or overnight. Slice; garnish with whipped cream if desired. **Yield:** 10-12 servings.

Fluffy Fruit Salad

"This salad's smooth sauce combined with all the colorful fruit makes it different than any other fruit salad I've tried," reports Anne Heinonen, Howell, Michigan.

- 2 cans (20 ounces *each*) crushed pineapple
- 2/3 cup sugar
- 2 tablespoons all-purpose flour
- 2 eggs, lightly beaten
- 1/4 cup orange juice
- 3 tablespoons lemon juice
- 1 tablespoon vegetable oil
- 2 cans (17 ounces *each*) fruit cocktail, drained
- 2 cans (11 ounces *each*) mandarin oranges, drained
- 2 bananas, sliced
- 1 cup heavy cream, whipped

Drain pineapple, reserving 1 cup juice in a small saucepan. Set pineapple aside. To saucepan, add sugar, flour, eggs, orange juice, lemon juice and oil. Bring to a boil, stirring constantly. Boil for 1 minute; remove from the heat and let cool. In a salad bowl, combine pineapple, fruit cocktail, oranges and bananas. Fold in the whipped cream and cooled sauce. Chill for several hours. **Yield:** 12-16 servings.

Four-Fruit Compote

(PICTURED ON THIS PAGE)

From Searcy, Arkansas, Donna Long writes, "This attractive compote spotlights wonderful fruit like bananas, apples, oranges and pineapple."

- **1 can (20 ounces) pineapple chunks**
- **1/2 cup sugar**
- **2 tablespoons cornstarch**
- **1/3 cup orange juice**
- **1 tablespoon lemon juice**
- **1 can (11 ounces) mandarin oranges, drained**
- **3 to 4 unpeeled apples, chopped**
- **2 to 3 bananas, sliced**

Drain pineapple, reserving 3/4 cup juice. In a saucepan, combine sugar and cornstarch. Add pineapple juice, orange juice and lemon juice. Cook and stir over medium heat until thickened and bubbly; cook and stir 1 minute longer. Remove from the heat; set aside. In a bowl, combine pineapple chunks, oranges, apples and bananas. Pour warm sauce over the fruit; stir gently to coat. Cover and refrigerate. **Yield:** 12-16 servings.

Pecan Sandies

(PICTURED ON THIS PAGE)

"Whenever Mother made these cookies, there never seemed to be enough! Even now, they disappear quickly," shares Debbie Carlson, San Diego, California.

- **2 cups butter *or* margarine, softened**
- **1 cup confectioners' sugar**
- **2 tablespoons water**
- **4 teaspoons vanilla extract**
- **4 cups all-purpose flour**
- **2 cups chopped pecans**
- **Additional confectioners' sugar**

In a mixing bowl, cream butter and sugar. Add water and vanilla; mix well. Gradually add flour; fold in pecans. Roll into 1-in. balls. Place on ungreased baking sheets and flatten with fingers. Bake at 300° for 20-25 minutes. Cool on a wire rack. When cool, dust with confectioners' sugar. **Yield:** about 5 dozen.

Ham-Stuffed Manicotti

(PICTURED ON THIS PAGE)

Dorothy Anderson of Ottawa, Kansas reveals, "Here's a fun and different use

for ham. The creamy cheese sauce makes this casserole perfect for chilly days."

- **8 manicotti shells**
- **1/2 cup chopped onion**
- **1 tablespoon vegetable oil**
- **3 cups (1 pound) ground fully cooked ham**
- **1 can (4 ounces) sliced mushrooms, drained**
- **1 cup (4 ounces) shredded Swiss cheese, *divided***
- **3 tablespoons grated Parmesan cheese**
- **1/4 to 1/2 cup chopped green pepper**
- **3 tablespoons butter *or* margarine**
- **3 tablespoons all-purpose flour**
- **2 cups milk**
- **Paprika**
- **Chopped fresh parsley**

Cook manicotti according to package directions; set aside. In a large skillet, saute onion in oil until tender. Remove from the heat. Add ham, mushrooms, half of the Swiss cheese and Parmesan; set aside. In a saucepan, saute green pepper in butter until tender. Stir in flour until thoroughly combined. Add milk; cook, stirring constantly, until thickened and bubbly. Mix a quarter of the sauce into ham mixture. Stuff shells with about 1/3 cup of filling each and place in a greased 11-in. x 7-in. x 2-in. baking dish. Top with remaining sauce; sprinkle with paprika. Cover and bake at 350° for 30 minutes or until heated through. Sprinkle with parsley and remaining Swiss cheese before serving. **Yield:** 8 servings. **Editor's Note:** Recipe can easily be doubled for a larger group.

Sauerkraut Soup

(PICTURED ON THIS PAGE)

"The medley of tomato, sauerkraut and smoked sausage gives this savory soup old-world flavor," says Jean Marie Cornelius of Whitesville, New York.

- **1 pound smoked Polish sausage, cut into 1/2-inch pieces**
- **5 medium potatoes, peeled and cubed**

CHASE AWAY HUNGER WITH comforting Ham-Stuffed Manicotti, tangy Sauerkraut Soup, colorful Four-Fruit Compote and melt-in-your-mouth Pecan Sandies (all recipes on this page).

2 medium onions, chopped
2 carrots, cut into 1/4-inch
  slices
3 cans (14-1/2 ounces *each*)
  chicken broth
1 can (32 ounces) sauerkraut,
  rinsed and drained
1 can (6 ounces) tomato paste

In a large saucepan or Dutch oven, combine sausage, potatoes, onions, carrots and chicken broth; bring to a boil. Reduce heat; cover and simmer for 30 minutes or until potatoes are tender. Add sauerkraut and tomato paste; mix well. Return to a boil. Reduce heat; cover and simmer 30 minutes longer. If a thinner soup is desired, add additional water or broth. **Yield:** 8-10 servings (2-1/2 quarts).

Turkey Tetrazzini

Gladys Waldrop of Calvert City, Kentucky reports, "This recipe comes from a cookbook our church compiled. It's convenient because it can be made ahead and frozen. After the holidays, we use leftover turkey to prepare a meal for university students. They clean their plates!"

1 box (7 ounces) spaghetti,
  broken into 2-inch pieces
2 cups cubed cooked turkey
1 cup (4 ounces) shredded
  cheddar cheese
1 can (10-3/4 ounces)
  condensed cream of
  mushroom soup, undiluted
1 medium onion, chopped
2 cans (4 ounces *each*) sliced
  mushrooms, drained
1/3 cup milk
1/4 cup chopped green pepper
1 jar (2 ounces) chopped
  pimientos, drained
1/4 teaspoon salt
1/8 teaspoon pepper
Additional shredded cheddar cheese,
  optional

Cook spaghetti according to package directions; drain. Transfer to a large bowl; add the next 10 ingredients and mix well. Spoon into a greased 2-1/2-qt. casserole; sprinkle with cheese if desired. Bake, uncovered, at 375° for 40-45 minutes or until heated through. **Yield:** 6-8 servings.

Baked Spaghetti

(PICTURED ON THIS PAGE)

"This cheesy dish puts a different spin on spaghetti and is great for any meal. The leftovers, if there are any, also

PASTA'S PERFECT. When you need to feed a hungry clan, take along easy-to-prepare Baked Spaghetti (recipe on this page). Its success lies in the creamy vegetable sauce.

freeze well for a quick meal later in the week," shares Ruth Koberna of Brecksville, Ohio.

1 cup chopped onion
1 cup chopped green pepper
1 tablespoon butter *or*
  margarine
1 can (28 ounces) tomatoes with
  liquid, cut up
1 can (4 ounces) mushroom
  stems and pieces, drained
1 can (2-1/4 ounces) sliced ripe
  olives, drained
2 teaspoons dried oregano
1 pound ground beef, browned
  and drained, optional
12 ounces spaghetti, cooked and
  drained
2 cups (8 ounces) shredded
  cheddar cheese
1 can (10-3/4 ounces)
  condensed cream of
  mushroom soup, undiluted
1/4 cup water
1/4 cup grated Parmesan cheese

In a large skillet, saute onion and green pepper in butter until tender. Add tomatoes, mushrooms, olives and oregano. Add ground beef if desired. Simmer, uncovered, for 10 minutes. Place half of the spaghetti in a greased 13-in. x 9-in. x 2-in. baking dish. Top with half of the vegetable mixture. Sprinkle with 1 cup of cheddar cheese. Repeat layers. Mix the soup and water until smooth; pour over the casserole. Sprinkle with Parmesan cheese. Bake, uncovered, at 350° for 30-35 minutes or until heated through. **Yield:** 12 servings.

SOUPS & SALADS

**Robust soups and refreshing salads make a perfect first course.
Or serve them alone for a light—yet pleasing—entree.**

Basic Turkey Soup

(PICTURED ON PAGE 71)

Katie Koziolek of Hartland, Minnesota notes, "For a rich broth, I simmer the turkey carcass, then add favorite vegetables and sometimes noodles."

TURKEY BROTH:
   1 turkey carcass
   2 quarts water
   1 chicken bouillon cube
   1 celery rib with leaves
   1 small onion, halved
   1 carrot
   3 whole peppercorns
   1 garlic clove
   1 teaspoon seasoned salt
   1/4 teaspoon dried thyme
TURKEY VEGETABLE SOUP:
   8 cups turkey broth (above)
   2 chicken bouillon cubes
   1/2 to 3/4 teaspoon pepper
   4 cups sliced carrots, celery *and/or* other vegetables
   3/4 cup chopped onion
   4 cups diced cooked turkey

Place all broth ingredients in a large soup kettle; cover and bring to a boil. Reduce heat; simmer for 25 minutes. Strain broth; discard bones and vegetables. Cool; skim fat. Use immediately for turkey vegetable soup or refrigerate and use within 24 hours. For soup, combine broth, bouillon, pepper, vegetables and onion in a large soup kettle. Cover and simmer for 15-20 minutes or until the vegetables are tender. Add turkey and heat through. **Yield:** 8-10 servings.

Sweetheart Salad

(PICTURED ON PAGE 72)

"The lightly sweet raspberry flavor of the vinaigrette really dresses up this salad. It's a lovely ruby color perfect to serve to someone special or just for yourself," shares Marcy Cella of L'Anse, Michigan.

RASPBERRY VINAIGRETTE:
   1/2 cup white wine vinegar
   3 tablespoons sugar
   1/2 cup fresh raspberries

   2 tablespoons water
   1 tablespoon vegetable oil
SALAD:
   1 medium tomato
Sweet red peppers
Assorted salad greens
Cherry tomatoes, halved
Pitted whole ripe olives

For dressing, combine vinegar and sugar in a pint glass jar. Microwave on high for 1 minute; stir. Add raspberries. Cover and let stand at room temperature for 1 hour. Refrigerate overnight. Just before serving, add water and oil; shake well. Make a "tomato rose" by taking a sharp knife and slowly peeling a continuous strip around tomato, keeping the peel in one piece. Turn the tomato skin in on itself, forming a rose (see diagram below). With a small heart-shaped metal cutter, cut out hearts from red peppers. Place salad greens on a serving platter; place tomato rose in the center and surround with the red pepper hearts, cherry tomatoes and olives. Serve dressing with salad. **Yield:** 3/4 cup dressing.

"Tomato rose"

Potato Cheese Soup

(PICTURED ON PAGE 74)

"My father was Swiss, so cheese has been a basic food in our family as long as I can remember," relates Carol Smith of New Berlin, Wisconsin. "With its big cheese taste, you'll want to prepare this soup often. A steaming bowl plus a salad and slice of bread makes a wonderful light meal."

   3 medium potatoes (about 1 pound), peeled and quartered
   1 small onion, finely chopped
   1 cup water
   1 teaspoon salt
   3 cups milk
   3 tablespoons butter *or* margarine, melted
   2 tablespoons all-purpose flour
   2 tablespoons minced fresh parsley
   1/8 teaspoon white pepper
   1 cup (4 ounces) shredded Swiss cheese

In a saucepan, bring potatoes, onion, water and salt to a boil. Reduce heat; cover and simmer until potatoes are tender. Do not drain; mash slightly. Stir in milk. In a small bowl, blend butter, flour, parsley and pepper; stir into the potato mixture. Cook and stir over medium heat until thickened and bubbly. Remove from the heat; add cheese and stir until almost melted. **Yield:** 6 servings (1-1/2 quarts).

Turkey Curry Salad

"Cucumbers, apples and curry make this salad distinctive," explains June Mullins, Livonia, Missouri.

   3/4 cup mayonnaise
   3/4 cup sour cream *or* plain yogurt
   1 to 2 teaspoons curry powder
   4 cups diced cooked turkey
   2 cups chopped apples
   1 cup chopped celery
   1 cup chopped peeled cucumber
   2 tablespoons chopped onion

In a large bowl, combine mayonnaise and sour cream or yogurt; stir in curry powder. Fold in remaining ingredients. Chill at least 2 hours before serving. **Yield:** 4-6 servings.

Low-Fat Potato Salad

"If you love potato salad but need to watch your diet, this low-fat version is for you," assures Paula Pelis of Rocky Point, New York. "Everyone loves this crunchy, refreshing salad."

✓ This tasty dish uses less sugar, salt and fat. Recipe includes *Diabetic Exchanges.*

   1-1/2 pounds small salad potatoes
   3/4 cup plain nonfat yogurt
   3 tablespoons white wine vinegar
   1 tablespoon minced fresh dill
   1 tablespoon minced fresh parsley
   2 teaspoons minced fresh tarragon
   1/2 medium onion, chopped
   1 celery rib, chopped

1 small carrot, coarsely
   shredded

Cook potatoes until tender but firm; cool
and slice. In a large bowl, combine remaining ingredients. Add potatoes and
stir until well coated. Chill for several
hours. **Yield:** 8 servings. **Diabetic Exchanges:** One serving equals 1 starch;
also, 78 calories, 19 mg sodium, trace
cholesterol, 17 gm carbohydrate, 3 gm
protein, trace fat.

Deluxe German Potato Salad

(PICTURED ON THIS PAGE)

*Betty Perkins of Hot Springs, Arkansas
shares, "I make this salad for all occasions— it goes well with any kind of meat.
The celery, carrots and dry mustard are
a special touch not usually found in traditional German potato salad."*

   1/2 **pound sliced bacon**
     1 **cup thinly sliced celery**
     1 **cup chopped onion**
     1 **cup sugar**
     2 **tablespoons all-purpose flour**
     1 **cup vinegar**
   1/2 **cup water**
     1 **teaspoon salt**
   3/4 **teaspoon dry mustard**
     5 **pounds unpeeled red new
        potatoes, cooked and sliced**
     2 **carrots, shredded**
     2 **tablespoons chopped fresh
        parsley**
Additional salt to taste

In a skillet, cook bacon until crisp. Drain,
reserving 1/4 cup drippings. Crumble
bacon and set aside. Saute the celery
and onion in drippings until tender.
Combine sugar and flour; add to skillet
with vinegar, water, salt and mustard.
Cook, stirring constantly, until mixture
thickens and bubbles. In a large bowl,
combine potatoes, carrots and parsley;
pour the sauce over and stir gently to
coat. Season to taste with additional
salt. Spoon into a serving dish; garnish
with the crumbled bacon. Serve warm.
Yield: 14-16 servings.

Baked Potato Soup

(PICTURED ON THIS PAGE)

*"This recipe was given to me by a dear
friend with whom I taught school,"
writes Loretha Bringle of Garland,
Texas. "I think of her whenever I make
this rich savory soup, which is a great
way to use up leftover baked potatoes."*

ONE POTATO, TWO. The ever-popular, practical spud is spotlighted in an updated version of
Deluxe German Potato Salad and classic creamy Baked Potato Soup (recipes on this page).

   2/3 **cup butter *or* margarine**
   2/3 **cup all-purpose flour**
     7 **cups milk**
     4 **large baking potatoes, baked,
        cooled, peeled and cubed
        (about 4 cups)**
     4 **green onions, sliced**
    12 **bacon strips, cooked and
        crumbled**
 1-1/4 **cups shredded cheddar
        cheese**
     1 **cup (8 ounces) sour cream**
   3/4 **teaspoon salt**
   1/2 **teaspoon pepper**

In a large soup kettle or Dutch oven,
melt the butter. Stir in flour; heat and stir
until smooth. Gradually add milk, stirring
constantly until thickened. Add potatoes
and onions. Bring to a boil, stirring constantly. Reduce heat; simmer for 10 minutes. Add remaining ingredients; stir until cheese is melted. Serve immediately.
Yield: 8-10 servings (2-1/2 quarts).

Festive Fruit Salad

(PICTURED ON PAGE 110)

*"This fruit salad disappears fast down
to the last spoonful. The light dressing
is perfect because it doesn't hide the refreshing flavors of the fruit. Pecans add
crunch and rich flavor I know you'll enjoy," says Julianne Johnson of Grove
City, Minnesota.*

     1 **can (20 ounces) pineapple
        chunks**
   1/2 **cup sugar**
     3 **tablespoons all-purpose flour**
     1 **egg, lightly beaten**
     2 **cans (11 ounces *each*)
        mandarin oranges, drained**
     1 **can (20 ounces) pears,
        drained
        and chopped**
     3 **kiwifruit, peeled and sliced**
     2 **large unpeeled apples,
        chopped**
     1 **cup pecan halves**

Drain pineapple, reserving juice. Set
pineapple aside. Pour juice into a small
saucepan; add sugar and flour. Bring to
a boil. Quickly stir in the egg; cook until
thickened. Remove from the heat; cool.
Refrigerate. In a large bowl, combine
pineapple, oranges, pears, kiwi, apples
and pecans. Pour dressing over and
blend well. Cover and chill for 1 hour.
Yield: 12-16 servings.

Buffalo Chili Con Carne

(PICTURED ON THIS PAGE)

Donna Smith of Victor, New York says, "This classic recipe of the American frontier is so meaty you can almost eat it with a fork. The zippy combination of ingredients is a perfect complement to the buffalo."

✓ This tasty dish uses less sugar, salt and fat. Recipe includes *Diabetic Exchanges*.

    1 pound cubed *or* coarsely
      ground buffalo meat
    2 tablespoons cooking oil
    1 to 2 cups diced onion
    1 to 2 cups diced green pepper
    2 cans (16 ounces *each*) diced
      tomatoes with liquid
1-1/2 to 2 cups tomato juice
    1 can (15-1/2 ounces) dark red
      kidney beans, rinsed and
      drained
    1 can (15 ounces) pinto beans,
      rinsed and drained
    1 can (4 ounces) chopped
      green chilies
    2 teaspoons chili powder
    1 teaspoon salt, optional
  1/2 teaspoon pepper

In a large kettle or Dutch oven, brown meat in oil; drain. Add onion and green pepper; saute for 5 minutes. Stir in remaining ingredients and bring to a boil. Reduce heat; cover and simmer 1-1/2 to 2 hours or until the meat is tender. **Yield:** 6 servings (1-1/2 quarts). **Diabetic Exchanges:** One 1-cup serving (prepared without added salt) equals 2 lean meat, 2 starch, 1 vegetable; also, 271 calories, 574 mg sodium, 27 mg cholesterol, 39 gm carbohydrate, 23 gm protein, 3 gm fat.

Easy Layered Salad

"Because I enjoy spending a fair amount of time in the kitchen, our kids have also learned to like cooking," reports Marsha Ransom of South Haven, Michigan. "All four kids make this salad together and take pride in serving it to the family."

    1 head lettuce, torn into
      bite-size pieces
    1 cup diced green pepper
  1/4 cup sliced green onions
    1 package (10 ounces) frozen
      peas, thawed
    2 cups salad dressing *or*
      mayonnaise
    2 to 4 cups (8 to 16 ounces)
      shredded cheddar cheese

In a 13-in. x 9-in. x 2-in. pan, layer lettuce, green pepper, onions and peas; do not toss. Spread salad dressing over all; sprinkle with cheese. Cover and refrigerate overnight. **Yield:** 8-10 servings.

Schoolhouse Chili

"When I was a cook at a school, the students loved my chili because they thought it didn't have beans in it," relates Mary Selner of Green Bay, Wisconsin. "They didn't know I pureed the beans, tomatoes, onions and green pepper to create a flavorful, vitamin-packed sauce!"

  1/2 cup chopped onion
  1/4 cup chopped green pepper
    1 can (16 ounces) tomatoes
      with liquid
    1 can (16 ounces) mild chili
      beans with sauce
    1 pound ground beef
    1 to 2 teaspoons chili powder
1-1/2 teaspoons salt
    1 teaspoon ground cumin
  1/2 teaspoon pepper
Cooked spaghetti, optional

Puree onion, green pepper, tomatoes and beans in a blender or food processor until smooth. In a large saucepan or Dutch oven, brown the beef; drain. Add seasonings and the pureed vegetables. Simmer over low heat for 1 hour. Add cooked spaghetti before serving if desired. **Yield:** 4-6 servings (1-1/2 quarts).

Cucumber Salad

"I like to cook and entertain for friends," comments Philip Stent of Leggett, Texas. "This cool, crunchy cucumber salad seems to go with whatever main dish I prepare."

    1 cup (8 ounces) sour cream
  1/4 cup chopped onion
    2 tablespoons lemon juice
    2 tablespoons cider vinegar
Salt and pepper to taste
    3 large cucumbers, peeled and
      thinly sliced

In a bowl, combine sour cream, onion, lemon juice, vinegar, salt and pepper. Add cucumbers and mix well. Chill for at least 1 hour. **Yield:** 6-8 servings.

Hamburger Vegetable Soup

"When my family's in the mood for soup, this is the recipe I reach for," admits Diana Frizzle of Knowlton, Quebec. "They love the unique combination of ground beef, tomatoes and carrots."

    1 pound ground beef
    1 cup chopped onion
    3 cups beef broth
    1 can (28 ounces) tomatoes
      with liquid, cut up
    1 cup sliced carrots

WARM UP family and friends with the full flavor of Buffalo Chili Con Carne (recipe on this page).

1 cup sliced celery
1 cup cubed peeled potatoes
2 bay leaves
1 teaspoon salt

In a large saucepan or Dutch oven, brown ground beef; drain. Add onion and cook until tender. Add remaining ingredients; bring to a boil. Reduce heat; cover and simmer until vegetables are tender, about 45-60 minutes. **Yield:** 8-10 servings (2-1/2 quarts).

Salmon Pasta Salad

(PICTURED ON THIS PAGE)

"This salad was one of my husband's favorite ways to enjoy salmon. It's a nice light meal for a hot summer day, and it lets the salmon flavor come through," shares Mary Dennis of Bryan, Ohio.

1 package (8 ounces) spiral pasta, cooked and drained
2 cups fully cooked salmon chunks *or* 1 can (14-3/4 ounces) pink salmon, drained, bones and skin removed
1-1/2 cups quartered cherry tomatoes
1 medium cucumber, quartered and sliced
1 small red onion, sliced
1/2 cup vegetable oil
1/3 cup fresh lemon *or* lime juice
1-1/2 teaspoons dill weed
1 garlic clove, minced
3/4 teaspoon salt
1/4 teaspoon pepper
1 head lettuce, torn

In a large bowl, toss the pasta, salmon, tomatoes, cucumber and onion. For dressing, combine the oil, lemon or lime juice, dill, garlic, salt and pepper; mix well. Pour over pasta. Cover and chill. Serve over lettuce. **Yield:** 6-8 servings.

Old-Fashioned Wilted Lettuce

"I remember my grandmother making this wonderful 'wilted' salad with leaf lettuce from her garden and serving it with a creamy dressing," recalls Rose Shawyer of Otterbein, Indiana.

2 eggs
1/2 cup milk
1/4 cup cider vinegar
1/2 teaspoon salt
1/4 teaspoon pepper
8 bacon strips, cut into 1-inch pieces

CATCH OF THE DAY. Salad lovers everywhere will be preparing this refreshing Salmon Pasta Salad (recipe on this page). And country cooks will be reeling in many compliments!

1 head iceberg *or* bunch leaf lettuce, torn
1 large onion, sliced into rings

In a small bowl, beat eggs, milk, vinegar, salt and pepper until smooth; set aside. In a skillet, cook bacon until crisp. Remove bacon to paper towels to drain, reserving drippings; reduce heat under skillet to medium. Whisk egg mixture into drippings; cook and stir until thickened, about 3-4 minutes. Place lettuce, onion and bacon in a large salad bowl. Pour dressing over and toss well. Serve immediately. **Yield:** 6-8 servings.

Chicken Soup With Spaetzle

"Here's a new and interesting twist to traditional chicken soup," assures Elaine Lange of Grand Rapids, Michigan. *"Everyone who samples it can't resist the delicious soup paired with homemade spaetzle."*

1 broiler-fryer chicken (2 to 3 pounds), cut up
2 tablespoons cooking oil
2 quarts chicken broth

2 bay leaves
1/2 teaspoon dried thyme
1/4 teaspoon pepper
1 cup sliced carrots
1 cup sliced celery
3/4 cup chopped onion
1 garlic clove, minced
1/3 cup medium barley
2 cups sliced fresh mushrooms
SPAETZLE:
1-1/4 cups all-purpose flour
1/8 teaspoon baking powder
1/8 teaspoon salt
1 egg, lightly beaten
1/4 cup water
1/4 cup milk

In a large kettle or Dutch oven, brown chicken pieces in oil. Add the broth, bay leaves, thyme and pepper. Simmer until chicken is tender. Cool broth and skim off fat. Skin and bone chicken and cut into bite-size pieces; return to broth along with carrots, celery, onion, garlic and barley. Bring to a boil. Reduce heat; cover and simmer for 35 minutes. Add mushrooms and simmer 8-10 minutes longer. Remove bay leaves. Combine first three spaetzle ingredients in a small bowl. Stir in egg, water and milk; blend well. Drop batter by 1/2 teaspoonfuls into simmering soup. Cook for 10 minutes. **Yield:** 8-10 servings (2-1/2 quarts).

Grandma's Potato Salad

(PICTURED ON THIS PAGE)

Remarks Sue Gronholz of Columbus, Wisconsin, "One taste and you'll agree the cooked dressing in this salad is well worth the little extra effort."

      1 cup water
    1/2 cup butter *or* margarine
    1/4 cup vinegar
      2 eggs
    1/2 cup sugar
  4-1/2 teaspoons cornstarch
    3/4 cup salad dressing *or* mayonnaise
    3/4 cup heavy cream, whipped
      6 pounds red salad potatoes, cooked, peeled and sliced
    1/2 cup chopped onion
    1/4 cup sliced green onions
      1 teaspoon salt
    1/2 teaspoon pepper
  Leaf lettuce, optional
      3 hard-cooked eggs, sliced
  Paprika

In the top of a double boiler over boiling water, heat water, butter and vinegar. In a bowl, beat eggs; add sugar and cornstarch. Add to butter mixture; cook and stir constantly until thick, about 5-7 minutes. Remove from the heat and allow to cool. Stir in the salad dressing; fold in the whipped cream. In a large bowl, toss potatoes, onion, green onions, salt and pepper. Pour the dressing over and mix gently. Chill. Serve in a lettuce-lined bowl if desired. Garnish with the hard-cooked eggs and sprinkle with paprika. **Yield:** 18 servings.

Patriotic Gelatin Salad

(PICTURED ON THIS PAGE)

"This salad is exciting to serve, and guests love the cool fruity and creamy layers," shares Sue.

      2 packages (3 ounces each) berry blue-flavored gelatin
      2 packages (3 ounces *each*) strawberry-flavored gelatin
      4 cups boiling water, *divided*
  2-1/2 cups cold water, *divided*
      2 envelopes unflavored gelatin
      2 cups milk
      1 cup sugar
      2 cups (16 ounces) sour cream
      2 teaspoons vanilla extract

In four separate bowls, dissolve each package of gelatin in 1 cup boiling water. Add 1/2 cup cold water to each and stir. Pour one bowl of blue gelatin into an oiled 10-in. fluted tube pan; chill until almost set, about 30 minutes. Set other three bowls of gelatin aside at room temperature. Soften unflavored gelatin in remaining cold water; let stand 5 minutes. Heat milk in a saucepan over medium heat just below boiling. Stir in softened gelatin and sugar until sugar is dissolved. Remove from heat; stir in sour cream and vanilla until smooth. When blue gelatin in pan is almost set, carefully spoon 1-1/2 cups sour cream mixture over it. Chill until almost set, about 30 minutes. Carefully spoon one bowl of strawberry gelatin over cream layer. Chill until almost set. Carefully spoon 1-1/2 cups cream mixture over strawberry layer. Chill until almost set. Repeat, adding layers of blue gelatin, cream mixture and strawberry gelatin, chilling in between each. Chill several hours or overnight. **Yield:** 16 servings.

Vegetable Bean Soup

Reports Laura Letobar of Livonia, Michigan, "This soup is packed with hearty vegetables and beans and has a unique robust flavor. It's no wonder this is a family favorite."

✓ **This tasty dish uses less sugar, salt and fat. Recipe includes *Diabetic Exchanges*.**

    2 cups chopped onion
    1 cup chopped carrots
    1 cup chopped celery
    6 cups water
    3 beef bouillon cubes
    1 can (28 ounces) tomatoes with liquid, cut up
    1 can (15 ounces) black beans, rinsed and drained
    1 cup quick-cooking barley
    1 teaspoon garlic powder
  3/4 teaspoon pepper
    1 package (10 ounces) frozen chopped spinach, thawed

In a large saucepan or Dutch oven coated with nonstick cooking spray, saute onion, carrots and celery over medium heat until onion is soft, about 8 minutes. Stir in water, bouillon, tomatoes, beans, barley, garlic powder and pepper; bring to a boil. Reduce heat; cover

FESTIVE FOURTH. A fabulous feast is sure to include favorites such as (clockwise from bottom) Grandma's Potato Salad, Patriotic Gelatin Salad (recipes this page), Red, White and Blue Dessert (recipe page 106) and All-American Barbecue Sandwiches (recipe page 78).

and simmer for 10 minutes. Add spinach; cover and simmer for 10-15 minutes or until the vegetables are tender. **Yield:** 14 servings. **Diabetic Exchanges:** One serving equals 1 starch, 1 vegetable; also, 113 calories, 442 mg sodium, 0 cholesterol, 23 gm carbohydrate, 6 gm protein, 1 gm fat.

Marinated Mushroom Salad

(PICTURED ON THIS PAGE)

"Packed with mushrooms and loads of crunchy colorful ingredients, this salad is perfect at picnics and parties," states Sandra Johnson of Tioga, Pennsylvania.

    2-1/2 quarts water
        3 tablespoons lemon juice
        3 pounds small fresh
          mushrooms
        2 carrots, sliced
        2 celery ribs, sliced
      1/2 medium green pepper,
          chopped
        1 small onion, chopped
        1 tablespoon minced fresh
          parsley
      1/2 cup sliced stuffed olives
        1 can (2-1/4 ounces) sliced ripe
          olives, drained
DRESSING:
      1/2 cup prepared Italian salad
          dressing
      1/2 cup red or white wine vinegar
        1 garlic clove, minced
      1/2 teaspoon dried oregano
      1/2 teaspoon salt

In a large saucepan, bring water and lemon juice to a boil. Add mushrooms and cook for 3 minutes, stirring occasionally. Drain; cool. Place mushrooms in a large bowl with the carrots, celery, green pepper, onion, parsley and olives. Combine all dressing ingredients in a small bowl or a jar with tight-fitting lid; shake or mix well. Pour over salad. Cover and refrigerate overnight. **Yield:** 6-8 servings.

Mushroom and Potato Chowder

(PICTURED ON THIS PAGE)

Romaine Wetzel of Lancaster, Pennsylvania writes, "My daughter shared this delightful recipe with me. The rich broth, big mushroom taste and medley of vegetables make this chowder a little different from ordinary mushroom soup."

'SHROOM STAPLES are (clockwise from bottom) Marinated Mushroom Salad, Mushroom and Potato Chowder (recipes this page) and Quick Mushroom Stew (recipe page 64).

      1/2 cup chopped onion
      1/4 cup butter or margarine
        2 tablespoons all-purpose flour
        1 teaspoon salt
      1/2 teaspoon pepper
        3 cups water
        1 pound fresh mushrooms,
          sliced
        1 cup chopped celery
        1 cup diced peeled potatoes
      1/2 cup chopped carrots
        1 cup light cream
      1/4 cup grated Parmesan cheese

In a large kettle, saute onion in butter until tender. Add flour, salt and pepper; stir to make a smooth paste. Gradually add water, stirring constantly. Bring to a boil; cook and stir for 1 minute. Add the mushrooms, celery, potatoes and carrots. Reduce heat; cover and simmer for 30 minutes or until vegetables are tender. Add cream and Parmesan cheese; heat through. **Yield:** 4-6 servings.

Fresh Tomato Soup

"When tomatoes are in season, my family knows they can expect to see this soup on the dinner table," says Hebron, Indiana cook Edna Hoffman.

      1/2 cup chopped onion
      1/4 cup butter or margarine
      1/4 cup all-purpose flour
        2 cups water
        6 medium tomatoes, peeled
          and diced
        1 tablespoon minced fresh
          parsley
    1-1/2 teaspoons salt
        1 teaspoon sugar
        1 teaspoon minced fresh thyme
          or 1/2 teaspoon dried thyme
        1 bay leaf
      1/4 teaspoon pepper
Thin lemon slices, optional

In a large saucepan, cook onion in butter until tender. Stir in flour to form a smooth paste. Gradually add water, stirring constantly until thickened. Add the tomatoes, parsley, salt, sugar, thyme, bay leaf and pepper; bring to a boil. Reduce heat; cover and simmer for 20-30 minutes or until tomatoes are tender. Remove bay leaf. Garnish with lemon if desired. **Yield:** 4 servings (5 cups).

14-CARROT IDEA. Try adding grated carrot to your clam chowder. The subtle color and flavor really enhance this creamy soup.

MAIN DISHES

This meaty assortment of oven meals, skillet suppers, hearty casseroles and more is sure to provide some mighty popular meals!

Roast Prime Rib

"When I prepared this roast for a family reunion, 'scrumptious' was the word used most to describe it," explains Wendell Obermeier of Charles City, Iowa.

  1 tablespoon dry mustard
1-1/2 teaspoons salt
  1/2 teaspoon paprika
  1/4 teaspoon ground allspice
  1/4 teaspoon pepper
  1 prime rib roast (4 to 5 pounds), rolled and tied
  1 small onion, cut into thin slivers
  2 garlic cloves, cut into slivers
Fresh parsley sprigs

In a small bowl, combine mustard, salt, paprika, allspice and pepper; set aside. Using a sharp knife, cut long deep slits in the top of the roast, approximately 1 in. apart. Stuff each slit with onion, garlic, parsley and a small amount of the spice mixture. Rub remaining spice mixture on the outside of the roast. Place on a rack in a deep roasting pan. Bake, uncovered, at 325° for 2 to 2-1/2 hours or until meat thermometer reads 160°. **Yield:** 8-10 servings.

Quick Mushroom Stew

(PICTURED ON PAGE 63)

"Even with chunky vegetables and tender meat, the mushrooms star in this stick-to-your-ribs main dish," shares Cherie Sechrist of Red Lion, Pennsylvania.

  1 can (10-3/4 ounces) condensed tomato soup, undiluted
  1 can (10-3/4 ounces) condensed cream of mushroom soup, undiluted
2-1/2 cups water
  2 pounds beef stew meat, cut into cubes
  2 bay leaves
  3 medium potatoes, peeled and cut into 1-inch chunks
  4 carrots, cut into 1/2-inch slices
  1 pound medium fresh mushrooms, halved

  1 tablespoon quick-cooking tapioca

In a Dutch oven, stir the soups and water until smooth. Add meat and bay leaves. Cover and bake at 325° for 1-1/2 hours. Stir in potatoes, carrots, mushrooms and tapioca. Cover and bake 1 hour longer or until the meat and vegetables are tender. Remove the bay leaves before serving. **Yield:** 6-8 servings.

Lasagna with White Sauce

"Unlike most lasagnas, this one doesn't call for precooking the noodles. It's so simple my children often make it," comments Angie Price, Bradford, Tennessee.

  1 pound ground beef
  1 large onion, chopped
  1 can (14-1/2 ounces) tomatoes with liquid, cut up
  2 tablespoons tomato paste
  1 beef bouillon cube
1-1/2 teaspoons Italian seasoning
  1 teaspoon salt
  1/2 teaspoon pepper
  1/4 teaspoon ground red *or* cayenne pepper
WHITE SAUCE:
  2 tablespoons butter *or* margarine
  3 tablespoons all-purpose flour
  1 teaspoon salt
  1/4 teaspoon pepper
  2 cups milk
1-1/4 cups shredded mozzarella cheese, *divided*
 10 to 12 uncooked lasagna noodles

In a Dutch oven, cook beef and onion until meat is browned and onion is tender; drain. Add tomatoes, tomato paste, bouillon and seasonings. Cover and cook over medium-low heat for 20 minutes, stirring occasionally. Meanwhile, melt butter in a medium saucepan; stir in flour, salt and pepper. Add milk gradually; bring to a boil, stirring constantly. Reduce heat and cook for 1 minute. Remove from the heat and stir in half of the cheese; set aside. Pour half of the meat sauce into an ungreased 13-in. x 9-in. x 2-in. baking dish. Cover with half of the lasagna noodles. Cover with remaining

meat sauce. Top with remaining noodles. Pour white sauce over noodles. Sprinkle with remaining cheese. Cover and bake at 400° for 40 minutes or until noodles are done. **Yield:** 10-12 servings.

Zesty Grilled Ham

"The mixture of sweet and tangy flavors in this recipe is mouth-watering on a grilled piece of ham," informs Mary Ann Lien of Tyler, Texas.

  1 cup packed brown sugar
  1/3 cup prepared horseradish
  1/4 cup lemon juice
  1 fully cooked ham steak (1 to 1-1/2 pounds and 1 inch thick)

In a small saucepan, bring brown sugar, horseradish and lemon juice to a boil. Brush over both sides of ham. Grill over medium-hot coals, turning once, until heated through and well glazed, about 20-25 minutes. **Yield:** 4 servings.

Tuna Mushroom Casserole

"I love to serve this dressed-up version of a tuna casserole. The green beans add color and flavor," relates Jone Furlong of Santa Rosa, California.

  1/2 cup water
  1 teaspoon chicken bouillon granules
  1 package (10 ounces) frozen green beans
  1 cup chopped onion
  1 cup sliced fresh mushrooms
  1/4 cup chopped celery
  1 garlic clove, minced
  1/2 teaspoon dill weed
  1/2 teaspoon salt
  1/8 teaspoon pepper
  4 teaspoons cornstarch
1-1/2 cups milk
  1/2 cup shredded Swiss cheese
  1/4 cup mayonnaise
2-1/2 cups medium noodles, cooked and drained
  1 can (12-1/4 ounces) tuna, drained and flaked
  1/3 cup dry bread crumbs
  1 tablespoon butter *or* margarine

In a large saucepan, bring water and bouillon to a boil, stirring to dissolve. Add the next eight ingredients; bring to a boil. Reduce heat; cover and simmer 5 minutes or until vegetables are tender. Dissolve cornstarch in milk; add to vegetable mixture, stirring constantly. Bring to a boil; boil 2 minutes or until thickened. Remove from the heat; stir in cheese and mayonnaise until the cheese is melted. Fold in noodles and tuna. Pour into a greased 2-1/2-qt. baking dish. Brown bread crumbs in butter; sprinkle on top of casserole. Bake, uncovered, at 350° for 25-30 minutes or until heated through. **Yield:** 4-6 servings.

Scrum-Delicious Burgers

(PICTURED ON THIS PAGE)

"I usually serve these burgers when we have company. The guests rave about the flavorful cheesy topping," says Wendy Sommers, West Chicago, Illinois.

- **1-1/2 pounds ground beef**
- **3 tablespoons finely chopped onion**
- **1/2 teaspoon garlic salt**
- **1/2 teaspoon pepper**
- **1 cup (4 ounces) shredded cheddar cheese**
- **1/3 cup canned sliced mushrooms**
- **6 bacon strips, cooked and crumbled**
- **1/4 cup mayonnaise**
- **6 hamburger buns, split**
- **Lettuce leaves and tomato slices, optional**

In a medium bowl, combine the beef, onion, garlic salt and pepper; mix well. Shape into six patties, 3/4 in. thick. In a small bowl, combine the cheese, mushrooms, bacon and mayonnaise; refrigerate. Grill burgers over medium-hot coals for 10-12 minutes, turning once. During the last 3 minutes, spoon 1/4 cup of the cheese mixture onto each burger. Serve on buns with lettuce and tomato if desired. **Yield:** 6 servings.

Teriyaki Shish Kabobs

(PICTURED ON THIS PAGE)

Suzanne Pelegrin of Ocala, Florida writes, "Growing up in Guam, we ate this delicious dish often."

- **1/2 cup ketchup**
- **1/2 cup sugar**
- **1/2 cup soy sauce**
- **1 teaspoon garlic powder**

- **1 teaspoon ground ginger**
- **2 pounds boneless beef sirloin steak (1-1/2 inches thick), cut into 1-1/2-inch cubes**
- **1/2 fresh pineapple, trimmed and cut into 1-inch chunks**
- **2 to 3 small zucchini, cut into 1-inch chunks**
- **1/2 pound whole fresh mushrooms (medium size work best)**
- **1/2 pound boiling onions, peeled**
- **1 large green *or* sweet red pepper, cut into 1-inch pieces**

Combine the first five ingredients; toss with beef. Cover and refrigerate overnight. Drain beef, reserving marinade. Thread meat, pineapple and vegetables alternately on long skewers. Grill over hot coals for 15-20 minutes, turning often, or until meat reaches desired doneness and vegetables are tender. Simmer marinade in a small saucepan over low heat for 15 minutes. Remove meat and vegetables from skewers; serve with marinade. **Yield:** 6-8 servings.

Spicy Pork Tenderloin

"This flavorful pork really sparks up a barbecue," assures Diana Steger of Prospect, Kentucky.

✓ This tasty dish uses less sugar, salt and fat. Recipe includes *Diabetic Exchanges*.

- **1 to 3 tablespoons chili powder**
- **1 teaspoon salt**
- **1/4 teaspoon ground ginger**
- **1/4 teaspoon ground thyme**
- **1/4 teaspoon pepper**
- **2 pork tenderloins (about 1 pound *each*)**

Combine the first five ingredients; rub over tenderloins. Cover and refrigerate for 2-4 hours. Grill over hot coals for 15 minutes per side or until juices run clear or a meat thermometer reads 160°. **Yield:** 8 servings. **Diabetic Exchanges:** One serving equals 3-1/2 lean meat; also, 173 calories, 328 mg sodium, 93 mg cholesterol, 1 gm carbohydrate, 29 gm protein, 5 gm fat.

GRILLSIDE GOODIES. Fire up the grill and invite friends and family over for warm-weather food like Scrum-Delicious Burgers and Teriyaki Shish Kabobs (both recipes on this page).

Quail in Mushroom Gravy

(PICTURED ON THIS PAGE)

"I cook this tasty dish with rich gravy often when my boys are home," shares Jean Williams of Hurtsboro, Alabama.

3/4 cup all-purpose flour, divided
1 teaspoon salt
1/2 teaspoon pepper
6 quail (1/3 to 1/2 pound each)
1/2 cup butter or margarine
1/2 pound fresh mushrooms, sliced
2 cups chicken broth
2 teaspoons minced fresh thyme or 3/4 teaspoon dried thyme
Hot cooked noodles, optional

Combine 1/2 cup flour, salt and pepper; coat each quail. Melt butter in a skillet; brown the quail. Transfer to an ungreased 2-1/2-qt. baking dish. In the pan drippings, saute the mushrooms until tender. Add remaining flour and stir to make a smooth paste. Add broth and thyme, stirring constantly. Bring to a boil; boil for 1 minute or until thickened. Pour over the quail. Cover and bake at 350° for 40-50 minutes or until tender and juices run clear. Serve over noodles if desired. **Yield:** 6 servings.

Matt's Mexican Pizza

"This pizza has a nice 'kick' to it as well as great flavor," remarks Matt Walter of Grand Rapids, Michigan.

2 flour tortillas (10 inches)
3 ounces sliced pepperoni
2 medium tomatoes, chopped
1/2 cup salsa
1 can (2-1/4 ounces) sliced ripe olives, drained
1 cup (4 ounces) shredded Monterey Jack cheese
1 cup shredded lettuce

Place one tortilla on a microwave-safe plate. Layer with half of the pepperoni, tomatoes, salsa, olives and cheese. Microwave on high for 1-1/2 to 2 minutes or until cheese melts. Top with half of the lettuce. Make a second pizza with remaining ingredients. **Yield:** 2 servings.

Potluck Special

"This hearty meal-in-a-dish is perfect for sauerkraut lovers and can easily be doubled," notes Reta Christensen, New Denmark, New Brunswick.

1 pound ground beef
1 medium onion, chopped

1 can (28 ounces) tomatoes with liquid, cut up
1 can (16 ounces) sauerkraut, rinsed and drained
1-1/2 cups cooked rice
1 medium green pepper, chopped

In a skillet, brown ground beef and onion; drain. Add remaining ingredients; transfer to a 2-qt. baking dish. Cover and bake at 350° for 1 hour. **Yield:** 6-8 servings.

Chicken with Mushroom Sauce

"Chicken is my meat of choice," reports Philip Stent of Leggett, Texas. "Besides barbecued chicken, this flavorful dish is one of my most tried-and-true."

1/2 pound fresh mushrooms, thinly sliced
1/2 cup butter or margarine
1/2 cup all-purpose flour
1/4 teaspoon ground nutmeg
Salt and pepper to taste
8 boneless skinless chicken breast halves
1/3 cup chicken broth or port wine
1-1/2 cups heavy cream
Minced fresh parsley, optional
Paprika, optional

In a skillet, saute mushrooms in butter until tender. With a slotted spoon, remove mushrooms and set aside. Reserve butter in the skillet. Combine flour, nutmeg, salt and pepper; coat chicken pieces and shake off excess. Brown chicken in skillet over medium heat. Add mushrooms. Add broth or wine to the remaining flour mixture; stir until smooth. Fold in cream. Pour over the chicken and mushrooms; bring to a boil. Reduce heat; cover and simmer for 20-25 minutes or until chicken is no longer pink. Garnish with parsley and paprika if desired. **Yield:** 4 servings.

"ABC" Sandwiches

"I love the combination of apple, bacon and cheddar—that's how these sandwiches got their name," informs Marilyn Dick of Centralia, Missouri.

2 cups (8 ounces) shredded cheddar cheese
1 medium apple, finely chopped
3/4 cup salad dressing or mayonnaise
1/2 cup finely chopped walnuts
12 slices bread, toasted and buttered
12 bacon strips, cooked
6 hard-cooked eggs, sliced
6 tomato slices, optional

HUNTING FOR FLAVORFUL FOOD? You'll receive a flock of recipe requests after family and friends sample this new and interesting Quail in Mushroom Gravy (recipe on this page).

In a bowl, combine the cheese, apple, salad dressing and walnuts. Spread on 6 slices of bread; place 2 slices of bacon on each. Cover with egg slices. Top with tomatoes if desired and remaining slices of bread. **Yield:** 6 servings.

Sheepherder's Breakfast

(PICTURED ON THIS PAGE)

"My sister-in-law always made this delicious dish when we were camping. It's a sure hit with the breakfast crowd!" says Pauletta Bushnell of Albany, Oregon.

> 1 pound sliced bacon, diced
> 1 medium onion, chopped
> 32 ounces frozen shredded hash brown potatoes, thawed
> 10 eggs
> Salt and pepper to taste
> 2 cups (8 ounces) shredded cheddar cheese, optional
> Chopped fresh parsley

In a large skillet, cook bacon and onion until bacon is crisp. Drain all but 1/2 cup of the drippings. Add hash browns to skillet; mix well. Cook over medium heat for 10 minutes, turning when browned. Make 10 "wells" evenly spaced in the hash browns. Place one egg in each well. Sprinkle with salt and pepper. Sprinkle with cheese if desired. Cover and cook over low heat for about 10 minutes or until eggs are set. Garnish with parsley; serve immediately. **Yield:** 10 servings.

Wheat Waffles

(PICTURED ON PAGE 87)

Phyllis Herlocker of Farlington, Kansas writes, "The whole wheat taste comes through in these waffles. Crispy and light, they make a great breakfast or supper."

> 1 egg, *separated*
> 3/4 cup milk
> 1/3 cup vegetable oil
> 1/4 cup orange juice
> 1 cup whole wheat flour
> 1 tablespoon sugar
> 1 to 1-1/2 teaspoons grated orange peel
> 1 teaspoon baking powder
> 1/4 teaspoon salt

In a small mixing bowl, beat the egg white until stiff peaks form; set aside. In another small mixing bowl, beat egg yolk, milk, oil and orange juice. Combine flour, sugar, orange peel, baking powder and salt; stir into milk mixture. Fold in egg white. Bake in a preheated waffle iron according to manufacturer's directions until golden brown. **Yield:** 5 waffles (6-1/2 inches).

MMM-MORNING MEALS begin with a hearty Sheepherder's Breakfast (recipe on this page).

Golden French Toast

"I was tired of making French toast... until I saw this recipe," says Karen Free of Overland Park, Kansas. "People are surprised it calls for cardamom."

> 1/3 cup fresh orange juice
> 1 teaspoon grated orange peel
> 4 eggs
> 1/2 teaspoon ground cardamom
> 1/4 cup butter *or* margarine
> 12 slices day-old French bread (cut 3/4 inch thick)
> Maple syrup

In a bowl, combine orange juice, peel, eggs and cardamom; beat well. Melt butter in a 13-in. x 9-in. x 2-in. pan in the oven. Remove pan from the oven. Dip the bread on both sides in egg mixture; place in a single layer in pan. Bake at 450° for 10 minutes, turning once. Serve with syrup. **Yield:** 6 servings.

Shipwreck

"I'm not sure of the origin of the name," admits Cary Letsche of Bradenton, Florida, "but we ate this inexpensive meal a lot while I was growing up."

> 1/2 pound sliced bacon
> 1 pound ground beef
> 1 large onion, chopped
> 1 cup ketchup
> 1/2 cup packed brown sugar
> 1 can (32 ounces) pork and beans

In a skillet, cook bacon until crisp. Remove to paper towels to drain; crumble and set aside. Drain drippings from skillet. Brown the beef; drain. Add onion and cook until tender, about 5 minutes. Combine ketchup and brown sugar; stir into beef mixture. Stir in pork and beans and all but 2 tablespoons of the bacon. Transfer to an 8-in. square baking dish. Top with the remaining bacon. Bake, uncovered, at 350° for 1 hour. **Yield:** 6-8 servings.

Monterey Spaghetti

"I rely on quick casseroles," states Janet Hibler of Cameron, Missouri. "This one's always a hit at home."

> 4 ounces spaghetti, broken into 2-inch pieces
> 1 egg
> 1 cup (8 ounces) sour cream
> 1/4 cup grated Parmesan cheese
> 1/4 teaspoon garlic powder
> 2 cups (8 ounces) shredded Monterey Jack cheese
> 1 package (10 ounces) frozen chopped spinach, thawed and drained
> 1 can (2.8 ounces) french-fried onions, *divided*

Cook spaghetti according to package directions. Meanwhile, in a medium bowl, beat egg. Add sour cream, Parmesan cheese and garlic powder. Drain spaghetti; add to egg mixture with Monterey Jack cheese, spinach and half of the onions. Pour into a greased 2-qt. baking dish. Cover and bake at 350° for 30 minutes or until heated through. Top with remaining onions; return to the oven for 5 minutes or until onions are golden brown. **Yield:** 6-8 servings.

FAMILY MEAL MAINSTAYS. Convenient, classic Cheese Potato Puff (recipe on page 83) and country-style Chicken and Dumpling Casserole (recipe on this page) are hard to resist.

Chicken and Dumpling Casserole

(PICTURED ON THIS PAGE)

"This savory casserole is one of my husband's favorites. He loves the fluffy dumplings with plenty of gravy poured over them," shares Sue Mackey of Galesburg, Illinois.

  1/2 cup chopped onion
  1/2 cup chopped celery
    2 garlic cloves, minced
  1/4 cup butter *or* margarine
  1/2 cup all-purpose flour
    2 teaspoons sugar
    1 teaspoon salt
    1 teaspoon dried basil
  1/2 teaspoon pepper
    4 cups chicken broth
    1 package (10 ounces) frozen
      green peas
    4 cups cubed cooked chicken
DUMPLINGS:
    2 cups buttermilk biscuit mix
    2 teaspoons dried basil
  2/3 cup milk

In a large saucepan, saute onion, celery and garlic in butter until tender. Add flour, sugar, salt, basil, pepper and broth; bring to a boil. Cook and stir for 1 minute; reduce heat. Add peas and cook for 5 minutes, stirring constantly. Stir in chicken. Pour into a greased 13-in. x 9-in. x 2-in. baking dish. For dumplings, combine biscuit mix and basil in a bowl. Stir in milk with a fork until moistened. Drop by tablespoonfuls onto casserole (12 dumplings). Bake, uncovered, at 350° for 30 minutes. Cover and bake 10 minutes more or until the dumplings are done. **Yield:** 6-8 servings.

Saucy Chicken and Asparagus

(PICTURED ON PAGE 83)

"You won't believe how delicious, yet how easy, this dish is. Even my grandmother likes to serve this creamy dish for luncheons with friends," says Vicki Schlechter of Davis, California.

1-1/2 pounds fresh asparagus
      spears, halved
    4 boneless skinless chicken
      breast halves
    2 tablespoons cooking oil
  1/2 teaspoon salt
  1/4 teaspoon pepper
    1 can (10-3/4 ounces) condensed
      cream of chicken soup,
      undiluted
  1/2 cup mayonnaise
    1 teaspoon lemon juice
  1/2 teaspoon curry powder
    1 cup (4 ounces) shredded
      cheddar cheese

If desired, partially cook the asparagus; drain. Place the asparagus in a greased 9-in. square baking dish. In a skillet over medium heat, brown the chicken in oil on both sides. Season with salt and pepper. Arrange chicken over asparagus. In a bowl, mix soup, mayonnaise, lemon juice and curry powder; pour over chicken. Cover and bake at 375° for 40 minutes or until the chicken is tender and juices run clear. Sprinkle with cheese. Let stand 5 minutes before serving. **Yield:** 4 servings.

Scalloped Potatoes and Pork Chops

"This dish is easy to prepare, and baking the chops with the potatoes gives the whole meal great flavor," reports Susan Chavez of Vancouver, Washington.

    5 cups thinly sliced peeled
      potatoes
    1 cup chopped onion
Salt and pepper to taste
    1 can (10-3/4 ounces)
      condensed cream of
      mushroom soup, undiluted
  1/2 cup sour cream
    6 pork loin chops (1 inch thick)
Chopped fresh parsley

In a greased 13-in. x 9-in. x 2-in. baking dish, layer half of the potatoes and onion; sprinkle with salt and pepper. Repeat layers. Combine the soup and sour cream; pour over potato mixture. Cover and bake at 375° for 30 minutes. Meanwhile, in a skillet, brown pork chops on both sides. Place chops on top of the casserole. Cover and return to the oven for 45 minutes or until chops are tender, uncovering during the last 15 minutes of baking. Sprinkle with parsley. **Yield:** 6 servings.

Applesauce Oatmeal Pancakes

(PICTURED ON THIS PAGE)

"This recipe makes light, fluffy pancakes that will have the entire family asking for seconds," reveals Martha Cage, from Wheeling, West Virginia. "They're wonderful for those on restricted diets. Try them topped with homemade sugarless applesauce."

✓ This tasty dish uses less sugar, salt and fat. Recipe includes *Diabetic Exchanges*.

  1 cup quick-cooking oats
1/4 cup whole wheat flour
1/4 cup all-purpose flour
  1 tablespoon baking powder
  1 cup skim milk
  2 tablespoons sugarless applesauce
  4 egg whites

In a bowl, combine the oats, flours and baking powder. In another bowl, combine milk, applesauce and egg whites; add to dry ingredients and mix well. Pour batter by 1/4 cupfuls onto a heated griddle coated with nonstick cooking spray. Cook until bubbles appear on the top; turn and cook until lightly browned. **Yield:** 5 servings (two pancakes each). **Diabetic Exchanges:** One serving equals 1 starch; also, 91 calories, 323 mg sodium, 1 mg cholesterol, 15 gm carbohydrate, 5 gm protein, trace fat.

Vegetable Quiche

(PICTURED ON THIS PAGE)

"I've made and served this tasty dish for a long time," informs Elnora Johnson of Union City, Tennessee. "It has a unique rice crust and really holds up well for cutting."

✓ This tasty dish uses less sugar, salt and fat. Recipe includes *Diabetic Exchanges*.

1-1/2 cups cooked brown rice, room temperature
  3/4 cup egg substitute, *divided*
  3/4 cup shredded low-fat mozzarella cheese, *divided*
1-1/2 cups chopped fresh broccoli
  3/4 cup sliced fresh mushrooms
1/4 cup skim milk
  1 tablespoon margarine, melted

In a bowl, combine rice, 1/4 cup egg substitute and half of the cheese; mix well. Pat into the bottom and up the sides of a 9-in. pie plate coated with nonstick cooking spray; set aside. In an-other bowl, combine the broccoli, mushrooms, milk, margarine and remaining egg substitute. Pour into crust. Bake, uncovered, at 375° for 20-25 minutes or until a knife inserted near the center comes out clean. Sprinkle with the remaining cheese. Return to the oven until cheese melts. **Yield:** 8 servings. **Diabetic Exchanges:** One serving equals 1 meat, 1 vegetable, 1/2 starch; also, 131 calories, 119 mg sodium, 7 mg cholesterol, 13 gm carbohydrate, 7 gm protein, 6 gm fat.

ARE YOU GAME? Soak red game meat in canned evaporated milk for 30 minutes before cooking. This tenderizes even the toughest cuts of meat.

Grilled Venison and Vegetables

"My husband enjoys hunting, and it's my challenge to find new ways to serve venison. This recipe makes hearty kabobs perfect for grilling. The marinade reduces the 'wild' taste, so guests often don't realize they're eating venison," notes Eva Miller-Videtich of Cedar Springs, Michigan.

1/2 cup red wine vinegar
1/4 cup honey
1/4 cup soy sauce
  2 tablespoons ketchup
Dash pepper
Dash garlic powder
1-1/2 pounds boneless venison steak, cut into 1-1/4-inch cubes
  8 to 12 cherry tomatoes
  8 to 12 fresh mushrooms, optional
1/2 medium green *or* sweet red pepper, cut into 1-1/2-inch pieces
  1 to 2 small zucchini, cut into 1-inch chunks
  1 large onion, cut into wedges
  8 to 12 small new potatoes, parboiled

In a glass bowl or plastic bag, combine vinegar, honey, soy sauce, ketchup, pepper and garlic powder; set aside 1/4 cup. Add meat to bowl or bag; stir or shake to coat. Cover (or close bag) and refrigerate for 4 hours. One hour before grilling, toss vegetables with 1/4 cup marinade. Drain meat, reserving marinade. Thread meat and vegetables alternately on skewers. Brush with marinade. Grill over medium-hot coals, turning and basting often, for 15-20 minutes or until meat and vegetables reach desired doneness. Remove from skewers and serve. **Yield:** 4-6 servings.

FABULOUS FIXIN'S. Sugarless Applesauce (recipe on page 83), Applesauce Oatmeal Pancakes and Vegetable Quiche (recipes on this page) are tasty dishes...and good for you, too!

♥🐘♥🐘♥🐘♥🐘♥🐘♥🐘♥

Slow-Cooked
Pepper Steak

(PICTURED ON THIS PAGE)

"After a long day in our greenhouse raising bedding plants for sale, I appreciate coming in to this hearty beef dish for supper," says Sue Gronholz of Columbus, Wisconsin.

 1-1/2 to 2 pounds beef round steak
 2 tablespoons cooking oil
 1/4 cup soy sauce
 1 cup chopped onion
 1 garlic clove, minced
 1 teaspoon sugar
 1/2 teaspoon salt
 1/4 teaspoon pepper
 1/4 teaspoon ground ginger
 4 tomatoes, cut into eighths *or*
  1 can (16 ounces) tomatoes
  with liquid, cut up
 2 large green peppers, cut into
  strips
 1/2 cup cold water
 1 tablespoon cornstarch
Cooked noodles *or* rice

Cut beef into 3-in. x 1-in. strips; brown in oil in a skillet. Transfer to a slow cooker. Combine the next seven ingredients; pour over beef. Cover and cook on low for 5-6 hours or until meat is tender. Add tomatoes and green peppers; cook on low for 1 hour longer. Combine the cold water and cornstarch to make a paste; stir into liquid in slow cooker and cook on high until thickened. Serve over noodles or rice. **Yield:** 6-8 servings.

♥🐘♥🐘♥🐘♥🐘♥🐘♥🐘♥

Wild Rice
Harvest Casserole

(PICTURED ON PAGE 110)

"Folks enjoy sitting down to a big helping of this hearty casserole, packed with wild rice and chicken and topped with cashews," notes Julianne Johnson of Grove City, Minnesota.

 4 to 5 cups diced cooked
  chicken
 1 cup chopped celery
 2 tablespoons butter *or*
  margarine
 2 cans (10-3/4 ounces *each*)
  condensed cream of
  mushroom soup, undiluted
 2 cups chicken broth
 1 jar (4-1/2 ounces) sliced
  mushrooms, drained
 1 small onion, chopped
 1 cup uncooked wild rice,
  rinsed and drained
 1/4 teaspoon poultry seasoning
 3/4 cup cashew pieces
Chopped fresh parsley

In a skillet, brown chicken and celery in butter. In a large bowl, combine soup and broth until smooth. Add the mushrooms, onion, rice, poultry seasoning and chicken mixture. Transfer to a greased 13-in. x 9-in. x 2-in. baking dish. Cover and bake at 350° for 1 hour. Uncover and bake for 30 minutes. Stir; sprinkle with cashews. Return to the oven for 15 minutes or until the rice is tender. Garnish with parsley. **Yield:** 10-12 servings.

> **SPREADING IT ON THIN.** Next time you make grilled cheese sandwiches, spread a thin layer of mustard on the cheese before toasting. The flavor is unbeatable!

♥🐘♥🐘♥🐘♥🐘♥🐘♥🐘♥

Heavenly Crab Cakes

"These crab cakes really are a piece of paradise," reveals Laura Letobar of Livonia, Michigan. *"Whenever I crave seafood, this is the dish I prepare."*

✓ This tasty dish uses less sugar, salt and fat.
Recipe includes *Diabetic Exchanges*.

 1 pound imitation crabmeat,
  flaked
 1 cup Italian bread crumbs,
  divided
 1/4 cup egg substitute
 2 tablespoons fat-free
  mayonnaise
 2 tablespoons Dijon mustard
 1 tablespoon dill weed
 1 tablespoon lime juice
 1 teaspoon lemon juice
 1 teaspoon Worcestershire
  sauce

Combine crabmeat, 1/2 cup of the bread crumbs, egg substitute, mayonnaise, mustard, dill, lime and lemon juices and Worcestershire sauce. Shape into eight patties. Place remaining bread crumbs in a shallow bowl; dip each patty into crumbs to cover. Refrigerate for 30 minutes. In a large skillet coated with nonstick cooking spray, cook patties over medium heat until browned on both sides. **Yield:** 8 servings. **Diabetic Exchanges:** One serving equals 1-1/2 lean meat, 1 starch; also, 150 calories, 108 mg sodium, 14 mg cholesterol, 22 gm carbohydrate, 11 gm protein, 2 gm fat.

SAVORY SLOW-COOKED Pepper Steak (recipe on this page) can save the day when you need to serve folks a satisfying meal, but a busy schedule keeps you away from the kitchen.

Toasted Turkey Sandwiches

(PICTURED ON THIS PAGE)

"This makes a yummy supper garnished with dill or sweet pickles," writes Patty Kile of Plymouth Meeting, Pennsylvania. "Or add a slice of American or cheddar cheese for another flavor."

- 12 slices buttered French bread (1/2 inch thick)
- 6 thin slices cooked turkey
- 6 thin slices fully cooked ham
- 2 eggs, lightly beaten
- 1/2 cup milk
- 2 tablespoons butter *or* margarine
- 1/2 cup salad dressing *or* mayonnaise
- 1/3 cup whole-berry cranberry sauce

Make six sandwiches, dividing turkey and ham evenly between bread. In a shallow bowl, beat eggs and milk. Dip sandwiches, turning to coat both sides. In a large skillet over medium heat, melt butter. Brown sandwiches on both sides. Combine the salad dressing and cranberry sauce; mix well. Serve with sandwiches. **Yield:** 6 servings.

Turkey Biscuit Stew

(PICTURED ON THIS PAGE)

"Served over biscuits, this chunky stew makes a hearty supper. And it's a great way to use extra turkey," says Lori Schlecht of Wimbledon, North Dakota.

- 1/3 cup chopped onion
- 1/4 cup butter *or* margarine
- 1/3 cup all-purpose flour
- 1/2 teaspoon salt
- 1/8 teaspoon pepper
- 1 can (10-1/2 ounces) condensed chicken *or* turkey broth, undiluted
- 3/4 cup milk
- 2 cups cubed cooked turkey
- 1 cup cooked peas
- 1 cup cooked whole baby carrots
- 1 tube (10 ounces) refrigerated buttermilk biscuits

In a 10-in. ovenproof skillet, saute onion in butter until tender. Stir in flour, salt and pepper until smooth. Gradually add broth and milk; cook, stirring constantly, until thickened and bubbly. Add the turkey, peas and carrots; heat through. Separate biscuits and arrange over the stew. Bake at 375° for 20-25 minutes

LEFTOVER TURKEY is finely featured in (clockwise from bottom) Toasted Turkey Sandwiches, Turkey Biscuit Stew (recipes on this page) and Basic Turkey Soup (recipe on page 58).

or until biscuits are golden brown. **Yield:** 6-8 servings.

Spaghetti Chop

"This is a delicious dish perfect for those who are watching their budget," explains Cary Letsche of Bradenton, Florida. "Plus, it's quick and easy to make."

- 2 pounds ground beef
- 1 large onion, chopped
- 1/2 teaspoon onion salt
- 1/2 teaspoon seasoned salt
- 8 ounces spaghetti, broken into 4-inch pieces
- 2 cans (10-3/4 ounces *each*) condensed tomato soup, undiluted
- 1 cup ketchup

In a skillet, brown ground beef; drain. Add onion, onion salt and seasoned salt; cook until onion is tender, about 5 minutes. Remove from the heat. In a large saucepan, cook spaghetti according to package directions; drain and return to pan. Add beef mixture, soup and ketchup; mix well. Simmer for 5-10 minutes. **Yield:** 6-8 servings.

Mix 'n' Match Squash Casserole

"Mix any kinds of summer squash you have on hand for this flavorful casserole," suggests June Mullins of Livonia, Missouri. "Served with a salad and hot rolls or homemade bread, it makes a meal my family enjoys."

- 4 cups cubed summer squash (yellow, zucchini, pattypan *and/or* sunburst)
- 1 pound bulk pork sausage, cooked and drained
- 1 cup dry bread crumbs
- 1/4 cup chopped green pepper
- 1/4 cup chopped onion
- 1/2 cup grated Parmesan cheese
- 2 eggs, beaten
- 1/2 cup milk
- 1/2 teaspoon salt

Place squash and a small amount of water in a large saucepan; cover and cook for 8-10 minutes or until tender. Drain. Add all remaining ingredients; mix well. Transfer to a greased 11-in. x 7-in. x 2-in. baking dish. Bake, uncovered, at 325° for 30-35 minutes. **Yield:** 6-8 servings.

STRAIGHT FROM THE HEART are Frosted Valentine Cookies (recipe p. 96), "Hearty" Lasagna (recipe this page), Sweetheart Salad (recipe p. 58), Heart-Shaped Herbed Rolls (recipe p. 86).

♥☎♥☎♥☎♥☎♥☎♥☎♥

"Hearty" Lasagna

(PICTURED ON THIS PAGE)

From L'Anse, Michigan, Marcy Cella writes, "Because you can make this lasagna ahead, you won't have to feel rushed when it's time to enjoy your meal."

- 1-1/2 pounds ground beef
- 1 medium onion, chopped
- 1 garlic clove, minced
- 3 tablespoons olive oil
- 1 can (28 ounces) Italian tomatoes with liquid, cut up
- 1 can (8 ounces) tomato sauce
- 1 can (6 ounces) tomato paste
- 1 teaspoon dried oregano
- 1 teaspoon sugar
- 1 teaspoon salt
- 1/4 teaspoon pepper
- 2 carrots, halved
- 2 celery ribs, halved
- 12 ounces lasagna noodles
- 1 carton (15 ounces) ricotta cheese
- 2 cups (8 ounces) shredded mozzarella cheese
- 1/2 cup grated Parmesan cheese

In a large skillet, cook beef, onion and garlic in oil until meat is browned and onion is tender; drain. Stir in tomatoes, tomato sauce, tomato paste, oregano, sugar, salt and pepper. Place carrots and celery in sauce. Simmer, uncovered, for 1-1/2 hours, stirring occasionally. Meanwhile, cook lasagna noodles according to package directions. Drain; rinse in cold water. Remove and discard carrots and celery. In a greased 13-in. x 9-in. x 2-in. baking dish, layer one-third of the noodles, one-third of the meat sauce, one-third of the ricotta, one-third of the mozzarella and one-third of the Parmesan. Repeat layers once. Top with the remaining noodles and meat sauce. Cut a heart out of aluminum foil and center on top of sauce. Dollop and spread remaining ricotta around heart. Sprinkle with remaining mozzarella and Parmesan. Bake, uncovered, at 350° for 45 minutes. Remove and discard foil heart. Let stand 10-15 minutes before cutting. **Yield:** 12 servings.

♥☎♥☎♥☎♥☎♥☎♥☎♥

4-H Corn Special

"When I came across this recipe during a 4-H cooking project, I liked it imme-diately," relates Donetta Brunner of Sa-vanna, Illinois. "The only change I've made to the original was to add extra seasonings."

- 1 pound ground beef
- 1 small onion, finely chopped
- 1-1/2 cups cooked rice
- 2 cups seeded chopped fresh tomatoes *or* 1 can (16 ounces) tomatoes with liquid, cut up
- 2 cups fresh, frozen *or* canned sweet corn
- Salt and pepper to taste
- 1 tablespoon Worcestershire sauce
- 1 teaspoon hot pepper sauce
- 1 cup crushed saltines
- 1/4 cup butter *or* margarine, melted

In a large skillet, brown beef and onion; drain. Stir in rice, tomatoes, corn, salt, pepper, Worcestershire sauce and hot pepper sauce. Pour into a greased 13-in. x 9-in. x 2-in. baking dish. Combine cracker crumbs and butter; sprinkle on top. Bake at 350° for 30 minutes. **Yield:** 6-8 servings.

♥☎♥☎♥☎♥☎♥☎♥

Beef Mushroom Stew

"When cold winter winds blow, there's nothing like sitting down to a steaming plate of savory stew," shares Marilyn Schroeder, St. Paul, Minnesota.

- 1/4 cup all-purpose flour
- 1 teaspoon salt
- 1/8 teaspoon pepper
- 2-1/2 to 3 pounds beef round steak, cut into cubes
- 2 tablespoons cooking oil
- 1 cup burgundy *or* beef broth
- 3/4 cup water
- 1 jar (8 ounces) whole mushrooms, drained
- 1/2 cup chopped onion
- 2 bay leaves
- 1 garlic clove, minced
- 1 tablespoon dried parsley flakes
- Cooked rice *or* noodles

Place flour, salt and pepper in a plastic bag; add beef cubes and shake to coat on all sides. Brown beef in oil in a large saucepan. Stir in burgundy or broth, wa-ter, mushrooms, onion, bay leaves, gar-lic and parsley; bring to a boil. Reduce heat; cover and simmer for 1-1/2 hours or until meat is tender. Thicken if de-sired. Serve over rice or noodles. **Yield:** 8-10 servings.

French Banana Pancakes

"These pancakes are a real breakfast favorite in our family. Our daughters make them all by themselves when they have friends stay over," reports Cheryl Sowers of Bakersfield, California.

PANCAKES:
- 1 cup all-purpose flour
- 1/4 cup confectioners' sugar
- 1 cup milk
- 2 eggs
- 3 tablespoons butter *or* margarine, melted
- 1 teaspoon vanilla extract
- 1/4 teaspoon salt

FILLING:
- 1/4 cup butter *or* margarine
- 1/4 cup packed brown sugar
- 1/4 teaspoon ground cinnamon
- 1/4 teaspoon ground nutmeg
- 1/4 cup light cream
- 5 to 6 firm bananas, halved lengthwise

Whipped cream and additional cinnamon, optional

Sift flour and confectioners' sugar into a mixing bowl. Add milk, eggs, butter, vanilla and salt; beat until smooth. Heat a lightly greased 6-in. skillet; add about 3 tablespoons batter, spreading to almost cover bottom of skillet. Cook until lightly browned; turn and brown the other side. Remove to a wire rack. Repeat with remaining batter (makes 10-12 pancakes), greasing skillet as needed. For filling, melt butter in a large skillet. Stir in brown sugar, cinnamon and nutmeg. Stir in cream and cook until slightly thickened. Add half of the bananas at a time to skillet; heat for 2-3 minutes, spooning sauce over them. Remove from the heat. Roll a pancake around each banana half and place on a serving platter. Spoon sauce over pancakes. Top with whipped cream and a dash of cinnamon if desired. **Yield:** 5-6 servings.

Marinated Flank Steak

"Whenever we make steak on the grill, this is the recipe we use," informs Debbie Bonczek of Tariffville, Connecticut.

✓ This tasty dish uses less sugar, salt and fat. Recipe includes *Diabetic Exchanges*.

- 1 beef flank steak (about 2 pounds)
- 3 tablespoons ketchup
- 1 tablespoon vegetable oil
- 1 tablespoon chopped onion
- 1 teaspoon brown sugar
- 1 teaspoon Worcestershire sauce
- 1 garlic clove, minced
- 1/8 teaspoon pepper

Place flank steak in an 11-in. x 7-in. x 2-in. glass dish. Combine remaining ingredients; pour over meat. Cover and refrigerate for at least 4 hours. Remove meat, discarding marinade. Grill over hot coals until meat reaches desired doneness, about 4 minutes per side for medium, 5 minutes per side for medium-well. Slice into thin strips across the grain to serve. **Yield:** 8 servings. **Diabetic Exchanges:** One serving equals 3 lean meat; also, 172 calories, 115 mg sodium, 43 mg cholesterol, 2 gm carbohydrate, 23 gm protein, 7 gm fat.

Pecan Waffles

"I've tried for years to duplicate a delicious waffle I ate at a restaurant chain here in the South. This is the closest I've come, and they're crisp and nutty," reveals Susan Jansen of Smyrna, Georgia.

- 1-3/4 cups all-purpose flour
- 1 tablespoon baking powder
- 1/2 teaspoon salt
- 2 eggs, *separated*
- 1-3/4 cups milk
- 1/2 cup vegetable oil
- 1 cup chopped pecans

Maple syrup

In a bowl, combine flour, baking powder and salt. Combine egg yolks, milk and oil; stir into dry ingredients. Beat egg whites until stiff; fold into batter. Sprinkle hot waffle iron with 2 tablespoons of pecans. Pour 1/4 to 1/3 cup of batter over pecans and bake according to manufacturer's directions until golden brown. Repeat with remaining pecans and batter. Serve with syrup. **Yield:** 8-10 waffles (4-1/2 inches).

Chicken 'n' Hash Brown Bake

Ruth Andrewson of Leavenworth, Washington states, "The first time I served this dish for company was to a family with five children. The kids and the adults loved it!"

- 1 package (32 ounces) frozen Southern-style hash brown potatoes
- 1 teaspoon salt
- 1/4 teaspoon pepper
- 4 cups diced cooked chicken
- 1 can (4 ounces) sliced mushrooms, drained
- 1 cup (8 ounces) sour cream
- 2 cups chicken broth *or* stock
- 1 can (10-3/4 ounces) condensed cream of chicken soup, undiluted
- 2 teaspoons instant chicken bouillon granules
- 2 tablespoons finely chopped onion
- 2 tablespoons finely chopped sweet red pepper
- 1 garlic clove, minced

Paprika
- 1/4 cup sliced almonds

Thaw hash browns overnight in refrigerator. Layer in an ungreased 13-in. x 9-in. x 2-in. baking dish. Sprinkle with salt and pepper. Place chicken and mushrooms over the hash browns. Stir together sour cream, broth, soup, bouillon, onion, red pepper and garlic; pour over all. Sprinkle with paprika and almonds. Bake, uncovered, at 350° for 50-60 minutes or until heated through. **Yield:** 8-10 servings.

Asparagus Cheese Strata

"We tried this egg casserole at our friends' house," says Betty Jacques from Hemet, California. "I use fresh asparagus and serve it with muffins and fruit."

- 1-1/2 pounds fresh asparagus, cut into 2-inch pieces
- 3 tablespoons butter *or* margarine, melted
- 1 loaf (1 pound) sliced bread, crusts removed
- 3/4 cup shredded cheddar cheese, *divided*
- 2 cups cubed fully cooked ham
- 6 eggs
- 3 cups milk
- 2 teaspoons dried minced onion
- 1/2 teaspoon salt
- 1/4 teaspoon dry mustard

In a saucepan, cover asparagus with water; cover and cook until just tender but still firm. Drain and set aside. Lightly brush butter over one side of bread slices. Place half of the bread, buttered side up, in a greased 13-in. x 9-in. x 2-in. baking dish. Sprinkle with 1/2 cup cheese. Layer with asparagus and ham. Cover with remaining bread, buttered side up. In a bowl, lightly beat eggs; add milk, onion, salt and mustard; pour over bread. Cover and refrigerate overnight. Bake, uncovered, at 325° for 50 minutes. Sprinkle with the remaining cheese. Return to the oven for 10 minutes or until cheese is melted and a knife inserted near the center comes out clean. **Yield:** 10-12 servings.

Mozzarella Meat Loaf

(PICTURED ON THIS PAGE)

"My children were not fond of meat loaf until I 'dressed up' this recipe with pizza flavor," shares Darlis Wilfer from Phelps, Wisconsin.

- 2 pounds lean ground beef
- 2 eggs, lightly beaten
- 1 cup saltine cracker crumbs
- 1 cup milk
- 1/2 cup grated Parmesan cheese
- 1/2 cup chopped onion
- 1-1/2 teaspoons salt
- 1 teaspoon dried oregano
- 1 can (8 ounces) pizza sauce
- 3 slices mozzarella cheese, halved

Green pepper rings, optional
Sliced mushrooms, optional
- 2 tablespoons butter *or* margarine, optional

Chopped fresh parsley, optional

Mix beef, eggs, crumbs, milk, Parmesan cheese, onion, salt and oregano. Shape into a loaf and place in a greased 9-in. x 5-in. x 3-in. loaf pan. Bake at 350° for 1-1/4 hours or until no pink remains; drain. Spoon pizza sauce over loaf and top with mozzarella cheese slices. Return to the oven for 10 minutes or until the cheese is melted. Meanwhile, if desired, saute green pepper and mushrooms in butter; arrange on top of meat loaf. Sprinkle with parsley if desired. **Yield:** 8-10 servings.

Apple-Topped Oatcakes

(PICTURED ON BACK COVER)

"On Saturdays, I like to make special breakfasts. The oatcakes and apple topping are a tasty, wholesome combination," says Lois Hofmeyer of Aurora, Illinois.

- 1-1/2 cups hot milk
- 3/4 cup old-fashioned oats
- 1 egg, beaten
- 2 tablespoons vegetable oil
- 2 tablespoons molasses
- 1 cup all-purpose flour
- 1-1/2 teaspoons baking powder
- 3/4 teaspoon ground cinnamon
- 1/4 teaspoon ground ginger
- 1/4 teaspoon baking soda
- 1/4 teaspoon salt
- 3 egg whites

LEMON APPLES:
- 2 tablespoons butter *or* margarine
- 5 medium tart apples, peeled and sliced
- 1 tablespoon lemon juice
- 1 teaspoon grated lemon peel
- 1/2 cup sugar
- 1 tablespoon cornstarch
- 1/8 teaspoon ground nutmeg

In a large bowl, combine milk and oats; let stand for 5 minutes. Stir in egg, oil and molasses. Combine dry ingredients; stir into the oat mixture just until moistened. Beat egg whites until soft peaks form; fold gently into batter. Set aside. Heat butter in a large skillet until foamy. Add apples, lemon juice and peel; cook, uncovered, for 8-10 minutes, stirring occasionally. Meanwhile, cook oatcakes: Pour batter by 1/4 cupfuls onto a hot greased griddle. Cook until bubbles form; turn and cook until browned on the other side. For apples, combine the sugar, cornstarch and nutmeg; add to apple mixture and cook 2 minutes longer or until tender. Serve warm over oatcakes. **Yield:** 6-8 servings.

Parsley Pasta Sauce

"My family was skeptical when I first presented this dish," admits Donna Barleen of Concordia, Kansas. *"But after one taste, they agreed it was even better than traditional tomato sauce."*

- 2 cups tightly packed fresh parsley leaves
- 1/2 cup vegetable oil
- 1 teaspoon dried basil
- 1 teaspoon dried oregano
- 1 teaspoon dried marjoram
- 1/2 teaspoon salt
- 1/2 teaspoon garlic powder
- 1/2 teaspoon pepper
- 1 cup (8 ounces) sour cream
- 1/2 cup grated Parmesan cheese

Hot cooked pasta *or* hot spaghetti squash
- 1/2 cup sunflower seeds, optional

In a blender, combine the first eight ingredients in order given; blend on high until smooth. Add sour cream and Parmesan cheese; blend on low just until mixed. Serve over pasta or spaghetti squash. Sprinkle with sunflower seeds if desired. **Yield:** 1-2/3 cups.

Cranberry Pork Roast

"Guests rave about this tender roast, and I love preparing it because it's so simple," relates Audrey Thibodeau of Mesa, Arizona.

- 1 boneless rolled pork loin roast (2-1/2 to 3 pounds)
- 1 can (16 ounces) jellied cranberry sauce
- 1/2 cup sugar
- 1/2 cup cranberry juice
- 1 teaspoon dry mustard
- 1/4 teaspoon ground cloves
- 2 tablespoons cornstarch

SATISFYING AND VERSATILE, cheese stars in Mozzarella Meat Loaf (recipe on this page), Potato Cheese Soup (recipe on page 58) and Cheesy Garlic Bread (recipe on page 86).

2 tablespoons cold water
Salt to taste

Place pork roast in a slow cooker. In a medium bowl, mash cranberry sauce; stir in sugar, cranberry juice, mustard and cloves. Pour over roast. Cover and cook on low for 6-8 hours or until meat is tender. Remove roast and keep warm. Skim fat from juices; measure 2 cups, adding water if necessary, and pour into a saucepan. Bring to a boil over medium-high heat. Combine the cornstarch and cold water to make a paste; stir into gravy. Cook and stir until thickened. Season with salt. Serve with sliced pork. **Yield:** 4-6 servings.

Stuffed Sole

(PICTURED ON THIS PAGE)

"Inspired by Mom's meals, I developed this recipe. The fish is moist and flavorful, and the sauce is so good over rice," assures Winnie Higgins of Salisbury, Maryland.

- 1 cup chopped onion
- 2 cans (4-1/4 ounces *each*) shrimp, rinsed and drained
- 1 jar (4-1/2 ounces) sliced mushrooms, drained
- 2 tablespoons butter *or* margarine
- 1/2 pound fresh cooked *or* canned crabmeat, drained and cartilage removed
- 8 sole *or* flounder fillets (2 to 2-1/2 pounds)
- 1/2 teaspoon salt
- 1/4 teaspoon pepper
- 1/4 teaspoon paprika
- 2 cans (10-3/4 ounces *each*) condensed cream of mushroom soup, undiluted
- 1/3 cup chicken broth
- 2 tablespoons water
- 2/3 cup shredded cheddar cheese
- 2 tablespoons minced fresh parsley
Cooked wild, brown *or* white rice *or* a mixture, optional

In a saucepan, saute onion, shrimp and mushrooms in butter until onion is tender. Add crabmeat; heat through. Sprinkle fillets with salt, pepper and paprika. Spoon crabmeat mixture on fillets; roll up and fasten with a toothpick. Place in a greased 13-in. x 9-in. x 2-in. baking dish. Combine the soup, broth and water; blend until smooth. Pour over fillets. Sprinkle with cheese. Cover and bake at 400° for 30 minutes. Sprinkle with parsley; return to the oven, uncovered, for 5 minutes or until the fish flakes easily with a fork. Serve over rice if desired. **Yield:** 8 servings.

SEAFOOD LOVERS will be delighted with from-scratch Stuffed Sole (recipe on this page).

Barbecued Trout

"Even those who aren't that fond of fish will like it prepared this way. The sauce prepared in this recipe really gives it a wonderful flavor," comments Vivian Wolfram of Mountain Home, Arkansas.

- 6 pan-dressed trout
- 2/3 cup soy sauce
- 1/2 cup ketchup
- 2 tablespoons lemon juice
- 2 tablespoons vegetable oil
- 1 teaspoon crushed dried rosemary
Lemon wedges, optional

Place trout in a single layer in a plastic bag or glass baking dish. Combine the soy sauce, ketchup, lemon juice, oil and rosemary; pour into bag or dish. Cover (or close bag) and let stand for 1 hour, turning once. Remove fish, reserving marinade. Place fish in a single layer in a well-greased hinged wire grill basket. Grill, covered, over medium coals for 8-10 minutes or until fish is browned on the bottom. Turn and baste with marinade; grill 5-7 minutes longer or until fish flakes easily with a fork. Serve with lemon if desired. **Yield:** 6 servings.

Thyme-Lime Chicken

"I like to find recipes that use the bounty of my herb garden," says Marge Clark of West Lebanon, Indiana. *"Thyme really enhances the flavor of chicken."*

- 2 tablespoons butter *or* margarine

- 2 tablespoons olive oil
- 2 tablespoons fresh lime juice
- 1 tablespoon minced fresh thyme *or* 1 teaspoon dried thyme
- 1 teaspoon grated lime peel
- 1 garlic clove, minced
- 1/2 teaspoon salt
- 1/4 teaspoon pepper
- 4 chicken breast halves
- 4 chicken thighs

In a small saucepan over low heat, melt butter in olive oil; add lime juice, thyme, lime peel, garlic, salt and pepper. Place chicken on a greased broiler pan. Brush with sauce. Broil, basting frequently, 6-7 in. from the heat for 15-20 minutes on each side or until the chicken juices run clear. **Yield:** 4-6 servings.

Chicken Salad Sandwiches

"Crisp cukes give a refreshing twist to the traditional in this recipe," explains Anna Mowan of Spencerville, Indiana.

- 2 cups diced cooked chicken
- 1 celery rib, diced
- 2 hard-cooked eggs, chopped
- 1 small cucumber, diced
- 1/3 cup salad dressing *or* mayonnaise
- 1/4 teaspoon salt
- 1/8 teaspoon dry mustard
- 1/8 teaspoon white pepper
Bread *or* pita bread

In a bowl, combine the first eight ingredients. Serve on bread or in pita bread. **Yield:** 4-6 servings.

SURELY SATISFYING Turkey Vegetable Skillet (recipe on this page) and Sugar-Free Strawberry Jam (recipe on page 93) fit needs of all folks, even those with special restrictions.

Turkey Vegetable Skillet

(PICTURED ON THIS PAGE)

"Everyone knows zucchini grows overnight!" declares June Formanek of Belle Plaine, Iowa. "I never like to let anything go to waste, so I try adding this hearty squash to every recipe I can."

✓ This tasty dish uses less sugar, salt and fat. Recipe includes *Diabetic Exchanges*.

- 1 pound ground turkey breast
- 1 small onion, chopped
- 1 garlic clove, minced
- 1 teaspoon vegetable oil
- 1 pound fresh tomatoes, chopped
- 1/4 pound zucchini, diced
- 1/4 cup chopped dill pickle
- 1 teaspoon dried basil
- 1/2 teaspoon pepper

In a skillet, brown turkey, onion and garlic in oil. Add remaining ingredients. Simmer, uncovered, for 5-10 minutes or until the turkey is cooked and zucchini is tender. **Yield:** 6 servings. **Diabetic Ex-**

changes: One serving equals 3 lean meat, 1 vegetable; also, 135 calories, 104 mg sodium, 47 mg cholesterol, 5 gm carbohydrate, 21 gm protein, 3 gm fat.

South Seas Chicken And Bananas

"Your taste buds get a tropical vacation when you prepare a platter of this chicken!" notes Wendy Smith of Eagleville, Pennsylvania.

- 1/4 cup lemon juice
- 1 can (14 ounces) sweetened condensed milk
- 1/3 cup milk
- 1/2 cup flaked coconut
- 1/8 teaspoon ground cardamom
- 6 very firm bananas, halved lengthwise
- 3 cups cornflake crumbs
- 5 to 6 pounds chicken pieces
- 3/4 cup butter *or* margarine, melted, *divided*

Sliced kiwifruit and starfruit, optional

In a food processor or blender, blend the lemon juice, condensed milk, milk, co-

conut and cardamom until smooth. Pour into a bowl. Dip bananas into milk mixture; roll in cornflakes and set aside. Dip chicken into remaining milk mixture; roll in the remaining cornflakes and place in two greased 13-in. x 9-in. x 2-in. baking pans. Drizzle with 1/2 cup of the melted butter. Bake, uncovered, at 350° for 1 hour. Arrange bananas over the chicken. Drizzle with remaining butter. Bake 15 minutes longer or until chicken juices run clear. Garnish with kiwi and starfruit if desired. **Yield:** 6-8 servings.

Cheddary Chicken Potpie

"This is a comforting chicken dish that features a medley of cheeses," comments Vicki Raatz of Waterloo, Wisconsin.

- 1 can (10-3/4 ounces) condensed cream of chicken soup, undiluted
- 1 cup milk, *divided*
- 1/2 cup chopped onion
- 1 package (3 ounces) cream cheese, softened
- 1/4 cup chopped celery
- 1/4 cup shredded carrots
- 1/4 cup grated Parmesan cheese
- 1/2 teaspoon salt
- 3 cups cubed cooked chicken
- 1 package (10 ounces) frozen chopped broccoli, cooked and drained
- 1 egg
- 1 tablespoon vegetable oil
- 1 cup buttermilk complete pancake mix
- 1 cup (4 ounces) shredded sharp cheddar cheese
- 1/4 cup sliced almonds, optional

In a large saucepan, combine soup, 1/2 cup of milk, onion, cream cheese, celery, carrots, Parmesan cheese and salt. Cook and stir until the mixture is hot and cream cheese is melted. Stir in the chicken and broccoli; heat through. Pour into an ungreased 2-qt. baking dish. In a medium bowl, combine the egg, oil and remaining milk. Add the pancake mix and cheddar cheese; blend well. Spoon over hot chicken mixture. Sprinkle with almonds if desired. Bake, uncovered, at 375° for 20-25 minutes or until golden brown. **Yield:** 6 servings.

Pan Burritos

"With this flavorful, satisfying casserole, you can get the taste of burritos and cut servings any size that you want," shares Joyce Kent of Grand Rapids, Michigan.

2 packages (1-1/2 ounces *each*)
enchilada sauce mix
3 cups water
1 can (12 ounces) tomato paste
1 garlic clove, minced
1/4 teaspoon pepper
Salt to taste
2 pounds ground beef
9 large flour tortillas (9 inches)
4 cups (16 ounces) shredded
cheddar cheese *or* taco
cheese
1 can (16 ounces) refried
beans, warmed
Taco sauce, sour cream, chili
peppers, chopped onion *and/or*
guacamole, optional

In a saucepan, combine the first six ingredients; simmer for 15-20 minutes. In
a skillet, brown the beef. Drain; stir in
one-third of the sauce. Spread another
third on the bottom of a greased 13-in. x
9-in. x 2-in. baking pan. Place three tortillas over sauce, tearing to fit bottom of
pan. Spoon half of meat mixture over
the tortillas; sprinkle with 1-1/2 cups
of cheese. Add three more tortillas.
Spread refried beans over tortillas; top
with remaining meat. Sprinkle with 1-1/2
cups of cheese. Layer remaining tortillas; top with the remaining sauce.
Sprinkle with remaining cheese. Bake,
uncovered, at 350° for 35-40 minutes.
Let stand 10 minutes before cutting.
Serve with taco sauce, sour cream, chili
peppers, chopped onion and/or guacamole if desired. **Yield:** 8-10 servings.

Howard's Sauerbraten

*"Cooking for family and friends is a
favorite pastime,"* offers Howard Koch
of Lima, Ohio. *"People always seem to
look forward to this tender beef roast
with traditional tangy gravy."*

2-1/2 cups water
1-1/2 cups red wine vinegar
1 carrot, finely chopped
1 celery rib, finely chopped
2 medium onions, sliced
8 whole cloves
4 bay leaves
1/2 teaspoon whole peppercorns
1 beef rump roast *or* eye of
round (about 3 pounds)
1/4 cup butter *or* margarine
GINGERSNAP GRAVY:
1/2 cup water
2 tablespoons sugar
1/2 cup gingersnap crumbs
(about 12 cookies)

In a medium saucepan, combine the first
eight ingredients; bring to a boil. Place
roast in a glass bowl. Pour hot marinade
over; cover and refrigerate for 48 hours,

turning meat twice each day. Remove
roast, reserving marinade; pat dry with
paper towel. In a Dutch oven, brown
the roast on all sides in butter. Strain
marinade; discard vegetables and seasonings. Add marinade to Dutch oven.
Cover and simmer until meat is tender,
about 3 hours. For gravy, remove 1-1/2
cups of the pan juices to a skillet; add
water and sugar. Bring to a boil, gradually dissolving sugar. Add gingersnap
crumbs; simmer until the gravy thickens.
Serve with sliced roast. **Yield:** 8 servings.

Herbed Pork Roast

*"This recipe proves pork roasts don't
have to be loaded with calories to be delicious,"* explains Dianne Bettin of Tru-
man, Minnesota. *"Even folks not on
restricted diets will find it appealing."*

✓ This tasty dish uses less sugar, salt and fat.
Recipe includes *Diabetic Exchanges*.

3 tablespoons finely chopped
fresh parsley, *divided*
2 teaspoons paprika
2 teaspoons dried basil
2 teaspoons salt, optional
1 teaspoon pepper
1 teaspoon garlic powder
1 teaspoon dried oregano
1/2 teaspoon crushed fennel
seed
1/2 teaspoon dried thyme
1 boneless extra-lean pork
roast (about 2 pounds)

Combine half of the parsley with the
herbs and seasonings. Rub over roast.
Place in a shallow pan; cover with remaining parsley. Roast, uncovered, at
325° for 35 minutes *per pound* or until
a meat thermometer reads 160°-170°.
Yield: 6 servings. **Diabetic Exchanges:**
One serving (prepared without added
salt) equals 4 lean meat; also, 239 calories, 86 mg sodium, 98 mg cholesterol,
2 gm carbohydrate, 32 gm protein, 11
gm fat.

Spanish Rice
And Chicken

*"My mother raised us on delicious cas-
seroles like this,"* recalls Cindy Clark of
Mechanicsburg, Pennsylvania. *"Now
I'm doing the same with my family."*

1 broiler-fryer chicken (2-1/2 to
3 pounds), cut up
1 teaspoon garlic salt
1 teaspoon celery salt

1 teaspoon paprika
1 cup uncooked rice
3/4 cup chopped onion
3/4 cup chopped green pepper
1/4 cup minced fresh parsley
1-1/2 cups chicken broth
1 cup chopped tomatoes
1-1/2 teaspoons salt
1-1/2 teaspoons chili powder

Place chicken in a greased 13-in. x 9-in.
x 2-in. baking pan. Combine garlic salt,
celery salt and paprika; sprinkle over
chicken. Bake, uncovered, at 425° for 20
minutes. Remove chicken from pan.
Combine rice, onion, green pepper and
parsley; spoon into the pan. In a saucepan, bring broth, tomatoes, salt and chili
powder to a boil. Pour over rice mixture;
mix well. Place chicken pieces on top.
Cover and bake for 45 minutes or until
chicken and rice are tender. **Yield:** 4-6
servings.

Inside Out Ravioli

*"With 10 children, I know the challenge
of finding a recipe everyone will eat,"*
attests Ethel Allbritton of Poplar Bluff,
Missouri. *"But the whole family loves
this spinach pasta."*

1 pound ground beef
1 medium onion, chopped
1 teaspoon salt
1/8 teaspoon pepper
1/8 teaspoon garlic powder
1 jar (14 ounces) spaghetti
sauce
1 can (8 ounces) tomato sauce
1 can (6 ounces) tomato paste
1 can (4 ounces) mushrooms,
drained
1 package (10 ounces) frozen
chopped spinach, thawed
and well drained
1 package (16 ounces)
corkscrew noodles, cooked
and drained
2 eggs, beaten
1/2 cup soft bread crumbs
2 cups (8 ounces) shredded
cheddar cheese
1-1/2 cups (6 ounces) shredded
mozzarella cheese

In a large skillet, cook beef with onion,
salt, pepper and garlic powder until the
onion is tender; drain. Stir in spaghetti
sauce, tomato sauce, tomato paste and
mushrooms; simmer 10 minutes. Combine the spinach, noodles, eggs, bread
crumbs and cheddar cheese; place half
in a greased 13-in. x 9-in. x 2-in. baking
dish. Top with half of the meat sauce.
Repeat layers. Cover and bake at 350°
for 40-45 minutes or until hot and bubbly. Sprinkle with mozzarella cheese; let
stand 10 minutes. **Yield:** 8-10 servings.

Light Chicken Kabobs

"These chicken kabobs are perfect because they can be prepared the night before," states Margaret Balley of Coffeeville, Mississippi.

✓ This tasty dish uses less sugar, salt and fat. Recipe includes *Diabetic Exchanges*.

    6 boneless skinless chicken
      breast halves
    2 large green peppers, cut into
      1-1/2-inch pieces
    2 large onions, cut into 18
      wedges
   18 medium fresh mushrooms
    1 bottle (8 ounces) low-fat
      Italian salad dressing
  1/4 cup light soy sauce
  1/4 cup Worcestershire sauce
    2 tablespoons lemon juice

Cut each chicken breast half into three lengthwise strips. Place all ingredients in a glass bowl or large plastic bag; cover or seal. Stir or turn to coat. Refrigerate 4 hours or overnight, turning occasionally. Remove chicken and vegetables, reserving marinade. Thread alternately on 18 short skewers. Grill over medium-hot coals, turning and basting with marinade occasionally, for 12-15 minutes or until chicken juices run clear. **Yield:** 6 servings. **Diabetic Exchanges:** One serving equals 3 lean meat, 2 vegetable; also, 210 calories, 673 mg sodium, 74 mg cholesterol, 13 gm carbohydrate, 29 gm protein, 4 gm fat.

Cordon Bleu Casserole

"Whenever I'm invited to attend a potluck, people usually ask me to bring this tempting casserole. The turkey, ham and cheese are delectable combined with the crunchy topping," comments Joyce Paul of Moose Jaw, Saskatchewan.

    4 cups cubed cooked turkey
    3 cups cubed fully cooked ham
    1 cup (4 ounces) shredded
      cheddar cheese
    1 cup chopped onion
  1/4 cup butter *or* margarine
  1/3 cup all-purpose flour
    2 cups light cream
    1 teaspoon dill weed

  1/8 teaspoon dry mustard
  1/8 teaspoon ground nutmeg
TOPPING:
    1 cup dry bread crumbs
    2 tablespoons butter *or*
      margarine, melted
  1/4 teaspoon dill weed
  1/4 cup shredded cheddar
      cheese
  1/4 cup chopped walnuts

In a large bowl, combine turkey, ham and cheese; set aside. In a saucepan, saute onion in butter until tender. Add flour; stir to form a paste. Gradually add cream, stirring constantly. Bring to a boil; boil 1 minute or until thick. Add dill, mustard and nutmeg; mix well. Remove from the heat and pour over the meat mixture. Spoon into a greased 13-in. x 9-in. x 2-in. baking dish. Toss bread crumbs, butter and dill; stir in cheese and walnuts. Sprinkle over the casserole. Bake, uncovered, at 350° for 30 minutes or until heated through. **Yield:** 8-10 servings.

Glazed Chicken with Lemon Relish

(PICTURED ON PAGE 111)

"This dish combines two elements I like in a recipe—herbs and citrus fruit," says Diane Hixon of Niceville, Florida.

  1/3 cup chicken broth
  1/4 cup butter *or* margarine
  1/4 cup chopped onion
    1 tablespoon honey
    1 teaspoon dried thyme
  1/2 teaspoon salt
  1/8 teaspoon pepper
    1 broiler-fryer chicken (about 3
      pounds), cut up
LEMON RELISH:
    1 lemon
  1/2 celery rib, chopped
  1/4 small sweet red pepper,
      chopped
    2 green onions, chopped
  1-1/2 teaspoons sugar
  1/2 teaspoon salt
  1/4 teaspoon hot pepper sauce

In a saucepan, combine the first seven ingredients; bring to a boil. Reduce heat and simmer, uncovered, for 5 minutes. Remove from the heat. Dip chicken pieces in glaze; place on broiler rack. Broil, approximately 5 in. from the heat, for 12 minutes, basting several times with the glaze. Turn chicken; broil 10-12 minutes more or until done. Meanwhile, trim outer portion of peel from lemon; set aside. Cut off and discard white membrane. Quarter lemon; discard seeds. Place lemon and peel in a food processor

or blender; process until peel is finely chopped. Add remaining relish ingredients; process until vegetables are finely chopped. Serve with the chicken. **Yield:** 4-6 servings (about 3/4 cup relish).

All-American Barbecue Sandwiches

(PICTURED ON PAGE 62)

Sue Gronholz of Columbus, Wisconsin writes, "This delicious recipe is my husband's favorite and a big hit with family and friends."

  4-1/2 pounds ground beef
  1-1/2 cups chopped onion
  2-1/4 cups ketchup
    3 tablespoons prepared mustard
    3 tablespoons Worcestershire
      sauce
    2 tablespoons vinegar
    2 tablespoons sugar
    1 tablespoon salt
    1 tablespoon pepper
   18 hamburger buns, split

In a Dutch oven, cook beef and onion until meat is browned and onion is tender; drain. Combine ketchup, mustard, Worcestershire, vinegar, sugar, salt and pepper; stir into beef mixture. Heat through. Serve on buns. **Yield:** 18 servings.

Catfish with Parsley Sauce

"Catfish is abundant here in Mississippi," informs Lee Bailey of Belzoni. *"So I was pleased to come across this new, interesting recipe. I hope you enjoy it as much as we do."*

SAUCE:
    2 cups tightly packed fresh
      parsley leaves
  1/2 cup olive oil
  1/2 cup chopped pecans
    1 garlic clove, minced
  1/2 cup grated Romano cheese
  1/2 cup grated Parmesan cheese
    2 tablespoons butter *or*
      margarine, cut into pieces
FILLETS:
    1 cup all-purpose flour
  1/2 to 1 teaspoon cayenne
      pepper
    1 teaspoon salt
    6 catfish fillets (6 to 8 ounces
      each)
    1 to 2 tablespoons vegetable oil
    1 to 2 tablespoons butter *or*
      margarine

In a food processor or blender, process

parsley until coarsely chopped. Add remaining sauce ingredients; process until smooth. Refrigerate. Combine the flour, cayenne pepper and salt in a bowl. Dredge each fillet; shake off excess. In a skillet, heat 1 tablespoon each of oil and butter. Fry fillets for 4-5 minutes or until golden brown. Turn fillets; add remaining oil and butter if necessary. Divide the sauce and spread evenly on the cooked side of each fillet. Cover and cook for 5 minutes or until fish flakes easily with a fork. **Yield:** 6 servings.

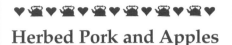

Herbed Pork and Apples

(PICTURED ON THIS PAGE)

"Whenever I make this roast, I'm reminded of the wonderful scent of apple orchards," shares Louise Keithley of Columbia, Missouri. "The aroma of the pork and apples certainly takes the chill out of the air."

> 1 teaspoon *each* dried sage, thyme, rosemary and marjoram, crushed
> 1 teaspoon salt
> 1 teaspoon pepper
> 1 pork loin roast with bone (about 6 pounds)
> 4 medium tart apples, cut into 1-inch chunks
> 1 large red onion, cut into 1-inch chunks
> 3 tablespoons brown sugar
> 1 cup apple juice
> 2/3 cup maple syrup

Combine herbs, salt and pepper; rub over roast. Cover and refrigerate for several hours or overnight. Bake, uncovered, at 325° for 1-1/2 hours. Drain fat. Mix apples and onion with brown sugar; spoon around roast. Continue to roast 1 hour or until meat thermometer reads 160°-170°. Transfer the roast, apples and onion to a serving platter and keep warm. Skim excess fat from meat juices; pour into a heavy skillet (or leave in the roasting pan if it can be heated on stovetop). Add apple juice and syrup. Cook and stir over medium-high heat until liquid has been reduced by half, about 1 cup. Slice the roast and serve with gravy. **Yield:** about 12 servings.

Overnight Apple French Toast

"This hearty breakfast combines fresh apples, apple jelly and applesauce in

MAKE SUNDAY DINNERS memorable with Herbed Pork and Apples (recipe on this page).

one recipe," states Debra Blazer of Hegins, Pennsylvania.

> 1 cup packed brown sugar
> 1/2 cup butter *or* margarine
> 2 tablespoons light corn syrup
> 2 large tart apples, peeled and sliced 1/4 inch thick
> 3 eggs
> 1 cup milk
> 1 teaspoon vanilla extract
> 9 slices day-old French bread (3/4 inch thick)

SYRUP:
> 1 cup applesauce
> 1 jar (10 ounces) apple jelly
> 1/2 teaspoon ground cinnamon
> 1/8 teaspoon ground cloves

In a small saucepan, cook brown sugar, butter and corn syrup until thick, about 5-7 minutes. Pour into an ungreased 13-in. x 9-in. x 2-in. baking pan; arrange apples on top. In a mixing bowl, beat eggs, milk and vanilla. Dip bread slices into the egg mixture for 1 minute; place over apples. Cover and refrigerate overnight. Remove from the refrigerator 30 minutes before baking. Bake, uncovered, at 350° for 35-40 minutes. Combine syrup ingredients in a medium saucepan; cook and stir until hot. Serve over French toast. **Yield:** 9 servings.

Farmhouse Barbecue Muffins

"Our daughter's friends all 'plowed' through a batch of these sandwiches at her birthday party. The tangy barbecue sauce, fluffy biscuits and cheddar cheese make them real kid-pleasers," says Karen Kenney of Harvard, Illinois.

> 1 tube (10 ounces) refrigerated buttermilk biscuits
> 1 pound ground beef
> 1/2 cup ketchup
> 3 tablespoons brown sugar
> 1 tablespoon cider vinegar
> 1/2 teaspoon chili powder
> 1 cup (4 ounces) shredded cheddar cheese

Separate dough into 10 biscuits; flatten into 5-in. circles. Press each into the bottom and up the sides of a greased muffin cup; set aside. In a skillet, brown ground beef; drain. In a small bowl, mix ketchup, brown sugar, vinegar and chili powder; stir until smooth. Add to meat and mix well. Divide the meat mixture among biscuit-lined muffins cups, using about 1/4 cup for each. Sprinkle with cheese. Bake at 375° for 18-20 minutes or until golden brown. Cool for 5 minutes before removing from tin and serving. **Yield:** 10 servings.

MERRY MENU. Snowdrifts can't dampen spirited dinner featuring Chicken Kiev (recipe this page), Buttery Crescents (recipe on page 88) and Snowflake Cake (recipe on page 104).

Chicken Kiev

(PICTURED ON THIS PAGE)

"A favorite aunt shared this special recipe with me. It makes attractive individual servings fancy enough to be served for company," says Lynne Peterson of Salt Lake City, Utah.

- 1/4 cup butter *or* margarine, softened
- 1 tablespoon grated onion
- 1 tablespoon chopped fresh parsley
- 1/2 teaspoon garlic powder
- 1/2 teaspoon dried tarragon
- 1/4 teaspoon pepper
- 6 boneless skinless chicken breast halves
- 1 egg
- 1 tablespoon milk
- 1 envelope (2-3/4 ounces) seasoned chicken coating mix

Combine the butter, onion, parsley, garlic powder, tarragon and pepper. Shape mixture into six pencil-thin strips about 2 in. long; place on waxed paper. Freeze until firm, about 30 minutes. Flatten each chicken breast to 1/4 in. Place one butter strip in the center of each chicken breast. Fold long sides over butter; fold ends up and secure with a toothpick. In a bowl, beat egg and milk; place coating mix in another bowl. Dip chicken in milk, then roll in coating mix. Place chicken, seam side down, in a greased 13-in. x 9-in. x 2-in. baking pan. Bake, uncovered, at 425° for 35-40 minutes or until the chicken is no longer pink and juices run clear. Remove toothpicks before serving. **Yield:** 6 servings.

Pork and Green Chili Casserole

"This zippy casserole was brought by a co-worker to a picnic at my house. People raved over it," writes Dianne Esposite of New Middletown, Ohio.

- 1-1/2 pounds boneless pork, cut into 1/2-inch cubes
- 1 tablespoon cooking oil
- 1 can (15 ounces) black beans, rinsed and drained
- 1 can (10-3/4 ounces) condensed cream of chicken soup, undiluted
- 1 can (14-1/2 ounces) diced tomatoes, undrained
- 2 cans (4 ounces *each*) chopped green chilies
- 1 cup quick-cooking brown rice
- 1/4 cup water
- 2 to 3 tablespoons salsa
- 1 teaspoon ground cumin
- 1/2 cup shredded cheddar cheese

In a large skillet, saute pork in oil until no pink remains; drain. Add the beans, soup, tomatoes, chilies, rice, water, salsa and cumin; cook and stir until bubbly. Pour into an ungreased 2-qt. baking dish. Bake, uncovered, at 350° for 30 minutes or until bubbly. Sprinkle with cheese; let stand a few minutes before serving. **Yield:** 6 servings.

"Humpty-Dumpty" Sandwiches

"Instead of ordinary egg salad, spark up brown-bag lunches with this hearty sandwich," suggests Cheryl Miller of Fort Collins, Colorado.

- 1 hard-cooked egg, chopped
- 1 celery rib, chopped
- 1/3 cup small curd cottage cheese
- 1/4 cup shredded cheddar cheese
- 1 to 1-1/2 teaspoons spicy brown mustard
- 1/4 teaspoon salt
- 1/8 teaspoon pepper
- 4 slices whole wheat bread

Lettuce leaves

In a bowl, combine the first seven ingredients. Spread on 2 slices of bread. Top with lettuce and remaining bread. **Yield:** 2 servings.

Spaghetti Squash Casserole

"Spaghetti squash, like zucchini, can take over a garden. This is an excellent way to put that abundance to good use," informs Mina Dyck of Boissevain, Manitoba.

- 1 small spaghetti squash (1-1/2 to 2 pounds)
- 1/2 cup water
- 1 pound ground beef
- 1/2 cup chopped onion
- 1/2 cup chopped sweet red pepper
- 1 garlic clove, minced
- 1 can (8 ounces) tomatoes with liquid, cut up
- 1/2 teaspoon dried oregano
- 1/4 teaspoon salt
- 1/8 teaspoon pepper
- 1 cup (4 ounces) shredded mozzarella *or* cheddar cheese

1 tablespoon chopped fresh
parsley

Cut squash in half lengthwise; scoop out seeds. Place with cut side down in a baking dish; add water. Cover and bake at 375° for 20-30 minutes or until it is easily pierced with a fork. When cool enough to handle, scoop out the squash, separating the strands with a fork. In a skillet, cook beef, onion, red pepper and garlic until the meat is browned and the vegetables are tender. Drain; add tomatoes, oregano, salt, pepper and squash. Cook and stir for 1-2 minutes or until liquid is absorbed. Transfer to an ungreased 1-1/2-qt. baking dish. Bake, uncovered, at 350° for 25 minutes. Sprinkle with cheese and parsley; let stand a few minutes. **Yield:** 6-8 servings.

Stromboli

(PICTURED ON THIS PAGE)

Offers Leigh Lauer of Hummelstown, Pennsylvania, "This is a nice recipe because you can add ingredients and spices to suit your taste."

  2 loaves (1 pound *each*) frozen
    bread dough, thawed
1/4 pound sliced ham
1/4 pound sliced pepperoni
1/4 cup chopped onion
1/4 cup chopped green pepper
  1 jar (14 ounces) pizza sauce,
    divided
1/4 pound sliced mozzarella
    cheese
1/4 pound sliced bologna
1/4 pound sliced hard salami
1/4 pound sliced Swiss cheese
  1 teaspoon dried basil
  1 teaspoon dried oregano
1/4 teaspoon garlic powder
1/4 teaspoon pepper
  2 tablespoons butter *or*
    margarine, melted

Let dough rise in a warm place until doubled. Punch down. Roll loaves together into one 15-in. x 12-in. rectangle. Layer ham and pepperoni on half of the dough (lengthwise). Sprinkle with onion and green pepper. Top with 1/4 cup of pizza sauce. Layer the mozzarella, bologna, salami and Swiss cheese over sauce. Sprinkle with basil, oregano, garlic powder and pepper. Spread another 1/4 cup of pizza sauce on top. Fold plain half of dough over filling and seal edges well. Place on a greased 15-in. x 10-in. x 1-in. baking pan. Bake at 375° for 30-35 minutes or until golden brown. Brush with melted butter. Heat the remaining pizza sauce and serve with sliced stromboli. **Yield:** 8-10 servings.

Easy Oven Stew

"I like to serve this beefy stew to guests because it can be made ahead," says Rita Zagrzebski, Eagle River, Wisconsin.
✓ **This tasty dish uses less sugar, salt and fat.**
Recipe includes *Diabetic Exchanges*.

3/4 pound boneless beef round
    steak, trimmed and cubed
  1 tablespoon cooking oil
  4 medium unpeeled potatoes,
    cut into 1-inch cubes
  5 medium carrots, cut into
    1-1/2-inch chunks
  1 celery rib, cut into 1-inch
    chunks
  1 large onion, cut into 1-inch
    chunks
  1 can (14-1/2 ounces) chunky
    stewed tomatoes
  3 tablespoons quick-cooking
    tapioca
  1 teaspoon browning sauce
1/8 to 1/4 teaspoon pepper
  1 cup frozen peas

In a Dutch oven, brown the steak in oil. Add the next eight ingredients; cover and bake at 300° for 4-5 hours, stirring twice. Add the peas during the last 30 minutes of baking. **Yield:** 6 servings. **Diabetic Exchanges:** One serving equals 2 starch, 2 vegetable, 1 meat; also, 263 calories, 257 mg sodium, 33 mg cholesterol, 38 gm carbohydrate, 17 gm protein, 5 gm fat.

Tangy Meatballs

"This recipe originally came from my mother-in-law, then I made a few adjustments," notes Ralph Wheat of Bedford, Texas. "These tender meatballs make a great entree."

  3 slices white bread, torn into
    small pieces
  1 cup milk
2-1/2 pounds ground beef
1/2 pound bulk pork sausage
  1 medium onion, finely chopped
  1 tablespoon mustard seed
  2 teaspoons seasoned salt
  2 garlic cloves, minced
  1 egg, beaten
Salt and pepper to taste
  3 tablespoons cooking oil
  2 bottles (10 ounces each) chili
    sauce
  1 jar (8 ounces) grape jelly
1-1/2 cups beef broth

In a large bowl, combine bread and milk. Squeeze excess milk out of bread; discard milk. To the bread, add beef, sausage, onion, mustard seed, seasoned salt, garlic, egg, salt and pepper; shape into 1-1/2-in. balls. In a large skillet, brown meatballs in oil; drain. In a large suacepan or Dutch oven, combine chili sauce, jelly and beef broth; slowly bring to a boil. Add meatballs; simmer for 30-45 minutes. **Yield:** 10 servings.

DELICIOUS DUO. Easy and Quick Guacamole (recipe on page 50) with tortilla chips and slices of hearty Stromboli (recipe on this page) are super snacks for family and friends.

SIDE DISHES

There's no better way to complement your main meal than with these delightful dishes and relishes featuring produce, pasta, potatoes and rice.

Oven Parmesan Chips

(PICTURED ON THIS PAGE)

"These delectable sliced potatoes get nice and crispy and give our meals a lift," explains Mary Lou Kelly of Scottdale, Pennsylvania.

 4 **medium unpeeled baking potatoes**
 1/4 **cup butter** *or* **margarine, melted**
 1 **tablespoon finely minced onion**
 1/2 **teaspoon salt**
 1/8 **teaspoon pepper**
Dash paprika
 2 **tablespoons grated Parmesan cheese**

Cut potatoes into 1/4-in. slices; place on a greased baking sheet in a single layer. Mix butter, onion, salt, pepper and paprika; brush on one side of potatoes, then turn and brush other side. Bake at 425° for 15-20 minutes or until potatoes are tender and golden. Sprinkle with Parmesan cheese; serve immediately. **Yield:** 4-6 servings.

Creamy Dilled Carrots

"This is a wonderfully different way to serve carrots," reports Howard Koch of Lima, Ohio. "They go with most any meal and add nice color to the table."

 4 **cups thinly sliced carrots**
 3/4 **cup water**
 1 **tablespoon butter** *or* **margarine**
 1/2 **teaspoon salt**
 1/4 **teaspoon sugar**
Pinch white pepper
 1 **tablespoon all-purpose flour**
 1/2 **cup light cream**
 2 **teaspoons dill weed** *or* 2 **tablespoons snipped fresh dill**

In a saucepan, combine carrots, water, butter, salt, sugar and pepper. Cover and simmer until carrots are crisp-tender, about 10 minutes. Drain liquid into a small saucepan; set the carrots aside and keep warm. Bring liquid to a boil. In a small bowl, combine flour and cream until smooth; slowly add to liquid, stirring constantly. Simmer for 10 minutes, stirring occasionally. Pour over the carrots; stir in dill. Cover and let stand for 15 minutes before serving. **Yield:** 6-8 servings.

Green Beans with Hazelnut-Lemon Butter

"Oregon is famous for hazelnuts," relates Woodburn, Oregon cook Earlene Ertelt. "Their crunch is delicious with fresh green beans."

 1 **pound fresh green beans, cut**
 1/4 **cup butter** *or* **margarine**
 1/2 **cup toasted chopped hazelnuts** *or* **almonds**
 1 **tablespoon lemon juice**
 1 **teaspoon minced fresh parsley**
 1/2 **teaspoon dried basil**
 1/2 **teaspoon salt**

In a saucepan, cover beans with water; cover and cook until crisp-tender, about 15 minutes. Meanwhile, in a small saucepan over medium-high heat, brown the butter. Add the hazelnuts, lemon juice, parsley, basil and salt; heat through. Drain beans; add the butter mixtrue and toss to coat. Serve immediately. **Yield:** 4 servings.

Sweet Broiled Grapefruit

(PICTURED ON PAGE 111)

"I was never a fan of grapefruit until I had it broiled at a restaurant—it was so tangy and delicious! I finally got the recipe and now make it often," contributes Terry Bray of Haines City, Florida.

 1 **large grapefruit, sliced in half**
 2 **tablespoons butter** *or* **margarine, softened**

AVOIDING FRIED FOODS? You'll really enjoy Oven Parmesan Chips (recipe on this page).

2 tablespoons sugar
1/2 teaspoon ground cinnamon
Maraschino cherry for garnish,
   optional

Cut membrane out of the center of each grapefruit half. Cut around each section so it will be easy to spoon out when eating. Place 1 tablespoon butter in the center of each half. Combine sugar and cinnamon; sprinkle over each. Broil until butter is melted and sugar is bubbly. Garnish with a cherry if desired. Serve immediately. **Yield:** 2 servings.

Sugared Asparagus

(PICTURED ON THIS PAGE)

"This tasty recipe is a simple way to dress up one of our favorite vegetables—asparagus!" shares Billie Moss of El Sobrante, California.

**3 tablespoons butter *or*
   margarine
2 tablespoons brown sugar
2 pounds fresh asparagus, cut
   into 2-inch pieces (about
   4 cups)
1 cup chicken broth**

In a skillet over medium-high, heat butter and brown sugar until sugar is dissolved. Add asparagus; saute for 2 minutes. Stir in chicken broth; bring to a boil. Reduce heat; cover and simmer for 8-10 minutes or until asparagus is crisp-tender. Remove asparagus to a serving dish and keep warm. Cook sauce, uncovered, until reduced by half. Pour over the asparagus and serve immediately. **Yield:** 4-6 servings.

Pasta with Asparagus

(PICTURED ON THIS PAGE)

"The garlic, asparagus, Parmesan cheese and red pepper flakes in this tempting dish create an irresistible taste combination," says Jean Fisher of Redlands, California.

**5 garlic cloves, minced
1 teaspoon crushed red pepper
   flakes
2 to 3 dashes hot pepper sauce
1/4 cup olive oil
1 tablespoon butter *or* margarine
1 pound fresh asparagus, cut
   into 1-1/2-inch pieces
Salt to taste
1/4 teaspoon pepper
1/4 cup shredded Parmesan
   cheese
1/2 pound mostaccioli *or* elbow
   macaroni, cooked and drained**

CRISP EARLY CROP is the basis for (clockwise from bottom) Saucy Chicken and Asparagus (recipe on page 68), Sugared Asparagus and Pasta with Asparagus (recipes on this page).

In a skillet, cook garlic, red pepper flakes and hot pepper sauce in oil and butter for 2-3 minutes. Add asparagus, salt and pepper; saute until asparagus is crisp-tender, about 8-10 minutes. Add Parmesan cheese; mix well. Pour over hot pasta and toss to coat. Serve immediately. **Yield:** 4-6 servings.

Cheese Potato Puff

(PICTURED ON PAGE 68)

Beverly Templeton of Garner, Iowa writes, "This comforting potato recipe is wonderful because it contains basic ingredients that everyone loves like milk and cheddar cheese."

**12 medium potatoes, peeled
   (about 5 pounds)
1 teaspoon salt, *divided*
3/4 cup butter *or* margarine
2 cups (8 ounces) shredded
   cheddar cheese
1 cup milk
2 eggs, beaten
Fresh *or* dried chives, optional**

Place potatoes in a large kettle; cover with water. Add 1/2 teaspoon of salt; cook until tender. Drain; mash potatoes until smooth. In a saucepan, cook and stir butter, cheese, milk and remaining salt until smooth. Stir into the potatoes; fold in the eggs. Pour into a greased 3-qt. baking dish. Bake, uncovered, at 350° for 40 minutes or until puffy and golden brown. Sprinkle with chives if desired. **Yield:** 8-10 servings.

Sugarless Applesauce

(PICTURED ON PAGE 69)

Informs Margery Bryan of Royal City, Washington, "A friend gave me this recipe some 20 years ago, and I've made applesauce this way ever since." (Try using this applesauce in the Applesauce Oatmeal Pancakes recipe on page 69.)

✓ This tasty dish uses less sugar, salt and fat.
Recipe includes *Diabetic Exchanges.*

**8 cups sliced peeled tart apples
1/2 to 1 can (12 ounces) diet
   white soda
1/2 to 1 teaspoon ground
   cinnamon**

In a saucepan over medium heat, cook apples, soda and cinnamon until apples are tender, about 45 minutes. Serve warm or cold. **Yield:** 8 servings. **Diabetic Exchanges:** One serving equals 1 fruit; also, 74 calories, 1 mg sodium, 0 cholesterol, 19 gm carbohydrate, trace protein, trace fat.

Hungarian Noodle Side Dish

(PICTURED ON THIS PAGE)

Betty Sugg of Akron, New York writes, "I first served this creamy, rich casserole at a meeting at church. Everyone liked it and many of the ladies wanted the recipe. The original recipe was from a friend, but I changed it a bit to suit our tastes."

    3 chicken bouillon cubes
1/4 cup boiling water
    1 can (10-3/4 ounces) condensed
       cream of mushroom soup,
       undiluted
1/2 cup chopped onion
    2 tablespoons Worcestershire
       sauce
    2 tablespoons poppy seeds
1/8 to 1/4 teaspoon garlic powder
1/8 to 1/4 teaspoon hot pepper
       sauce
    2 cups (16 ounces) cottage
       cheese
    2 cups (16 ounces) sour cream
    1 package (16 ounces) medium
       noodles, cooked and drained
1/4 cup shredded Parmesan
       cheese
Paprika

In a large bowl, dissolve bouillon in water. Add the next six ingredients; mix well. Stir in cottage cheese, sour cream and noodles and mix well. Pour into a greased 2-1/2-qt. baking dish. Sprinkle with the Parmesan cheese and paprika. Cover and bake at 350° for 45 minutes or until heated through. **Yield:** 8-10 servings. **Editor's Note:** Casserole may be covered and refrigerated overnight. Allow to stand at room temperature for 30 minutes before baking.

Polish Sausage Patties

"I like to prepare these patties when I'm serving a special breakfast for family or friends," explains Loretta Ruda of Kennesaw, Georgia. "Everyone loves their down-home flavor."

    5 pounds pork butt *or* steak,
       trimmed
    5 teaspoons dried marjoram
    5 teaspoons salt
    1 teaspoon garlic powder
1/4 teaspoon pepper
    2 cups water

In a food processor, process pork until coarsely ground (or have your butcher grind the meat); place in a large bowl.

Add marjoram, salt, garlic powder and pepper; mix well. Add water and mix well. Shape into 20 patties, 4 in. each. Fry in a skillet over medium heat for 20-25 minutes or until thoroughly cooked. **Yield:** 20 servings. **Editor's Note:** Patties can be frozen. Sausage can also be stuffed into casings to make links.

Sweet Potatoes With Apples

"This satisfying dish is very welcome at any meal at our house, especially on holidays. The tart apple slices taste so good baked on top of the mild sweet potatoes," says Jean Winfree of Merrill, Wisconsin.

    3 to 3-1/2 pounds sweet potatoes
    2 tart apples, peeled, cored and
       cut into 1/4-inch rings
1/2 cup orange juice
1/4 cup packed brown sugar
1/4 teaspoon ground ginger
1/4 teaspoon ground cinnamon

    2 tablespoons butter *or*
       margarine

In a large saucepan, cover sweet potatoes with water; bring to a boil. Reduce heat; cover and simmer for 30 minutes or until just tender. Drain and cool slightly. Peel and cut into 1/4-in. slices. Alternate layers of potatoes and apples in a greased 13-in. x 9-in. x 2-in. baking dish. Pour orange juice over. Mix brown sugar, ginger and cinnamon; sprinkle over potatoes and apples. Dot with butter. Bake, uncovered, at 350° for 35-45 minutes or until apples have reached desired doneness. **Yield:** 8 servings.

Tomatoes Supreme

"After I retired, I persuaded my wife to let me do most of the food preparation," Wendell Obermeier of Charles City, Iowa reveals. "This refreshing side dish is simple to put together, but the results are fantastic."

    8 thick tomato slices
    1 teaspoon salt
1/2 teaspoon pepper
    2 teaspoons sugar
    8 thin sweet onion slices

ARE YOU HUNGRY FOR PASTA? Creamy Hungarian Noodle Side Dish (recipe on this page) is guaranteed to please. It can be made ahead and goes well with meaty main dishes.

1/2 cup vinegar
8 green pepper rings
Chopped fresh parsley

Place tomato slices on paper towel to drain excess moisture; place on serving plate. Combine salt, pepper and sugar; lightly sprinkle half over tomatoes. Top each tomato with an onion slice. Sprinkle 1 tablespoon of vinegar over each onion. Sprinkle remaining salt mixture over onions. Cover and refrigerate at least 30 minutes before serving. Garnish with green pepper rings and parsley. **Yield:** 8 servings.

Paradise Cran-Applesauce

(PICTURED ON THIS PAGE AND BACK COVER)

Sallie McQuay of Sayre, Pennsylvania shares, "Whether I use this recipe for a holiday dinner or to spark up a Sunday supper, it wouldn't be a feast without a bowl of beautiful and delicious cran-applesauce!"

**4 cups fresh *or* frozen
   cranberries
1/4 cup water
8 cups sliced peeled cooking
   apples
2 cups sugar**

In a covered saucepan, simmer cranberries and water for 20-25 minutes or until tender. Press through a sieve or food mill; return to the saucepan. Add apples; cover and simmer for 35-40 minutes or until apples are tender but retain their shape. Add sugar. Simmer for 5 minutes, stirring occasionally. **Yield:** 8-10 servings.

Summer Squash Saute

"Yes, my family loves squash of all kinds," confirms Shelbyville, Tennessee's Jane Chartrand, who shares this fresh-tasting dish sparked with flavors of bacon and Parmesan cheese.

**1 large red onion, sliced
2 tablespoons cooking oil
2 cups halved small sunburst
   or pattypan squash
2 small yellow squash, cut into
   1/2-inch slices
1 medium sweet red pepper,
   julienned
1 medium green pepper,
   julienned
2 teaspoons minced fresh basil
   or 1/2 teaspoon dried basil
2 tablespoons red wine vinegar**

SIMPLY EXTRAORDINARY SIDE DISH. Eye-catching tart apple slices peek through a tangy ruby-red cranberry sauce in one-of-a-kind Paradise Cran-Applesauce (recipe on this page).

**4 bacon strips, cooked and
   crumbled
1/4 cup grated Parmesan cheese**

In a large skillet, saute onion in oil until tender. Stir in the squash, peppers and basil. Cover and cook until vegetables are crisp-tender. Remove from the heat; stir in vinegar and bacon. Sprinkle with Parmesan cheese. **Yield:** 8-10 servings.

Parsley Rice Casserole

"Who says rice has to be plain?" asks Mary Alice Stefancik of Westlake, Ohio. "Everyone will rave about the subtle flavors in this rice casserole."

**2 eggs, beaten
2 cups milk
2 cups cooked rice
1 cup chopped fresh parsley
1/2 cup butter *or* margarine,
   melted
1 tablespoon finely chopped
   onion
1 teaspoon celery salt
1/2 teaspoon salt
3/4 cup shredded cheddar
   cheese**

In a bowl, combine eggs, milk and rice. Stir in parsley, butter, onion, celery salt and salt. Pour into a greased 2-qt. baking dish; sprinkle with cheese. Set dish

in a 13-in. x 9-in. x 2-in. pan; add 1 in. of hot water to pan. Bake at 350° for 50-60 minutes or until a knife inserted in the center comes out clean. **Yield:** 4-6 servings.

> **WINTERTIME TREAT.** You can enjoy fresh-tasting corn on the cob throughout the year. Just freeze fresh ears with the husks on in plastic freezer bags.

Freezer Sweet Corn

"Whenever I serve this corn, people can't believe that it's frozen, not fresh," states Judi Oudekerk of St. Michael, Minnesota. "It's always crisp! I got the recipe from my daughter's mother-in-law, who lives on an Iowa farm."

**4 quarts fresh-cut sweet corn
   (18 to 20 ears)
1 quart hot water
2/3 cup sugar
1/2 cup butter *or* margarine
2 teaspoons salt**

Combine all ingredients in a large kettle; simmer for 5-7 minutes, stirring occasionally. Pour into large shallow containers to cool; stir occasionally. Spoon into freezer bags or containers; freeze. **Yield:** 3 quarts.

BREADS, ROLLS & MUFFINS

You'll savor these oven-fresh quick breads, coffee cakes, muffins and yeast breads topped with jam or jelly.

Heart-Shaped Herbed Rolls

(PICTURED ON PAGE 72)

"Refrigerated crescent rolls give you a head start on these festive rolls," reveals Marcy Cella of L'Anse, Michigan. "You'll love their convenience!"

- 1 tube (8 ounces) refrigerated crescent rolls
- 1 tablespoon butter *or* margarine, softened
- 1 teaspoon Italian seasoning

Cut crescent roll dough apart along the perforations. Spread all eight triangles with butter and sprinkle with Italian seasoning. Make four stacks by placing two pieces of dough on top of each other, stretching as needed to match the shapes. Using a 2-1/2-in. cookie cutter, cut two heart shapes out of each stack. Place on an ungreased baking sheet. Bake at 375° for 11-13 minutes. Serve warm. **Yield:** 8 rolls.

Cheesy Garlic Bread

(PICTURED ON PAGE 74)

Judy Skaar of Pardeeville, Wisconsin writes, "I find this crisp bread smothered in a full-flavored topping adds zip to an ordinary meal. It's also a satisfying snack or appetizer. A friend shared this recipe a while back. I always come home with an empty plate when I take it to a gathering."

- 1-1/2 cups mayonnaise
- 1 cup (4 ounces) shredded sharp cheddar cheese
- 1 cup thinly sliced green onions with tops
- 3 garlic cloves, minced
- 1 loaf French bread (about 20 inches), halved lengthwise
- 1/3 cup minced fresh parsley, optional
- Paprika, optional

Mix mayonnaise, cheese, onions and garlic; spread on bread halves. If desired, sprinkle with parsley and paprika. Wrap each half in foil. Refrigerate for

1-2 hours or freeze. Unwrap and place on a baking sheet. Bake at 400° for 8-10 minutes (20-25 minutes if frozen) or until puffed but not brown. Cut into slices. **Yield:** 12-15 servings.

Monkey Bread

"When our boys hear me preparing this sweet bread, they're eager to help," informs Carol Allen of McLeansboro, Illinois. "It always seems to taste twice as good when they help fix it."

- 1 package (3-1/2 ounces) cook and serve butterscotch pudding mix
- 3/4 cup sugar
- 1 tablespoon ground cinnamon
- 1/2 cup finely chopped pecans, optional
- 1/2 cup butter *or* margarine, melted
- 3 tubes (10 ounces *each*) refrigerated biscuits

In a plastic bowl with tight-fitting lid, combine pudding mix, sugar, cinnamon and pecans if desired. Pour the butter into a shallow bowl. Cut the biscuits into quarters. Dip several pieces into the butter, then place in bowl; cover and shake. Remove to a greased 10-in. fluted tube pan. Continue until all the biscuit pieces are coated. Bake at 350° for 30-35 minutes. Cool in pan for 30 minutes before inverting onto a serving plate. **Yield:** 10-12 servings.

Easy Bran Muffins

"Granddaughter Kelsey entered these muffins in a baking contest at age 4," declares Vergennes, Vermont cook Peggy Reed. "Because the ingredients are measured in whole amounts, it's a perfect recipe for kids."

- 6 cups bran cereal (not flakes)
- 2 cups boiling water
- 1 cup butter *or* margarine, softened
- 3 cups sugar
- 4 eggs
- 5 cups all-purpose flour

- 5 teaspoons baking soda
- 1 teaspoon salt
- 1 quart buttermilk

Combine cereal and water; let stand 10 minutes. In a mixing bowl, cream butter and sugar. Add the eggs, one at a time, beating well after each addition. Combine flour, baking soda and salt; add to creamed mixture alternately with buttermilk. Fold in cereal mixture. Fill greased or paper-lined muffin cups two-thirds full. Bake at 400° for 15-20 minutes. **Yield:** 5-6 dozen.

Grandma's Orange Rolls

(PICTURED ON PAGE 111)

"Both our two children and grandchildren love these fine-textured sweet rolls. We have our own orange, lime and grapefruit trees, and it's such a pleasure to go out and pick fruit right off the tree," states Norma Poole of Auburndale, Florida.

- 1 package (1/4 ounce) active dry yeast
- 1/4 cup warm water (110° to 115°)
- 1 cup warm milk (110° to 115°)
- 1/4 cup shortening
- 1/4 cup sugar
- 1 teaspoon salt
- 1 egg, lightly beaten
- 3-1/2 to 3-3/4 cups all-purpose flour
- FILLING:
- 1 cup sugar
- 1/2 cup butter *or* margarine, softened
- 2 tablespoons grated orange peel
- GLAZE:
- 1 cup confectioners' sugar
- 4 teaspoons butter *or* margarine, softened
- 4 to 5 teaspoons milk
- 1/2 teaspoon lemon extract

In a small bowl, dissolve yeast in water. In a large mixing bowl, mix milk, shortening, sugar, salt and egg. Add yeast mixture and blend. Stir in enough flour to form a soft dough. Knead on a lightly floured board until smooth and elastic, about 6-8 minutes. Place in a greased bowl, turning once to grease top. Cover and let rise in a warm place until doubled, about 1 hour. Punch dough down; divide in half. Roll each half into a 15-in. x 10-in. rectangle. Mix filling ingredients until smooth. Spread half the filling on each rectangle. Roll up, jelly-roll style, starting with a long end. Cut each into 15 rolls. Place in two greased 11-in. x 7-in. x 2-in. baking pans. Cover and let rise until doubled, about 45 minutes. Bake at 375° for 20-25 minutes or until lightly browned. Mix glaze ingredients; spread over warm rolls. **Yield:** 30 rolls.

Cheese Twists

(PICTURED ON THIS PAGE)

Michelle Beran of Claflin, Kansas admits, "These impressive loaves take a little time to prepare, but they're well worth the effort. I've used the recipe for several years. I love making bread—there's no better way to work out life's little frustrations and with such yummy results!"

> 3-1/4 cups all-purpose flour
> 2 packages (1/4 ounce *each*) active dry yeast
> 1-1/2 cups buttermilk
> 3/4 cup butter *or* margarine
> 1/2 cup sugar
> 1/2 teaspoon salt
> 5 eggs
> 3-1/2 to 4 cups whole wheat flour, *divided*
> 2 cups (8 ounces) shredded cheddar cheese

In a large mixing bowl, combine all-purpose flour and yeast. In a saucepan, heat buttermilk, butter, sugar and salt to 120°-130°; add to flour mixture. Blend on low speed until moistened. Add eggs; beat on low for 30 seconds. Beat on high for 3 minutes. Stir in enough whole wheat flour to make a soft dough. Turn onto a floured board; knead until smooth and elastic, about 6-8 minutes. Place in a greased bowl, turning once to grease top. Cover and let rise in a warm place until nearly doubled, about 1 hour. Punch dough down; divide in half. On a lightly floured board, roll each into a 12-in. x 9-in. rectangle. Cut each into three 12-in. x 3-in. strips. Combine cheese with 2 tablespoons of the remaining whole wheat flour; sprinkle 1/3 cup down the

WONDERFUL WHEAT is basic, hearty ingredient in many satisfying recipes like Wheat Waffles (recipe on page 67), Cheese Twists and Honey Wheat Bread (recipes on this page).

center of each strip. Bring long edges together over cheese and pinch to seal. Place three strips seam side down on greased baking sheets. Braid strips together; secure ends. Cover and let rise until doubled, about 45 minutes. Bake at 375° for 20-25 minutes or until golden. Immediately remove from baking sheets to wire racks; cool. **Yield:** 2 loaves.

KEEP THEM HANDY. If you freeze berries or rhubarb for future baking projects, pre-measure the amounts called for in your favorite recipes. This allows you to quickly whip up sweet treats later without messy measuring of frozen ingredients.

Honey Wheat Bread

(PICTURED ON THIS PAGE)

"This recipe produces two beautiful, high loaves that have wonderful texture and slice very well. The tempting aroma of this bread baking can cut the chill from a cool day. It's a tribute to the goodness of wheat," confirms Dorothy Anderson, Ottawa, Kansas.

✓ **This tasty dish uses less sugar, salt and fat. Recipe includes** *Diabetic Exchanges.*

> 3-1/2 cups whole wheat flour, *divided*

> 2-1/2 to 3 cups all-purpose flour
> 2 packages (1/4 ounce *each*) active dry yeast
> 1 cup milk
> 1-1/4 cups water
> 1/4 cup honey
> 3 tablespoons butter *or* margarine
> 1 tablespoon salt

In a large mixing bowl, combine 2 cups whole wheat flour, 2 cups all-purpose flour and yeast. In a saucepan, heat milk, water, honey, butter and salt to 120°-130°; add to flour mixture. Blend on low speed until moistened; beat on medium for 3 minutes. Gradually stir in remaining whole wheat flour and enough of the remaining all-purpose flour to form a soft dough. Turn onto a floured board; knead until smooth and elastic, about 6-8 minutes. Place in a greased bowl, turning once to grease top. Cover and let rise in a warm place until doubled, about 1 hour. Punch dough down. Shape into two loaves; place in greased 8-in. x 4-in. x 2-in. loaf pans. Cover and let rise until doubled, about 1 hour. Bake at 375° for 40-45 minutes. Remove from pans to cool on wire racks. **Yield:** 2 loaves. **Diabetic Exchanges:** One 1/2-inch slice (prepared with skim milk and margarine) equals 1 starch; also, 99 calories, 216 mg sodium, 0 cholesterol, 19 gm carbohydrate, 3 gm protein, 1 gm fat.

Apricot Banana Bread

(PICTURED ON THIS PAGE)

"Making this delightfully different twist on traditional banana bread is fun. It tastes excellent spread with cream cheese or butter. When I take this bread to bake sales, it really goes fast. I also make it in small loaf pans to give as gifts. I discovered the recipe in 1955 and have been making it since," reports Betty Hull of Stoughton, Wisconsin.

      1/3 cup butter *or* margarine,
          softened
      2/3 cup sugar
        2 eggs
        1 cup mashed ripe bananas
          (2 to 3 medium)
      1/4 cup buttermilk
    1-1/4 cups all-purpose flour
        1 teaspoon baking powder
      1/2 teaspoon baking soda
      1/2 teaspoon salt
        1 cup bran cereal (not flakes)
      3/4 cup chopped dried apricots
          (about 6 ounces)
      1/2 cup chopped walnuts

In a mixing bowl, cream butter and sugar. Add eggs; mix well. Combine bananas and buttermilk. Combine the flour, baking powder, baking soda and salt; add to creamed mixture alternately with banana mixture. Stir in bran, apricots and nuts. Pour into a greased 9-in. x 5-in. x 3-in. loaf pan. Bake at 350° for 55-60 minutes or until bread tests done. Cool 10 minutes before removing from pan to a wire rack. **Yield:** 1 loaf.

Jam-Filled Muffins

"Kids and adults love the sweet surprise inside each muffin," assures Jessie MacLeod of St. Stephen, New Brunswick. "They go great in any lunch."

    1-3/4 cups all-purpose flour
      1/2 cup sugar
        1 tablespoon baking powder
      1/2 teaspoon salt
        2 eggs
      2/3 cup milk
      1/3 cup butter *or* margarine,
          melted
        1 teaspoon grated lemon peel
      1/2 cup raspberry *or* strawberry
          jam

In a large bowl, combine flour, sugar, baking powder and salt. In a small bowl, lightly beat eggs; add milk, butter and lemon peel. Pour into dry ingredients and stir just until moistened. Spoon half of the batter into 12 greased or paper-lined muffin cups. Make a well in the center of each; add jam. Spoon remaining batter over jam. Bake at 400° for 20-25 minutes or until golden. **Yield:** 1 dozen.

Buttery Crescents

(PICTURED ON PAGE 80)

"I learned this recipe 28 years ago, when I was a new bride and my grandmother taught me how to make these rolls. They're crusty outside and tender inside," shares Lynne Peterson of Salt Lake City, Utah.

        2 packages (1/4 ounce *each*)
          active dry yeast
        2 cups warm milk (110° to 115°)
    6-1/2 to 7 cups all-purpose flour
        2 eggs, lightly beaten
      1/4 cup butter *or* margarine,
          melted and cooled
        3 tablespoons sugar
        1 teaspoon salt
    Additional melted butter *or*
        margarine, optional

In a large mixing bowl, dissolve yeast in milk. Add 4 cups flour, eggs, butter, sugar and salt; beat until smooth. Add enough remaining flour to form a soft dough. Turn onto a floured board; knead until smooth and elastic, about 6-8 minutes. Place in a greased bowl, turning once to grease top. Cover and let rise in a warm place until doubled, about 1 hour. Punch the dough down and divide in thirds. Roll each portion into a 12-in. circle; cut each circle into 12 wedges. Roll up wedges from the wide end and place with pointed end down on greased baking sheets. Cover and let rise until doubled, about 30 minutes. Bake at 400° for 12-14 minutes or until golden brown. Brush with butter if desired. **Yield:** 3 dozen.

Chocolate Zucchini Bread

"I shred and freeze zucchini from my garden each summer so that I can make this bread all winter long," explains Shari McKinney from Birney, Montana. "Our family loves this bread."

        3 eggs
        1 cup vegetable oil
        2 cups sugar
        1 tablespoon vanilla extract
        2 cups shredded peeled
          zucchini (about 1 medium)
    2-1/2 cups all-purpose flour
      1/2 cup baking cocoa
        1 teaspoon salt
        1 teaspoon baking soda
        1 teaspoon ground cinnamon
      1/4 teaspoon baking powder

In a mixing bowl, beat eggs, oil, sugar and vanilla. Stir in zucchini. Combine dry ingredients; add to zucchini mixture and

NUTRITIOUS SNACKING is made simple with Apricot Banana Bread (recipe on this page).

mix well. Pour into two greased 8-in. x 4-in. x 2-in. loaf pans. Bake at 350° for 1 hour or until bread tests done. **Yield:** 2 loaves.

♥☎♥☎♥☎♥☎♥☎♥☎♥

Cranberry Canes

In shape for the holidays, these confections from Sublimity, Oregon's Darlene Markel are made from a recipe her mother handed down. "I still think her breads are better than mine even when we're using the same recipe!" Darlene admits.

FILLING:
 1-1/2 cups chopped fresh *or* frozen cranberries
 1/2 cup sugar
 1/2 cup raisins
 1/3 cup chopped walnuts
 1/3 cup honey
DOUGH:
 1 package (1/4 ounce) active dry yeast
 1/4 cup warm water (110° to 115°)
 4 cups all-purpose flour
 1/4 cup sugar
 1 teaspoon salt
 1 cup butter *or* margarine
 1 cup warm milk (110° to 115°)
 2 eggs, lightly beaten
Confectioners' sugar icing, optional

In a saucepan, combine all filling ingredients; bring to a boil. Reduce heat and simmer, uncovered, for 5 minutes. Cool. For dough, dissolve yeast in water; set aside. In a large bowl, combine flour, sugar and salt. Cut in butter until mixture resembles coarse crumbs. Add yeast mixture, milk and eggs; stir to form a soft dough. Place in a greased bowl; cover with plastic wrap. Refrigerate at least 2 hours. Divide dough in half. On a well-floured board, roll each half into an 18-in. x 15-in. rectangle. Spoon filling down the center of each rectangle widthwise. Fold into thirds so finished rectangles are 15 in. x 6 in. Cut each into 15 strips. Twist strips and shape into candy canes. Place on greased baking sheets. Bake at 375° for 15-18 minutes or until golden. Cool. Frost with confectioners' sugar icing if desired. **Yield:** 30 rolls.

♥☎♥☎♥☎♥☎♥☎♥☎♥

Pumpkin Bread

"I keep my freezer stocked with home-baked goodies. This recipe is a winner with our harvest crew," relates Joyce Jackson of Bridgetown, Nova Scotia.

 1-1/2 cups sugar
 1 cup cooked *or* canned pumpkin
 1/2 cup vegetable oil

 1/2 cup water
 2 eggs
1-2/3 cups all-purpose flour
 1 teaspoon baking soda
 1 teaspoon ground cinnamon
 3/4 teaspoon salt
 1/2 teaspoon baking powder
 1/2 teaspoon ground nutmeg
 1/4 teaspoon ground cloves
 1/2 cup chopped walnuts
 1/2 cup raisins, optional

In a mixing bowl, combine sugar, pumpkin, oil, water and eggs; beat well. Combine dry ingredients; gradually add to pumpkin mixture and mix well. Stir in nuts and raisins if desired. Pour into a greased 9-in. x 5-in. x 3-in. loaf pan. Bake at 350° for 65-70 minutes or until bread tests done. Cool 10 minutes in pan before removing to a wire rack. **Yield:** 1 loaf.

HARVEST a bushel of compliments with tasty Nutty Apple Muffins (recipe on this page).

♥☎♥☎♥☎♥☎♥☎♥☎♥

Nutty Apple Muffins

(PICTURED ON THIS PAGE)

Gloria Kaufmann of Orrville, Ohio contributes, "I teach quick-bread making for 4-H, and I'm always on the lookout for good new recipes. My sister-in-law shared this recipe with me for a slightly different kind of muffin. With apples and coconut, they are moist, chewy and tasty."

 1-1/2 cups all-purpose flour
 1-1/2 teaspoons baking soda
 3/4 teaspoon salt
 1/2 teaspoon ground nutmeg
 2 eggs

 1 cup plus 2 tablespoons sugar
 1/3 cup vegetable oil
 2 cups diced peeled apples
 1-1/2 cups chopped walnuts
 3/4 cup flaked coconut

In a large bowl, combine the flour, baking soda, salt and nutmeg. In another bowl, beat eggs, sugar and oil. Stir in apples, nuts and coconut. Stir into dry ingredients just until moistened. Fill 18 greased muffin cups three-fourths full. Bake at 350° for 25-30 minutes. Cool in pan 10 minutes before removing to a wire rack. **Yield:** 1-1/2 dozen.

♥☎♥☎♥☎♥☎♥☎♥☎♥

Chive Garden Rolls

"I never seem to have enough of these flavorful rolls on hand," remarks Joanie Elbourn of Gardner, Massachusetts. "Folks like the subtle taste of chives."

✓ This tasty dish uses less sugar, salt and fat. Recipe includes *Diabetic Exchanges.*

 1 egg
 1 cup (8 ounces) nonfat cottage cheese
 1/4 cup vegetable oil
 2 teaspoons honey
 1 teaspoon salt
 1 package (1/4 ounce) active dry yeast
 1/2 cup warm water (110° to 115°)
 1/4 cup wheat germ
2-3/4 to 3-1/4 cups all-purpose flour
 3 tablespoons chopped fresh *or* dried chives
TOPPING:
 1 egg, beaten
 1 small onion, finely chopped

In a mixing bowl, combine the egg, cottage cheese, oil, honey and salt. Dissolve yeast in warm water; add to egg mixture. Add wheat germ and 1-1/2 cups flour. Mix on medium speed for 3 minutes. Add chives and enough remaining flour to form a soft dough. Turn onto a floured board; knead until smooth and elastic, about 10 minutes. Place in a greased bowl, turning once to grease top. Cover and let rise in a warm place until doubled, about 1 hour. Punch dough down; roll out to 3/4-in. thickness. Cut with a 3-in. round cutter and place on greased baking sheets. Cover and let rise until doubled, about 45 minutes. Brush tops with egg and sprinkle with onion. Bake at 350° for 15-20 minutes or until the rolls are golden brown. **Yield:** about 1 dozen. **Diabetic Exchanges:** One serving (1 roll) equals 2 starch, 1 fat; also, 205 calories, 270 mg sodium, 35 mg cholesterol, 29 gm carbohydrate, 8 gm protein, 6 gm fat.

Any Way You Slice It, Bread Machines Save Time

AUTOMATIC bread-baking with machine frees Mary Jane Cantrell for other activities.

YOU'LL have more time for loafing with an automatic bread machine!

The popular new kitchen appliance is fascinating home bakers with the prospect of simply measuring ingredients, pushing a button and later removing a luscious loaf of fresh bread.

But are the automatic home bakeries all they're cracked up to be? Is the bread as good as that made by more traditional (and time-consuming) methods?

We asked field editors for comments and favorite bread machine recipes, which they enthusiastically supplied.

"When my husband originally asked me if I'd like a bread machine, I said no!" admits Ruth Andrewson of Leavenworth, Washington. "I love making bread, but it takes a lot of time.

"So, 3 years ago, I got a bread machine. I love mine so much that we've bought them for our children, too."

Old-Fashioned Daily Bread

Of all the recipes Ruth's tried in her DAK machine, Oatmeal Bread is her favorite. It has a lightly sweet flavor with good texture and crust. "I make it every third day, sometimes adding part whole wheat flour," she says.

Another loaf Ruth often makes is Onion Dill Bread. Moist and flavorful, it owes its richness to cottage cheese and sour cream. (See her recipes at far right.)

Like Ruth, Mary Jane Cantrell had baked bread traditionally for years before buying a Zojirushi machine.

"I've always enjoyed making bread, but finding the time was a problem," conveys this Turlock, California contributing editor.

"I do miss not being able to knead the bread—to me that's one of the most enjoyable parts of making it. However, the time saved can really be put to good use...and I can still offer my family fresh-baked bread."

Topping Mary Jane's list of favorite recipes is Buttermilk Wheat Bread (above right). "It has a golden crust, wonderful texture and taste that's as close to homemade as any recipe I've tried," she contends.

Here at *Taste of Home*, we tested Ruth's and Mary Jane's recipes in a Hitachi Home Bakery—adjusting the crust setting to obtain the desired color —with good results.

Food Editor Mary Beth Jung advises, "Since every bread machine is a little different, be sure to carefully read the instructions for yours regarding its operation and features.

"If you are dissatisfied with how a recipe turns out, you can consult references like *The Bread Machine Magic Book of Helpful Hints* by Linda Rehberg and Lois Conway, which discusses common problems, causes and cures."

Red Star Yeast has a hotline staffed by home economists familiar with bread machines (1-800/445-4746 ext. 4) as well as a handy brochure, "Helpful Hints for Bread Machines from Red Star", that includes tips like these:

● White sugar, brown sugar, honey and molasses may be interchanged equally in most bread machine recipes. When substituting honey or molasses for sugar, decrease another liquid ingredient in recipe by the same amount.

● Yeast functions best in an automatic bread machine when the liquid temperature is between 75° and 85°.

● Use bread flour for best results.

BUTTERMILK WHEAT BREAD

    1-1/2 cups buttermilk
    1-1/2 tablespoons butter *or*
       margarine
       2 tablespoons sugar
       1 teaspoon salt

    3 cups bread flour
    1/3 cup whole wheat flour
    1 package (1/4 ounce) active
       dry yeast

In bread machine pan, place all ingredients in order given. Select "white bread" setting. Bake according to bread machine directions. **Yield:** 1 loaf (1-1/2 pounds).

ONION DILL BREAD

       1 package (1/4 ounce) active
          dry yeast
    3-1/2 cups bread flour
       1/4 teaspoon salt
       1 unbeaten egg, room
          temperature
       1/4 cup water
       3/4 cup cream-style cottage
          cheese
       3/4 cup sour cream
       3 tablespoons sugar
       3 tablespoons minced dried
          onion
       2 tablespoons dill seed
    1-1/2 tablespoons butter *or*
          margarine

In bread machine pan, place first four ingredients in order given. In a saucepan, combine remaining ingredients and heat just until warm (do not boil). Pour into bread pan. Select "white bread" setting. Bake according to bread machine directions. **Yield:** 1 loaf (1-1/2 pounds).

OATMEAL BREAD

       1 package (1/4 ounce) active
          dry yeast
       1 cup quick-cooking oats
       3 cups bread flour
       1 teaspoon salt
       1/2 cup molasses
       1 tablespoon vegetable oil
    1-1/4 cups plus 1 tablespoon warm
          water

In bread machine pan, place ingredients in order given. Select "white bread" setting. Bake according to bread machine directions. **Yield:** 1 loaf (1-1/2 pounds).

APPETIZING aroma advertises fresh bread from Ruth Andrewson's well-used machine.

Upside-Down Peach Muffins

"These novel muffins make pretty individual servings for breakfast, a snack or even dessert," comments Geraldine Grisdale, Mt. Pleasant, Michigan.

    2 cups all-purpose flour
1-1/2 cups sugar
    1 tablespoon baking powder
1/2 teaspoon salt
1/4 cup shortening, melted
    2 eggs, lightly beaten
    1 cup milk
    6 tablespoons butter *or*
       margarine
    1 cup plus 2 tablespoons
       packed brown sugar
    3 cups sliced peeled ripe
       peaches

In a mixing bowl, combine flour, sugar, baking powder and salt. Add shortening, eggs and milk; mix until smooth. In the bottom of 18 greased muffin cups, place 1 teaspoon of butter and 1 tablespoon brown sugar. Place in a 375° oven for 5 minutes. Arrange peaches in the muffin cups. Fill each half full with batter. Bake at 375° for 25 minutes or until browned. Turn out of pans immediately. **Yield:** 1-1/2 dozen.

Cardamom Holiday Bread

"Don't limit this festive bread to the holidays," says Sheryl Olstad from her Rochester, New Hampshire home. *"Family and friends will be delighted to see it on the table year-round."*

    2 packages (1/4 ounce *each*)
       active dry yeast
3/4 cup warm water (110° to 115°)
    1 can (12 ounces) evaporated
       milk
    1 cup sugar
    1 teaspoon salt
1/2 cup butter *or* margarine,
       softened
    4 eggs, beaten
    1 to 1-1/2 teaspoons ground
       cardamom
7-1/2 to 8 cups all-purpose flour
Confectioners' sugar glaze
Candied cherries and sliced
    almonds

In a mixing bowl, dissolve yeast in water. Add milk, sugar, salt, butter, eggs, cardamom and 2 cups flour; beat until smooth. Add enough remaining flour to form a soft dough. Turn onto a floured board; knead until smooth and elastic, 6-

8 minutes. Place in greased bowl, turning once to grease top. Cover and let rise in a warm place until doubled, about 1-1/2 hours. Punch dough down; let rest 10 minutes. Divide into nine portions; shape each into a 12-in. strip. Place three strips on a greased baking sheet and braid, sealing ends. Repeat with remaining strips. Cover and let rise until nearly doubled, about 45 minutes. Bake at 375° for 20-25 minutes or until golden. Cool. Glaze and decorate with cherries and almonds. **Yield:** 3 loaves.

Applesauce Muffins

"This batter keeps in the refrigerator for 2 weeks, so you can quickly bake these moist, cake-like muffins whenever you want," comments Linda Williams of Lafayette, Alabama.

    1 cup butter *or* margarine,
       softened
    2 cups sugar
    2 eggs
    1 teaspoon vanilla extract
    2 cups applesauce
    4 cups all-purpose flour
    2 teaspoons baking soda
    1 teaspoon ground cinnamon
    1 teaspoon ground allspice
1/2 teaspoon ground cloves
    1 cup chopped walnuts,
       optional
Cinnamon-sugar, optional

In a mixing bowl, cream butter and sugar. Add eggs and vanilla; mix well. Stir in applesauce. Combine flour, baking soda and spices; stir into creamed mixture. Fold in nuts. Fill greased or paper-lined muffin cups three-fourths full. Bake at 350° for 25 minutes or until muffins test done. Sprinkle with cinnamon-sugar if desired. **Yield:** about 2 dozen.

Rhubarb Coffee Cake

"My daughter gave me the recipe for this moist coffee cake. It mixes up quickly and is ideal for the family's weekend breakfast. The tangy rhubarb and crunchy nuts are nice accents," writes Page Alexander of Baldwin City, Kansas.

1/2 cup butter *or* margarine,
       softened
1/2 cup packed brown sugar
1/4 cup sugar
    1 egg
    1 teaspoon vanilla extract
1-1/4 cups all-purpose flour
3/4 cup whole wheat flour
    1 teaspoon baking powder

1/2 teaspoon baking soda
1/4 teaspoon salt
1/4 teaspoon ground cinnamon
    1 cup buttermilk
    2 cups diced fresh *or* frozen
       rhubarb
TOPPING:
1/4 cup packed brown sugar
1-1/2 teaspoons ground cinnamon
1/2 cup chopped walnuts

In a mixing bowl, cream butter and sugars. Add egg and vanilla; beat until fluffy. Combine flours, baking powder, baking soda, salt and cinnamon; add to creamed mixture alternately with buttermilk, mixing well after each addition. Stir in rhubarb. Pour into a greased 13-in. x 9-in. x 2-in. baking pan. Combine the topping ingredients; sprinkle evenly over batter. Bake at 350° for 35 minutes or until a wooden pick inserted near the center comes out clean. Serve warm or at room temperature. **Yield:** 12-16 servings.

Whole Wheat Hamburger Buns

"I never baked much bread—much less hamburger buns—until I worked as a baker at a ranch camp," shares Dawn Fagerstrom of Warren, Minnesota. *"This recipe from the camp files has become a favorite of mine."*

    2 packages (1/4 ounce *each*)
       active dry yeast
1-3/4 cups warm water (110° to 115°)
1-1/4 cups whole wheat flour
1/4 cup nonfat dry milk powder
    3 tablespoons sugar
    2 teaspoons salt
    2 teaspoons lemon juice
    5 tablespoons butter *or*
       margarine, melted, *divided*
3-1/2 to 4 cups all-purpose flour

In a large mixing bowl, dissolve yeast in warm water; let stand 5 minutes. Add wheat flour, dry milk, sugar, salt, lemon juice, 3 tablespoons butter and 1 cup all-purpose flour. Beat until smooth. Add enough of the remaining all-purpose flour to form a soft dough. Turn onto a floured board; knead until smooth and elastic, about 10 minutes. Place in a greased bowl, turning once to grease top. Cover and let rise in a warm place until doubled, about 1 hour. Punch down. Shape into 14 buns, about 3-1/2 in. in diameter. Place on greased baking sheets; brush with 1 tablespoon of the remaining butter. Cover and let rise until doubled, about 30 minutes. Bake at 375° for 14-16 minutes. Remove from baking sheets; brush with remaining butter. Cool on wire racks. **Yield:** 14 buns.

Delicious Potato Doughnuts

(PICTURED ON THIS PAGE)

"I first tried these treats at my sister's house. The fudge frosting tops them off well," says Pat Davis of Beulah, Michigan.

2 cups hot mashed potatoes (mashed with milk and butter)
2-1/2 cups sugar
2 cups buttermilk
2 eggs, lightly beaten
2 tablespoons butter *or* margarine, melted
2 teaspoons baking soda
2 teaspoons baking powder
1 teaspoon ground nutmeg
1/2 teaspoon salt
6-1/2 to 7 cups all-purpose flour
Cooking oil
FAST FUDGE FROSTING:
4 cups (1 pound) confectioners' sugar
1/2 cup baking cocoa
1/4 teaspoon salt
1/3 cup boiling water
1/3 cup butter *or* margarine, melted
1 teaspoon vanilla extract

In a large bowl, combine potatoes, sugar, buttermilk and eggs. Stir in butter, baking soda, baking powder, nutmeg, salt and enough of the flour to form a soft dough. Turn onto a lightly floured surface; pat out to 3/4-in. thickness. Cut with a 2-1/2-in. floured doughnut cutter. In an electric skillet, heat 1 in. of oil to 350°. Fry the doughnuts for 2 minutes per side or until browned. Place on paper towels. For frosting, sift sugar, cocoa and salt into a large bowl. Stir in water, butter and vanilla. Dip tops of warm doughnuts in frosting. **Yield:** 4 dozen.

Poppy Seed Snack Bread

"A slice of this bread is a great between-meal snack," assures Kathy Scott of Hemingford, Nebraska.

1 package (18-1/2 ounces) white cake mix without pudding
1 package (3.4 ounces) instant coconut cream pudding mix
4 eggs, lightly beaten
1 cup hot water
1/2 cup vegetable oil
2 tablespoons poppy seeds

In a mixing bowl, combine the cake and pudding mixes, eggs, water and oil; beat for 2 minutes. Fold in poppy seeds. Pour into two greased and floured 8-1/2-in. x 4-1/2-in. x 2-1/2-in. loaf pans. Bake at 350° for 35-40 minutes or until golden. **Yield:** 2 loaves.

Cranberry Nut Bread

"This moist, dark sweet bread is chock full of old-fashioned, spicy goodness," notes Maxine Smith of Owanka, South Dakota.

2-1/2 cups halved fresh *or* frozen cranberries, *divided*
2/3 cup sugar
2 teaspoons grated orange peel
2-1/4 cups all-purpose flour
3/4 cup packed light brown sugar
1 tablespoon baking soda
1/2 teaspoon salt
2 teaspoons ground cinnamon
1/4 teaspoon ground cloves
2 eggs, lightly beaten
3/4 cup sour cream
1/4 cup butter *or* margarine, melted
1 cup chopped pecans

In a saucepan, combine 1-1/2 cups cranberries, sugar and orange peel. Bring to a boil; reduce heat and cook for 6-8 minutes or until the cranberries are soft. Remove from the heat; stir in the remaining berries and set aside. In a bowl, combine flour, brown sugar, baking soda, salt, cinnamon and cloves. Combine eggs, sour cream and butter; stir into dry ingredients until blended. Fold in cranberries and pecans. Pour into two greased 8-1/2-in. x 4-1/2-in. x 2-1/2-in. loaf pans. Bake at 350° for 55-60 minutes or until the bread tests done. **Yield:** 2 loaves.

Nutty Sweet Potato Biscuits

"Mom often left a plate of these warm wonderful biscuits waiting for us when we got home from school. What a treat!" shares Mrs. India Thacker of Clifford, Virginia.

2-3/4 cups all-purpose flour
4 teaspoons baking powder
1-1/4 teaspoons salt
1/2 teaspoon ground cinnamon
1/2 teaspoon ground nutmeg
3/4 cup chopped nuts
2 cups mashed sweet potatoes
3/4 cup sugar
1/2 cup butter *or* margarine, melted
1 teaspoon vanilla extract

In a large mixing bowl, combine flour, baking powder, salt, cinnamon, nutmeg and nuts. In another bowl, combine sweet potatoes, sugar, butter and vanilla; add to flour mixture and mix well. Turn onto a lightly floured surface and knead

DELICIOUS Potato Doughnuts (recipe on this page) make a sweet addition to all your breakfasts.

slightly. Roll dough to 1/2-in. thickness. Cut with a 2-1/2-in. biscuit cutter and place on lightly greased baking sheets. Bake at 450° for 12 minutes or until golden brown. **Yield:** 1-1/2 to 2 dozen.

Pecan Cranberry Muffins

(PICTURED ON THIS PAGE)

"I store these muffins in the freezer and reheat them when we want them," comments Suzanne McKinley of Lyons, Georgia.

- 1-1/2 cups chopped fresh *or* frozen cranberries
- 1-1/4 cups sugar, *divided*
- 3 cups all-purpose flour
- 4-1/2 teaspoons baking powder
- 1/2 teaspoon salt
- 1/2 cup butter *or* margarine
- 2 eggs, lightly beaten
- 1 cup milk
- 1 cup chopped pecans
- 1 tablespoon grated lemon peel

In a bowl, toss cranberries with 1/4 cup sugar; set aside. Combine flour, baking powder, salt and remaining sugar. Cut in butter until the mixture resembles coarse crumbs. Combine the eggs and milk; stir into the flour mixture just until moistened. Fold in pecans, lemon peel and cranberries. Fill greased or paper-lined muffin cups two-thirds full. Bake at 400° for 20-25 minutes or until muffins test done. **Yield:** about 1-1/2 dozen.

Easy Potato Rolls

Jeanette McKinney of Belleview, Missouri writes, *"I make this dough ahead of time when company is coming and keep some in the refrigerator to make for 'hay hands' on our cattle ranch."*

- 2/3 cup sugar
- 2/3 cup shortening
- 1 cup mashed potatoes
- 2-1/2 teaspoons salt
- 2 eggs
- 2 packages (1/4 ounce *each*) active dry yeast
- 1-1/3 cups warm water (110° to 115°), *divided*
- 6 to 6-1/2 cups all-purpose flour

In a large mixing bowl, cream sugar and shortening. Add the potatoes, salt and eggs. In a small bowl, dissolve yeast in 2/3 cup of warm water; add to creamed mixture. Beat in 2 cups of flour and remaining water. Add enough remaining flour to form a soft dough. Shape into a ball; do not knead. Place in a greased

BAKE AND FREEZE pleasing Pecan Cranberry Muffins (recipe on this page) for a fast treat.

bowl, turning once to grease top. Cover and let rise in a warm place until doubled, about 1 hour. Punch dough down; divide into thirds. Shape each portion into 15 balls and arrange in three greased 9-in. round baking pans. Cover and let rise until doubled, about 30 minutes. Bake at 375° for 20-25 minutes. Remove from pans to cool on wire racks. **Yield:** 45 rolls.

IT'S A JAM-BOREE!

Try these sweet tasty toppings on all of your fresh-from-the-oven breads.

Wild Plum Jelly

"Each year when wild plums are ripe, I'll fill my pail and make this jelly," informs Ludell Heuser from her Mt. Horeb, Wisconsin home. *"It's so good!"*

- 5 pounds wild plums, halved and pitted
- 4 cups water
- 1 package (1-3/4 ounces) powdered fruit pectin
- 7-1/2 cups sugar

In a large kettle, simmer plums and water until tender, about 30 minutes. Pour through a damp jelly bag, allowing juice to drip into a bowl. Measure 5-1/2 cups of juice; return to the kettle. Add pectin; stir and bring to a boil. Add sugar; bring to a full rolling boil. Boil for 1 minute, stirring constantly. Remove from the heat; skim off any foam. Pour hot into hot jars, leaving 1/4-in. headspace. Adjust caps. Process for 5 minutes in a boiling-water bath. **Yield:** about 8 half-pints.

Sugar-Free Strawberry Jam

(PICTURED ON PAGE 76)

"My husband was tired of eating flavorless jams and jellies for diabetics, so I came up with this," explains Rita Christ of Wauwatosa, Wisconsin. *"It also makes a nice gift."*

✓ This tasty dish uses less sugar, salt and fat. Recipe includes *Diabetic Exchanges*.

- 3/4 cup diet lemon-lime soda
- 1 package (.3 ounce) sugar-free strawberry-flavored gelatin
- 1 cup mashed fresh *or* unsweetened frozen strawberries
- 1-1/2 teaspoons lemon juice

In a saucepan, bring soda to a boil. Remove from the heat; stir in gelatin until dissolved. Stir in strawberries and lemon juice. Pour into jars or plastic containers; cover and refrigerate up to 3 weeks. Do not freeze. **Yield:** 1-3/4 cups. **Diabetic Exchanges:** One serving (1 tablespoon) equals a free food; also, 4 calories, 9 mg sodium, 0 cholesterol, 1 gm carbohydrate, trace protein, trace fat.

COOKIES & BARS

Tempt your family with a cookie jar full of tasty morsels—
or a platter stacked with a bounty of bars.

Apricot Bars

(PICTURED ON PAGE 51)

Sioux Falls, South Dakota cook Helen Cluts explains, "My family likes snacking on these rich bars. This recipe's one I've used and shared for over 30 years."

- 1 cup all-purpose flour
- 1 teaspoon baking powder
- 1/2 cup butter *or* margarine
- 1 egg
- 1 tablespoon milk
- 1 cup apricot preserves
TOPPING:
- 1 egg, lightly beaten
- 2/3 cup sugar
- 1/4 cup butter *or* margarine, melted
- 1 teaspoon vanilla extract
- 2 cups shredded coconut

In a bowl, combine flour and baking powder. Cut in butter until the mixture resembles coarse crumbs. Beat the egg and milk; stir into flour mixture. Spread in a greased 9-in. square baking pan. Spread preserves over crust. Combine topping ingredients; carefully drop by tablespoonfuls over apricot layer. Bake at 350° for 25-30 minutes or until golden brown. Cool; cut into small bars. **Yield:** 2 to 2-1/2 dozen.

Turtle Bars

"I always have good intentions of taking some of these bars to parties, but my family finishes them too soon!" admits Faye Hintz of Springfield, Missouri.

- 2 cups all-purpose flour
- 1 cup packed brown sugar
- 1/2 cup butter *or* margarine, softened
- 1 cup pecan halves
TOPPING:
- 2/3 cup butter *or* margarine
- 1/2 cup packed brown sugar
- 1 cup (6 ounces) semisweet chocolate chips

In a mixing bowl, beat flour, sugar and butter on medium speed for 2-3 minutes. Press firmly into an ungreased 13-in. x

9-in. x 2-in. baking pan. Arrange pecans over crust. Combine butter and brown sugar in a heavy saucepan. Bring to a boil; boil for 1 minute, stirring constantly. Pour over pecans. Bake at 350° for 18-22 minutes or until bubbly. Sprinkle chocolate chips on top; let stand for 3 minutes. Spread chocolate but allow some chips to remain whole. Cool completely; cut into small squares. **Yield:** about 8 dozen.

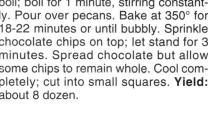

Mom's Chocolate Chip Cookies

"My mom often brightened my lunch with these yummy cookies," recalls Tammy Orr of Wharton, New Jersey.

- 1 cup butter *or* margarine, softened
- 3/4 cup packed brown sugar
- 1/4 cup sugar
- 1 package (3.4 ounces) instant vanilla pudding mix
- 2 eggs, lightly beaten
- 1 teaspoon vanilla extract
- 2-1/4 cups all-purpose flour
- 1 teaspoon baking soda
- 2 cups (12 ounces) semisweet chocolate chips

In a mixing bowl, cream butter and sugars. Add pudding mix, eggs and vanilla. Combine flour and baking soda; add to creamed mixture and mix well. Fold in chocolate chips. Drop by teaspoonfuls onto ungreased baking sheets. Bake at 375° for 10-12 minutes or until lightly browned. **Yield:** 4 dozen.

Sour Cream Cutouts

"These soft cookies make a comforting anytime snack," pledges Marlene Jackson of Kingsburg, California. "They have a delicious, delicate flavor and cake-like texture."

- 1 cup butter *or* margarine, softened
- 1-1/2 cups sugar
- 3 eggs

- 1 cup (8 ounces) sour cream
- 2 teaspoons vanilla extract
- 3-1/2 cups all-purpose flour
- 2 teaspoons baking powder
- 1 teaspoon baking soda
FROSTING:
- 1/3 cup butter *or* margarine, softened
- 2 cups confectioners' sugar
- 2 to 3 tablespoons milk
- 1-1/2 teaspoons vanilla extract
- 1/4 teaspoon salt

In a mixing bowl, cream butter and sugar. Beat in eggs. Add sour cream and vanilla; mix well. Combine flour, baking powder and baking soda; add to the creamed mixture and mix well. Chill dough at least 2 hours or overnight. Roll on a heavily floured board to 1/4-in. thickness. Cut with a 3-in. cutter. Place on lightly greased cookie sheets. Bake at 350° for 10-12 minutes or until cookie springs back when lightly touched. Cool. Mix all frosting ingredients until smooth; spread over cookies. **Yield:** about 3-1/2 dozen.

Frosted Banana Bars

"I like to provide these moist bars for coffee hour after church," states Karen Dryak of Niobrara, Nebraska.

- 1/2 cup butter *or* margarine, softened
- 2 cups sugar
- 3 eggs
- 1-1/2 cups mashed ripe bananas (about 3 medium)
- 1 teaspoon vanilla extract
- 2 cups all-purpose flour
- 1 teaspoon baking soda
Pinch salt
FROSTING:
- 1/2 cup butter *or* margarine, softened
- 1 package (8 ounces) cream cheese, softened
- 4 cups confectioners' sugar
- 2 teaspoons vanilla extract

In a mixing bowl, cream butter and sugar. Beat in eggs, bananas and vanilla. Combine the flour, baking soda and salt; add to creamed mixture and mix well. Pour into a greased 15-in. x 10-in. x 1-in. baking pan. Bake at 350° for 25 minutes or until bars test done. Cool. For frosting, cream butter and cream cheese in a mixing bowl. Gradually add confectioners' sugar and vanilla; beat well. Spread over bars. **Yield:** 3 dozen.

Deluxe Sugar Cookies

(PICTURED ON THIS PAGE)

"Usually I 'paint' these cutouts with colorful icing—or if time's short, I simply sprinkle them with colored sugar," relates Dawn Fagerstrom of Warren, Minnesota.

    1 cup butter *or* margarine,
      softened
1-1/2 cups confectioners' sugar
    1 egg, beaten
    1 teaspoon vanilla extract
  1/2 teaspoon almond extract
2-1/2 cups all-purpose flour
    1 teaspoon baking soda
    1 teaspoon cream of tartar

In a mixing bowl, cream butter and sugar. Add egg and extracts. Combine flour, baking soda and cream of tartar; gradually add to the creamed mixture and mix well. Chill for at least 1 hour. On a surface lightly sprinkled with confectioners' sugar, roll out a quarter of the dough to 1/8-in. thickness. Cut into desired shapes. Place on ungreased baking sheets. Repeat with the remaining dough. Bake at 350° for 7-8 minutes or until the edges begin to brown. **Yield:** 5 dozen (2-inch cookies). **Editor's Note:** Cookies may be sprinkled with colored sugar before baking or frosted after being baked and cooled.

Gingerbread Cutouts

(PICTURED ON THIS PAGE)

"I decorate gingerbread cookies to use for gifts and always serve them during the holidays," explains Camden, Alabama cook LaJunta Malone.

    1 cup butter *or* margarine,
      softened
    1 cup sugar
  1/2 cup dark corn syrup
    1 teaspoon *each* ground
      cinnamon, nutmeg, cloves
      and ginger
    2 eggs, beaten
    1 teaspoon vinegar
    5 cups all-purpose flour
    1 teaspoon baking soda
Red-hot candies

In a large saucepan, combine the butter, sugar, corn syrup and spices; bring to a

FESTIVE SHAPES distinguish tasty Deluxe Sugar Cookies and Gingerbread Cutouts. Sugar-dusted Pecan Meltaways (bottom) will disappear fast (all recipes on this page).

boil, stirring constantly. Remove from the heat and cool to lukewarm. Stir in eggs and vinegar. Combine the flour and baking soda; stir into sugar mixture to form a soft dough. Chill for several hours. On a lightly floured surface, roll dough to 1/4-in. thickness. Cut with a floured 2-1/2-in. gingerbread man cookie cutter and place on greased baking sheets. Use red-hots for eyes and buttons. Bake at 350° for 8-10 minutes. Remove to wire racks to cool. **Yield:** about 6 dozen.

Pecan Meltaways

(PICTURED ON THIS PAGE)

Says Alberta McKay from her Bartlesville, Oklahoma home, "These attractive sugared, nut-filled balls are true to their name—they really do melt in your mouth!"

    1 cup butter *or* margarine,
      softened
  1/2 cup confectioners' sugar
    1 teaspoon vanilla extract
2-1/4 cups all-purpose flour
  1/4 teaspoon salt
  3/4 cup finely chopped pecans
  Additional confectioners' sugar

In a mixing bowl, cream the butter, sugar and vanilla; mix well. Combine the flour and salt; add to creamed mixture. Stir in pecans. Chill. Roll into 1-in. balls and place on ungreased baking sheets. Bake at 350° for 10-12 minutes. Roll in confectioners' sugar while warm. Cool; roll in sugar again. **Yield:** about 4 dozen.

Cow Pies

"My daughter's barnyard birthday party just wouldn't have been complete without cow pies! All the kids loved 'em!" shares Karen Kenney of Harvard, Illinois.

    2 cups (12 ounces) milk
      chocolate chips
    1 tablespoon shortening
  1/2 cup raisins
  1/2 cup chopped slivered almonds

In a double boiler over simmering water, melt the chocolate chips and shortening, stirring until smooth. Remove from the heat; stir in raisins and almonds. Drop by tablespoonfuls onto waxed paper. Chill until ready to serve. **Yield:** 2 dozen.

Pecan Tarts

(PICTURED ON THIS PAGE)

Jean Rhodes of Tignall, Georgia writes, "The flaky crust combined with a rich center makes these little tarts a satisfying snack to serve and eat."

    1 package (3 ounces) cream cheese, softened
  1/2 cup butter *or* margarine, softened
    1 cup all-purpose flour
  1/4 teaspoon salt
FILLING:
    1 egg
  3/4 cup packed dark brown sugar
    1 tablespoon butter *or* margarine, melted
    1 teaspoon vanilla extract
  2/3 cup chopped pecans
Maraschino cherry halves, optional

In a mixing bowl, beat cream cheese and butter; blend in flour and salt. Chill for 1 hour. Shape into 1-in. balls; press into the bottom and up the sides of greased mini-muffin cups. For filling, beat the egg in a small mixing bowl. Add brown sugar, butter and vanilla; mix well. Stir in pecans. Spoon into shells. Bake at 325° for 25-30 minutes. Cool in pan on a wire rack. Decorate with cherries if desired. **Yield:** about 20.

Apple Cutout Sugar Cookies

"Not only are these pretty cookies fun to serve, but they taste wonderful," shares Marlys Benning of Wellsburg, Iowa.

1-1/2 cups confectioners' sugar
    1 cup butter *or* margarine, softened
    1 egg
1-1/2 teaspoons vanilla extract
2-1/4 cups all-purpose flour
    1 teaspoon baking soda
    1 teaspoon cream of tartar
FROSTING:
    2 cups confectioners' sugar
  1/4 cup light corn syrup
    2 tablespoons water
Red and green food coloring

In a large mixing bowl, combine the first seven ingredients in order given and mix well. Chill dough 2-3 hours or until easy to handle. Roll out on a lightly floured surface to 1/4-in. thickness. Cut with an apple-shaped cookie cutter dipped in flour. Place on greased baking sheets. Bake at 375° for 7-8 minutes or until lightly browned. Cool on

wire racks. For frosting, combine sugar, corn syrup and water in a small bowl. Transfer three-fourths of the frosting into another bowl; add red food coloring for apples. Add green food coloring to remaining frosting for stems. Frost cookies. Allow to sit overnight for frosting to harden. **Yield:** 4 dozen.

Double Chocolate Chip Cookies

(PICTURED ON PAGE 103)

"Who doesn't like chocolate chip cookies?" inquires Diane Hixon. These disappear fast from the cookie jar in her Niceville, Florida home!

    1 cup butter *or* margarine, softened
    1 cup sugar
  1/2 cup packed dark brown sugar
    1 teaspoon vanilla extract
    1 egg
  1/3 cup baking cocoa
    2 tablespoons milk
1-3/4 cups all-purpose flour
  1/4 teaspoon baking powder
    1 cup chopped walnuts
    1 cup (6 ounces) semisweet chocolate chips

In a large mixing bowl, cream the butter, sugars and vanilla. Beat in egg. Add cocoa and milk. Combine flour and baking powder; fold into creamed mixture

with walnuts and chocolate chips. Roll teaspoonfuls of dough into balls; place 2 in. apart on ungreased baking sheets. Bake at 350° for 10-12 minutes. Cool for 5 minutes before removing to wire racks to cool. **Yield:** 3-4 dozen.

Frosted Valentine Cookies

(PICTURED ON PAGE 72)

"It's easy to demonstrate your love to family and friends with a batch of these buttery cookies," says Marcy Cella of L'Anse, Michigan.

    2 cups butter *or* margarine, softened
    1 cup confectioners' sugar
    4 cups all-purpose flour
    2 cups quick-cooking oats
    2 teaspoons vanilla extract
  1/2 teaspoon almond extract
  1/2 teaspoon salt
  1/2 pound semisweet *or* milk chocolate confectionery coating, melted
Confectioners' sugar icing, optional

In a mixing bowl, cream butter and sugar. Add flour, oats, extracts and salt; mix well. Roll out dough to 1/4-in. thickness. Cut with a 3-in. heart-shaped cookie cutter; place on ungreased baking sheets. Bake at 350° for 12-15 minutes. While cookies are warm, spread melted chocolate on tops. Cool. Using a pastry tube,

SWEET FINGER TREATS. Pecan Tarts (recipe on this page) are packed with fantastic flavor.

decorate with confectioners' sugar icing if desired. **Yield:** 3-1/2 dozen.

Chocolate Marshmallow Cookies

(PICTURED ON THIS PAGE)

"In these double-chocolaty delights, marshmallow peeks out under the chocolate icing," explains June Formanek, Belle Plaine, Iowa.

     1/2 cup butter *or* margarine, softened
       1 cup sugar
       1 egg
     1/4 cup milk
       1 teaspoon vanilla extract
   1-3/4 cups all-purpose flour
     1/3 cup baking cocoa
     1/2 teaspoon baking soda
     1/2 teaspoon salt
      16 to 18 large marshmallows
ICING:
       6 tablespoons butter *or* margarine
       2 tablespoons baking cocoa
     1/4 cup milk
   1-3/4 cups confectioners' sugar
     1/2 teaspoon vanilla extract
Pecan halves

In a mixing bowl, cream butter and sugar. Add egg, milk and vanilla; mix well. Combine flour, cocoa, baking soda and salt; beat into creamed mixture. Drop by rounded teaspoonfuls onto ungreased cookie sheets. Bake at 350° for 8 minutes. Meanwhile, cut marshmallows in half. Press a marshmallow half, cut side down, onto each cookie. Return to the oven for 2 minutes. Cool completely on a wire rack. For icing, combine butter, cocoa and milk in a saucepan. Bring to a boil; boil for 1 minute, stirring constantly. Cool slightly; transfer to a small mixing bowl. Add confectioners' sugar and vanilla; beat well. Spread over the cooled cookies. Top each with a pecan half. **Yield:** about 3 dozen.

Fudge Brownies

(PICTURED ON THIS PAGE)

"These rich frosted bars are BIG on fudgy chocolate flavor," assures Inez Orsburn from DeMotte, Indiana.

   1-1/4 cups butter *or* margarine, softened
       4 cups sugar
       8 eggs
       2 cups all-purpose flour
   1-1/4 cups baking cocoa
       1 teaspoon salt
       2 teaspoons vanilla extract

CHOCOLATE shines in treats like (clockwise from bottom) tantalizing Chocolate Marshmallow Cookies, nutty Fudge Brownies (recipes on this page) and impressive Chocolate Trifle (p. 100).

       2 cups chopped walnuts
ICING:
     1/2 cup butter *or* margarine
   1-1/2 squares (1-1/2 ounces) unsweetened chocolate
       3 cups confectioners' sugar
       5 tablespoons milk
       1 teaspoon vanilla extract
Additional chopped walnuts, optional

In a mixing bowl, cream butter and sugar. Add eggs. Combine flour, cocoa and salt; add to creamed mixture and mix well. Stir in vanilla and walnuts. Spread into a greased 15-in. x 10-in. x 1-in. baking pan. Bake at 325° for 40-45 minutes or until brownies test done. Cool for 10 minutes. Meanwhile, for icing, melt the butter and chocolate. Place in a mixing bowl. Add half of the confectioners' sugar; mix well. Add milk, vanilla and remaining sugar and beat until smooth. Spread immediately over warm brownies. Sprinkle with nuts if desired. **Yield:** about 3 dozen.

Chewy Snack Squares

States Cheryl Miller, Fort Collins, Colorado, *"Peanuts and cereals combine to make a tasty snack."*

       5 cups cornflakes
       4 cups crisp rice cereal
       1 cup salted peanuts

       1 cup flaked coconut
       1 cup light corn syrup
       1 cup sugar
     1/2 cup butter *or* margarine
     1/2 cup light cream

In a large bowl, combine cereal, peanuts and coconut; set aside. In a saucepan, combine corn syrup, sugar, butter and cream; cook and stir over medium heat until the mixture reaches soft-ball stage (240°), about 25-30 minutes. Pour over cereal mixture and toss to coat evenly. Pat into a greased 15-in. x 10-in. x 1-in. baking pan. Cool before cutting. **Yield:** 2-1/2 to 3 dozen.

Crispy Coconut Balls

"For satisfying a sweet tooth, nothing can compare to these light bite-size snacks," contributes Elaine Wilkins of Jasper, Alabama.

     1/4 cup butter *or* margarine
      40 large marshmallows *or* 4 cups miniature marshmallows
       5 cups crisp rice cereal
       1 cup flaked coconut

Melt butter in a saucepan over low heat. Add marshmallows and cook, stirring constantly, until marshmallows are melted. Remove from heat; stir in cereal until well coated. With buttered hands, shape into 1-in. balls. Roll in coconut, pressing gently to coat. **Yield:** about 3 dozen.

Black-Bottom Banana Bars

(PICTURED ON THIS PAGE)

"The rich banana and chocolate flavor of these bars is even better the second day," shares Renee Wright of Ferryville, Wisconsin.

- 1/2 cup butter *or* margarine, softened
- 1 cup sugar
- 1 egg
- 1 teaspoon vanilla extract
- 1-1/2 cups mashed ripe bananas (about 3 medium)
- 1-1/2 cups all-purpose flour
- 1 teaspoon baking powder
- 1 teaspoon baking soda
- 1/2 teaspoon salt
- 1/4 cup baking cocoa

In a mixing bowl, cream butter and sugar. Add egg and vanilla; beat until thoroughly combined. Blend in the bananas. Combine the flour, baking powder, baking soda and salt; add to creamed mixture and mix well. Divide batter in half. Add cocoa to half; spread into a greased 13-in. x 9-in. x 2-in. baking pan. Spoon remaining batter on top and swirl with a knife. Bake at 350° for 25 minutes or until the bars test done. Cool. **Yield:** 2-1/2 to 3 dozen.

Chewy Brownie Cookies

(PICTURED ON PAGE 108)

"You'll agree these chocolaty cookies really do resemble a chewy brownie," reveals Jonie Adams, Albion, Michigan.

- 2/3 cup shortening
- 1-1/2 cups packed brown sugar
- 1 tablespoon water
- 1 teaspoon vanilla extract
- 2 eggs
- 1-1/2 cups all-purpose flour
- 1/3 cup baking cocoa
- 1/2 teaspoon salt
- 1/4 teaspoon baking soda
- 2 cups (12 ounces) semisweet chocolate chips
- 1/2 cup chopped walnuts *or* pecans, optional

In a large mixing bowl, cream shortening, sugar, water and vanilla. Beat in the eggs. Combine flour, cocoa, salt and baking soda; gradually add to creamed mixture and beat just until blended. Stir in chocolate chips and nuts if desired. Drop by rounded teaspoonfuls 2 in. apart on ungreased baking sheets. Bake at 375° for 7-9 minutes; do not overbake. Cool 2

minutes before removing to wire racks. **Yield:** 3 dozen.

Praline Brownies

"These brownies pay a nice tribute to that luscious candy so popular in the Deep South," says Mindy Weiser of Southport, North Carolina.

- 1/2 cup packed dark brown sugar
- 3/4 cup butter *or* margarine, *divided*
- 2 tablespoons evaporated milk
- 1/2 cup coarsely chopped pecans
- 2 cups packed light brown sugar
- 2 eggs
- 1-1/2 cups all-purpose flour
- 1 teaspoon vanilla extract
- 1/2 teaspoon salt

In a saucepan, combine the dark brown sugar, 1/4 cup butter and milk. Stir over low heat just until butter is melted. Pour into an ungreased 8-in. square baking pan; sprinkle evenly with pecans. In a mixing bowl, cream light brown sugar and remaining butter; add eggs. Stir in flour, vanilla and salt until moistened. Spread over pecans. Bake at 350° for 45-50 minutes or until brownies test done. Cool 5 minutes in pan; invert onto a tray or serving plate. Cool slightly before cutting. **Yield:** 16 brownies.

Raisin Bran Chewies

"I created this recipe when I was trying to use up some Raisin Bran cereal," explains Ione Perkins, Rawlins, Wyoming.

- 1 cup shortening
- 1 cup packed brown sugar
- 1/2 cup sugar
- 2 eggs, lightly beaten
- 2 tablespoons honey
- 2 teaspoons vanilla extract
- 2-1/4 cups all-purpose flour
- 1/2 teaspoon baking soda
- 1/4 teaspoon salt
- 3 cups Raisin Bran cereal
- 3/4 cup raisins
- 1/2 cup chopped walnuts

In a mixing bowl, cream shortening and sugars. Add eggs, honey and vanilla; mix well. Combine flour, baking soda and salt; add to creamed mixture. Stir in cereal. Fold in raisins and walnuts. Drop by teaspoonfuls onto greased baking sheets. Bake at 350° for 12-14 minutes or until done. **Yield:** 4 dozen.

Scott's Peanut Cookies

"These cookies are packed with oatmeal for a hearty, satisfying taste," says Scott Walter of Little Rock, Arkansas.

DELIGHTFUL COMBINATION of chocolate and bananas in Black-Bottom Banana Bars (recipe on this page) is hard to resist. Plus, this dessert is perfect for potlucks and picnics.

1 cup shortening
1 cup sugar
1 cup packed brown sugar
2 eggs
1-1/2 cups all-purpose flour
1 teaspoon baking powder
1 teaspoon baking soda
3 cups quick-cooking oats
1 cup salted peanuts

In a mixing bowl, cream shortening and sugars; beat in eggs. Combine the flour, baking powder and baking soda; stir into creamed mixture. Add the oats and peanuts. Drop by heaping tablespoonfuls onto greased baking sheets. Dip the bottom of a glass in sugar and slightly flatten cookies. Bake at 350° for 7-10 minutes. **Yield:** 4 dozen.

Cookie Jar Gingersnaps

(PICTURED ON THIS PAGE)

"One of Grandma's cookie jars always had these crisp and chewy gingersnaps in it," recalls Deb Handy of Pomona, Kansas.

3/4 cup shortening
1 cup sugar
1 egg
1/4 cup molasses
2 cups all-purpose flour
2 teaspoons baking soda
1-1/2 teaspoons ground ginger
1 teaspoon ground cinnamon
1/2 teaspoon salt
Additional sugar

In a large mixing bowl, cream shortening and sugar. Beat in egg and molasses. Combine flour, baking soda, ginger, cinnamon and salt; gradually add to creamed mixture. Roll teaspoonfuls of dough into balls. Dip one side of each ball into sugar; place with sugar side up on a greased baking sheet. Bake at 350° for 12-15 minutes or until lightly browned and crinkly. **Yield:** 3-4 dozen.

Icebox Cookies

(PICTURED ON THIS PAGE)

States Chris Paulsen, Glendale, Arizona, "I love to make a fresh batch of these cookies when company drops in."

1/2 cup butter *or* margarine,
    softened
1 cup packed brown sugar
1 egg, beaten
1/2 teaspoon vanilla extract
2 cups all-purpose flour
1/2 teaspoon baking soda
1/2 teaspoon cream of tartar
1/2 teaspoon salt

REMEMBER GRANDMA with desserts like (clockwise from bottom) Cookie Jar Gingersnaps, Icebox Cookies (recipes on this page), Old-Fashioned Raisin Pie (recipe on page 103).

1 cup chopped walnuts,
    optional

In a mixing bowl, cream the butter and brown sugar. Add egg and vanilla; beat well. Combine dry ingredients; add to creamed mixture. Stir in nuts if desired. On a lightly floured surface, shape the dough into three 10-in. x 1-in. rolls. Tightly wrap each roll in waxed paper. Freeze for at least 12 hours. Cut into 3/8-in. slices and place on greased baking sheets. Bake at 350° for 6-8 minutes. Remove to a wire rack to cool. **Yield:** about 7 dozen.

Chewy Maple Bars

"Husband Bill has been making maple syrup for over 50 years, so I've collected many maple recipes," relates Sue Clark of Wells, Vermont. "Bill says these bars are some of the best he's ever eaten."

1/2 cup sugar
1/2 cup shortening
1/2 cup maple syrup
1 egg
2/3 cup all-purpose flour
1/2 teaspoon baking powder
1 teaspoon vanilla extract
1 cup rolled oats
1 cup chopped walnuts

In a mixing bowl, cream sugar and shortening. Add the syrup and egg; beat well. Combine flour and baking powder; add to creamed mixture. Add vanilla and mix well. Stir in oats and walnuts. Pour into a greased 9-in. square baking pan. Bake at 350° for 35 minutes. Cut into squares while warm. Cool on a wire rack. **Yield:** about 2 dozen.

Oatmeal Chip Cookies

Ruth Ann Stelfox, Raymond, Alberta reports, "These delicious, nutritious cookies use lots of oatmeal. They're crisp on the outside and sweet and chewy inside."

2 cups butter *or* margarine,
    softened
2 cups sugar
2 cups packed brown sugar
4 eggs
2 teaspoons vanilla extract
6 cups quick-cooking oats
3 cups all-purpose flour
2 teaspoons baking soda
1 teaspoon salt
2 cups (12 ounces) semisweet
    chocolate chips

In a mixing bowl, cream butter, sugars, eggs and vanilla. Combine oats, flour, baking soda and salt; stir into creamed mixture. Add chocolate chips and mix well. Chill dough for 1 hour or until firm. Roll dough into 1-1/2-in. balls; place on greased cookie sheets. Bake at 350° for 11-13 minutes or until lightly browned. **Yield:** about 7 dozen.

SWEET TREATS

For a flavorful finale to any meal, present your family with these scrumptious cakes, pies, pudding, candies...and more!

Chocolate Trifle

(PICTURED ON PAGE 97)

"This do-ahead dessert is perfect for a group, and it even tastes great the next day," comments Pam Botine from Goldsboro, North Carolina.

- 1 package (18-1/4 ounces) chocolate fudge cake mix
- 1 package (6 ounces) instant chocolate pudding mix
- 1/2 cup strong coffee
- 1 carton (12 ounces) frozen whipped topping, thawed
- 6 Heath bars (1.4 ounces *each*), crushed

Bake cake according to package directions. Cool. Prepare pudding according to package directions; set aside. Crumble cake; reserve 1/2 cup. Place half of the remaining cake crumbs in the bottom of a 4-1/2- or 5-qt. trifle dish or decorative glass bowl. Layer with half of the coffee, half of the pudding, half of the whipped topping and half of the crushed candy bars. Repeat the layers of cake, coffee, pudding and whipped topping. Combine remaining crushed candy bars with reserved cake crumbs; sprinkle over top. Refrigerate 4-5 hours before serving. **Yield:** 8-10 servings.

Butterscotch Pie

"I've been cooking since I was a young boy. Now I enjoy preparing foods like this pie for my wife," explains Cary Letsche of Bradenton, Florida.

- 6 tablespoons butter *or* margarine
- 6 tablespoons all-purpose flour
- 1-1/2 cups packed brown sugar
- 2 cups milk
- 1/4 teaspoon salt
- 3 eggs yolks, beaten
- 1 teaspoon vanilla extract
- 1 pastry shell (9 inches), baked

MERINGUE:
- 3 egg whites
- 1/4 teaspoon cream of tartar
- 1/2 cup sugar

In a saucepan, melt the butter. Remove from the heat; add flour and stir until smooth. Stir in brown sugar. Return to heat; gradually add milk and salt, stirring constantly. Cook and stir over medium-high heat until thickened and bubbly. Reduce heat; cook and stir 2 minutes more. Remove from the heat. Stir about 1 cup into the egg yolks; return all to saucepan. Bring to a gentle boil. Cook and stir for 2 minutes. Remove from the heat and add vanilla. Pour into pie shell. Immediately make the meringue: In a small bowl, beat egg whites with cream of tartar until soft peaks form. Gradually add sugar, about 1 tablespoon at a time, beating until stiff and glossy. Spread evenly over filling, sealing meringue to crust. Bake at 350° for 12-15 minutes or until golden. Cool on a wire rack. Store, covered, in the refrigerator. **Yield:** 6-8 servings.

Layered Banana Pudding

"My mother gave me this recipe, which an old friend had shared with her. When my children were still at home, we enjoyed this satisfying pudding often, and now I make it for company," writes Esther Matteson of Bremen, Indiana.

- 1/3 cup all-purpose flour
- 2/3 cup packed brown sugar
- 2 cups milk
- 2 egg yolks, beaten
- 2 tablespoons butter *or* margarine
- 1 teaspoon vanilla extract
- 1 cup heavy cream, whipped
- 4 to 6 firm bananas, sliced

Chopped walnuts, optional

In a medium saucepan, combine the flour and brown sugar; stir in milk. Cook and stir over medium heat until thickened and bubbly; cook and stir 1 minute more. Remove from the heat. Gradually stir about 1 cup hot mixture into egg yolks. Return all to the saucepan. Bring to a gentle boil; cook and stir for 2 minutes. Remove from the heat; stir in butter and vanilla. Cool to room temperature, stirring occasionally. Fold in the whipped cream. Layer a third of the pudding in a 2-qt. glass bowl; top with half of the bananas. Repeat layers. Top with remaining pudding. Sprinkle with nuts if desired. Cover and chill at least 1 hour before serving. **Yield:** 8 servings.

Perfect Peppermint Patties

"Calling for just a few ingredients, this is one candy that's simple to prepare. I make lots of different candy at Christmas to give as gifts. It's time consuming, but worth it to see the delight it brings to people," says Joanne Adams, Bath, Maine.

- 1 box (1 pound) confectioners' sugar
- 3 tablespoons butter *or* margarine, softened
- 2 to 3 teaspoons peppermint extract
- 1/2 teaspoon vanilla extract
- 1/4 cup evaporated milk
- 2 cups (12 ounces) semisweet chocolate chips
- 2 tablespoons shortening

In a bowl, combine first four ingredients. Add milk and mix well. Roll into 1-in. balls and place on a waxed paper-lined cookie sheet. Flatten with a glass to 1/4 in.; cover and freeze for 30 minutes. In a double boiler or microwave-safe bowl, melt chocolate chips and shortening. Dip patties; place on waxed paper to harden. **Yield:** about 5 dozen.

Marshmallow Puffs

"With peanut butter, chocolate and marshmallows, these treats were very popular with our children. They're perfect for the holidays," reports Dody Cagenello of Simsbury, Connecticut.

- 36 large marshmallows
- 1-1/2 cups semisweet chocolate chips
- 1/2 cup chunky peanut butter
- 2 tablespoons butter (no substitutes)

Line a 9-in. square pan with foil; butter the foil. Arrange marshmallows in pan. In a double boiler or microwave-safe bowl, melt chocolate chips, peanut butter and butter at 50% power. Pour and spread over the marshmallows. Chill completely. Cut between marshmallows. **Yield:** 3 dozen. **Editor's Note:** This recipe was tested in a 700-watt microwave.

Peach Shortcake

(PICTURED ON THIS PAGE)

With blushing fresh peaches in plentiful supply, Karen Owen of Rising Sun, Indiana thinks this appealing layered dessert can't be beat. "Brown sugar and ginger give the shortcake its mellow, sweet-spicy flavor," she notes.

     2 cups all-purpose flour
     2 tablespoons brown sugar
     1 tablespoon baking powder
 1/2 teaspoon salt
 1/2 teaspoon ground ginger
 1/2 cup butter *or* margarine
 2/3 cup milk
FILLING:
 1-1/2 pounds ripe fresh peaches *or* nectarines, peeled and thinly sliced
     6 tablespoons brown sugar, *divided*
 1/4 teaspoon ground ginger
     1 cup heavy cream
 1/4 cup chopped pecans, toasted

Combine the first five ingredients in a bowl; cut in butter until mixture resembles coarse crumbs. Add milk, stirring only until moistened. Turn onto a lightly floured surface; knead 10 times. Pat evenly into a greased 8-in. round baking pan. Bake at 425° for 20-25 minutes or until golden brown. Remove from pan to cool on a wire rack. Just before serving, combine peaches, 4 tablespoons brown sugar and ginger. Whip cream with remaining brown sugar until stiff. Split shortcake into two layers; place bottom layer on a serving platter. Spoon half of the peach mixture over cake; top with half of the cream. Cover with second cake layer and remaining peach mixture. Garnish with remaining cream; sprinkle with pecans. **Yield:** 8-10 servings.

Vanilla Custard Ice Cream

(PICTURED ON THIS PAGE)

"When we were growing up on the farm, homemade ice cream was our favorite dessert," recalls Lucile Proctor of Panguitch, Utah, who now makes it for her own family. "Enjoy this recipe 'solo' or topped with chocolate sauce, fruit or nuts for a spectacular sundae."

     1 tablespoon butter *or* margarine
     6 cups milk
 2-1/4 cups sugar, *divided*

SCRUMPTIOUS, showy medley of tempting treats includes (clockwise from the bottom) Peach Shortcake, Vanilla Custard Ice Cream and Turtle Sundae Dessert (all recipes on this page).

     6 tablespoons all-purpose flour
     6 eggs, *separated*
     3 cups heavy cream
     1 tablespoon vanilla extract
Sliced strawberries *or* **other fresh fruit, optional**

In a large kettle, melt butter to coat the bottom. Pour in milk and 1 cup of sugar. Bring to a boil over medium-high heat, stirring occasionally. Combine flour and remaining sugar; add to kettle. Bring to a boil, stirring constantly. Cook and stir for 2 minutes; remove from the heat. In a mixing bowl, beat egg whites until stiff peaks form. While beating, gradually add yolks. Stir in 1 cup of hot milk mixture. Return all to kettle; cook and stir for 2 minutes (do not boil). Chill. Add cream and vanilla; mix well. Freeze in an ice cream maker according to manufacturer's directions. Serve with fruit if desired. **Yield:** about 3 quarts.

Turtle Sundae Dessert

(PICTURED ON THIS PAGE)

Bethel Walters of Willow River, Minnesota pledges, "This treat is sure to please children and chocolate lovers of all ages!" A convenient cake mix starts the stellar surprise her six grandchildren endorse.

     1 package (18-1/4 ounces) German chocolate cake mix
     1 package (14 ounces) caramels
 1/2 cup evaporated milk
     6 tablespoons butter *or* margarine
     1 cup chopped pecans
     1 cup (6 ounces) semisweet chocolate chips
Vanilla ice cream and pecan halves, optional

Mix cake according to package directions. Set aside half of the batter; pour remaining batter into a greased and floured 13-in. x 9-in. x 2-in. baking pan. Bake at 350° for 18 minutes. Meanwhile, in a saucepan over low heat, melt the caramels, milk and butter. Remove from the heat and add nuts. Pour over cake. Sprinkle with chocolate chips. Pour reserved batter over top. Bake 20-25 minutes more or until cake springs back when lightly touched. Cool. Cut into squares. If desired, top each with a scoop of ice cream and a pecan half. **Yield:** 20 servings.

Layered Lemon Dessert

(PICTURED ON THIS PAGE)

"This cool and creamy refrigerator dessert adds sunshine to any meal and golden color to the table," comments Dorothy Pritchett from her Wills Point, Texas home.

- 6 tablespoons butter *or* margarine
- 1 cup all-purpose flour
- 1/2 cup finely chopped pecans

FILLING:
- 1 package (8 ounces) cream cheese, softened
- 1-1/2 cups confectioners' sugar
- 1-1/2 cups whipped topping
- 2 cups sugar
- 1/3 cup cornstarch
- 1/4 teaspoon salt
- 2 cups water, *divided*
- 3 eggs
- 1/4 cup vinegar
- 1/4 cup lemon juice
- 1 tablespoon butter *or* margarine
- 1 teaspoon lemon extract

Cut butter into flour until crumbly. Stir in pecans. Press into the bottom of an ungreased 13-in. x 9-in. x 2-in. baking pan. Bake at 350° for 15 minutes. Cool. Beat cream cheese and confectioners' sugar until fluffy. Fold in whipped topping. Spread over crust; chill. In a saucepan, combine sugar, cornstarch and salt. Add 1/4 cup water and stir until smooth. Add eggs and mix well. Add vinegar, lemon juice and the remaining water; stir until smooth. Bring to a boil over medium heat, stirring constantly; boil for 1 minute. Remove from the heat; add butter and extract. Cool. Spread over cream cheese layer. Chill 2 hours or overnight. **Yield:** 12-16 servings.

Creamy Chocolate Cupcakes

(PICTURED ON THIS PAGE)

"The 'surprise' inside these rich chocolate cupcakes is their smooth cream cheese filling," reports Mrs. Walter Jacobson of Ashland, Ohio.

- 1-1/2 cups all-purpose flour
- 1 cup sugar
- 1/4 cup baking cocoa
- 1 teaspoon baking soda
- 1/2 teaspoon salt
- 2 eggs, lightly beaten
- 3/4 cup water
- 1/3 cup vegetable oil
- 1 tablespoon vinegar
- 1 teaspoon vanilla extract

FILLING:
- 1 package (8 ounces) cream cheese, softened
- 1/3 cup sugar
- 1 egg, lightly beaten
- 1/8 teaspoon salt
- 1 cup (6 ounces) semisweet chocolate chips
- 1 cup chopped walnuts

In a large mixing bowl, combine the dry ingredients. Add the eggs, water, oil, vinegar and vanilla; mix well. Pour into 18 greased or paper-lined muffin cups. For filling, beat cream cheese and sugar in another mixing bowl. Add egg and salt; mix well. Fold in chocolate chips. Drop by tablespoonfuls into center of each cupcake. Sprinkle with nuts. Bake at 350° for 25-30 minutes. **Yield:** 1-1/2 dozen.

Cherry Pie

(PICTURED ON THIS PAGE)

"Whenever I want to treat family and friends to a traditional type of dessert, I make this cherry pie," shares Frances Poste of Wall, South Dakota. *"People are pleased to see a slice set in front of them!"*

PASTRY:
- 1-1/2 cups all-purpose flour
- 1/2 teaspoon salt
- 1/2 cup shortening
- 1/4 cup ice water

FILLING:
- 2 cans (16 ounces *each*) tart cherries
- 1 cup sugar
- 3 tablespoons quick-cooking tapioca
- 1/4 teaspoon almond extract
- 1/4 teaspoon salt
- Red food coloring, optional
- 1 tablespoon butter *or* margarine

In a bowl, combine flour and salt; cut in the shortening until crumbly. Gradually add ice water, tossing with a fork until dough forms a ball. Divide dough in half. Roll out one half to fit a 9-in. pie plate for bottom crust. Drain cherries, reserving 1/4 cup juice. Mix cherries, juice, sugar, tapioca, extract, salt and food coloring if desired; pour into the crust. Dot with butter. Top with a lattice crust. Bake at 375° for 55-60 minutes. **Yield:** 6-8 servings.

WHAT'S FOR DESSERT TONIGHT? Why not answer (top to bottom) with luscious Layered Lemon Dessert, Creamy Chocolate Cupcakes or Cherry Pie? (All recipes on this page.)

Soda Cracker Chocolate Candy

(PICTURED ON THIS PAGE)

"My husband and I make several batches of these easy, chocolaty nut squares for holiday gifts," notes Margery Bryan of Royal City, Washington. *"Most people are surprised to learn the recipe includes soda crackers."*

    35 to 40 soda crackers
     1 cup butter *or* margarine
     1 cup packed brown sugar
 1-1/2 cups semisweet chocolate
        chips
 1-1/2 cups coarsely chopped
        walnuts

Line a 15-in. x 10-in. x 1-in. baking pan with foil and coat with nonstick cooking spray. Place crackers in rows on foil. In a saucepan, melt butter; add the brown sugar and bring to a boil. Boil for 3 minutes. Pour over crackers and spread until completely covered. Bake at 350° for 5 minutes (crackers will float). Remove from the oven. Turn oven off. Sprinkle chocolate chips and walnuts over crackers. Return to the oven until chocolate is melted, about 3-5 minutes. Remove from the oven; using a greased spatula, press walnuts into chocolate. Cut into 1-in. squares while warm. Cool completely; remove candy from foil. **Yield:** about 5 dozen.

Sandy's Chocolate Cake

(PICTURED ON THIS PAGE)

"Topping 59 other entries, this velvety cake with creamy frosting took first place in a local cake contest," reveals Sandy Johnson of Tioga, Pennsylvania. *"It's an impressive dessert that's perfect for special occasions."*

     3 cups packed brown sugar
     1 cup butter *or* margarine,
        softened
     4 eggs
     2 teaspoons vanilla extract
 2-2/3 cups all-purpose flour
   3/4 cup baking cocoa
     1 tablespoon baking soda
   1/2 teaspoon salt
 1-1/3 cups sour cream
 1-1/3 cups boiling water
FROSTING:
   1/2 cup butter *or* margarine
     3 squares (1 ounce *each*)
        unsweetened chocolate
     3 squares (1 ounce *each*)
        semisweet chocolate

SWEET FINALES. Top off your meals with (clockwise from bottom) Soda Cracker Chocolate Candy, Sandy's Chocolate Cake (recipes this page) and Double Chocolate Chip Cookies (p. 96).

     5 cups confectioners' sugar
     1 cup (8 ounces) sour cream
     2 teaspoons vanilla extract

In a mixing bowl, cream brown sugar and butter. Add eggs, one at a time, beating well after each addition. Beat on high speed until light and fluffy. Blend in vanilla. Combine flour, cocoa, baking soda and salt; add alternately with sour cream to creamed mixture. Mix on low just until combined. Stir in water until blended. Pour into three greased and floured 9-in. round baking pans. Bake at 350° for 35 minutes. Cool in pans 10 minutes; remove to wire racks to cool completely. For frosting, in a medium saucepan, melt butter and chocolate over low heat. Cool several minutes. In a mixing bowl, combine sugar, sour cream and vanilla. Add chocolate mixture and beat until smooth. Frost cooled cake. **Yield:** 12-14 servings.

FOR FAST, FABULOUS FROSTING, break up two and a half chocolate candy bars and place them on top of a still-warm cake. When the chocolate has melted a bit, spread it evenly over the cake. If you like, sprinkle with nuts.

Old-Fashioned Raisin Pie

(PICTURED ON PAGE 99)

"This is a timeless recipe for two reasons," relates Debra Ayers from Cheyenne, Wyoming. *"It's been in the family since just after the Civil War, plus it can be prepared in no time!"*

     2 eggs
     1 cup (8 ounces) sour cream
     2 cups raisins
     1 cup packed brown sugar
     1 teaspoon ground cinnamon
   1/2 teaspoon ground nutmeg
   1/4 teaspoon salt
Pastry for double-crust pie (9
   inches)
Additional nutmeg, optional

In a bowl, beat eggs. Add sour cream. Stir in raisins, brown sugar, cinnamon, nutmeg and salt. Place bottom pastry in a pie plate; pour in filling. Top with a lattice crust. Bake at 450° for 10 minutes. Reduce the heat to 350°; bake for about 25 minutes more or until filling is set. If desired, sprinkle with nutmeg. **Yield:** 8 servings.

Creamy Banana Pie

(PICTURED ON THIS PAGE)

"This delectable pie is from a recipe I found years ago. Everyone who tastes it enjoys its old-fashioned flavor," shares *Rita Pribyl, Indianapolis, Indiana.*

   1 envelope unflavored gelatin
   1/4 cup cold water
   3/4 cup sugar
   1/4 cup cornstarch
   1/2 teaspoon salt
2-3/4 cups milk
   4 egg yolks, beaten
   2 tablespoons butter *or* margarine
   1 tablespoon vanilla extract
   4 medium firm bananas
   1 cup heavy cream, whipped
   1 pastry shell (10 inches), baked
Juice and grated peel of 1 lemon
   1/2 cup apple jelly

Soften gelatin in cold water; set aside. In a saucepan, combine sugar, cornstarch and salt. Blend in the milk and egg yolks; cook over low heat, stirring constantly, until thickened and bubbly, about 20-25 minutes. Remove from the heat; stir in softened gelatin until dissolved. Stir in butter and vanilla. Cover the surface of custard with plastic wrap and chill until no longer warm. Slice 3 bananas; fold into custard with whipped cream. Spoon into pie shell. Chill until set, about 4-5 hours. Shortly before serving time, place lemon juice in a small bowl and slice the remaining banana into it. Melt jelly in a saucepan over low heat. Drain banana; pat dry and arrange on top of pie. Brush banana with the jelly. Sprinkle with grated lemon peel. Serve immediately. **Yield:** 8 servings. **Editor's Note:** The filling is very light in color. It is not topped with additional whipped cream.

Banana Bread Pudding

(PICTURED ON THIS PAGE)

"With its crusty golden top, custard-like inside and smooth vanilla sauce, this bread pudding is a real homespun dessert," attests *Mary Detweiler of West Farmington, Ohio.*

   4 cups cubed day-old French *or* sourdough bread (1-inch pieces)
   1/4 cup butter *or* margarine, melted
   3 eggs
   2 cups milk
   1/2 cup sugar
   2 teaspoons vanilla extract
   1/2 teaspoon ground cinnamon
   1/2 teaspoon ground nutmeg
   1/2 teaspoon salt
   1 cup sliced firm bananas (1/4-inch pieces)
SAUCE:
   3 tablespoons butter *or* margarine
   2 tablespoons sugar
   1 tablespoon cornstarch
   3/4 cup milk
   1/4 cup light corn syrup
   1 teaspoon vanilla extract

Place the bread cubes in a greased 2-qt. casserole; pour butter over and toss to coat. In a medium bowl, lightly beat eggs; add milk, sugar, vanilla, cinnamon, nutmeg and salt. Stir in bananas. Pour over bread cubes and stir to coat. Bake, uncovered, at 375° for 40 minutes or until a knife inserted near the center comes out clean. Meanwhile, for sauce, melt butter in a small saucepan. Combine sugar and cornstarch; add to butter. Stir in milk and corn syrup. Cook and stir over medium heat until the mixture comes to a full boil. Boil for 1 minute. Remove from the heat; stir in the vanilla. Serve warm sauce over warm pudding. **Yield:** 6 servings.

Snowflake Cake

(PICTURED ON PAGE 80)

Lynne Peterson of Salt Lake City, Utah

writes, *"The coconut sprinkled on this old-fashioned white cake gives the impression of snow inside the house without the cold!"*

   2 eggs plus 4 egg yolks
1-1/2 cups sugar
   1 cup milk
   1/2 cup butter *or* margarine
2-1/2 cups all-purpose flour
   1 tablespoon baking powder
   1 teaspoon vanilla extract
   1/2 cup chopped nuts, optional
FROSTING:
1-3/4 cups sugar
   1/2 cup water
   4 egg whites
   1/2 teaspoon cream of tartar
   1 teaspoon vanilla extract
   2 cups flaked coconut

In a mixing bowl, beat eggs, yolks and sugar until light and fluffy, about 5 minutes. In a saucepan, heat milk and butter until butter melts. Combine flour and baking powder; add to egg mixture alternately with milk mixture. Beat until well mixed. Add vanilla. Fold in nuts if desired. Pour into three greased 9-in. round baking pans. Bake at 350° for 15-18 minutes or until cakes test done. Cool in pans 10 minutes before removing to a wire rack to cool completely. For frosting, in a saucepan, bring sugar and water to a boil. Boil 3-4 minutes or until a candy

FRUITFUL FAVORITES like Creamy Banana Pie and Banana Bread Pudding (recipes on this page) add sunny color and tropical taste to your dessert table...any way you slice it!

thermometer reads 242° (firm-ball stage). Meanwhile, beat egg whites and cream of tartar in a mixing bowl until foamy. Slowly pour in the hot sugar mixture and continue to beat on high for 6-8 minutes or until stiff peaks form. Add vanilla. Frost the tops of two cake layers and sprinkle with coconut; stack on a cake plate with plain layer on top. Frost sides and top of cake; sprinkle with coconut. Refrigerate for several hours. **Yield:** 12-16 servings.

Seven-Minute Pudding

(PICTURED ON PAGE 50)

"This rich, smooth pudding couldn't be quicker to make, and it has such nice homemade flavor," promises Renee Schwebach of Dumont, Minnesota.

> 1/3 cup sugar
> 2 tablespoons cornstarch
> 2 cups milk
> 2 egg yolks
> 2 tablespoons butter *or* margarine
> 1 teaspoon vanilla extract

In a microwave-safe mixing bowl, combine sugar and cornstarch. With a hand mixer, beat in milk and egg yolks until smooth. Microwave on medium for 5 minutes. Beat well with mixer. Microwave on high for 2 minutes; stir. Blend in butter and vanilla. Pour into serving dishes; cool. **Yield:** 3-4 servings.

Spice Cake

"I enjoy baking and decorating cakes for people's birthdays," informs Robin Perry of Seneca, Pennsylvania. *"I like to start with a sure-to-please cake like this moist spice cake."*

> 2 cups sugar
> 1 cup butter *or* margarine, softened
> 4 eggs, beaten
> 3 cups all-purpose flour
> 1 teaspoon baking powder
> 1 teaspoon baking soda
> 1 teaspoon ground cinnamon
> 1 teaspoon ground cloves
> 1 teaspoon ground nutmeg
> 1 cup buttermilk
> **BUTTER CREAM FROSTING:**
> 1/2 cup shortening
> 1/2 cup butter *or* margarine, softened
> 1 teaspoon vanilla extract
> 4 cups confectioners' sugar
> 3 tablespoons milk

In a mixing bowl, cream sugar and butter. Add eggs; beat well. Combine dry

ingredients; add to creamed mixture alternately with buttermilk. Mix well. Pour into a greased and floured 13-in. x 9-in. x 2-in. baking pan. Bake at 350° for 35-40 minutes or until the cake tests done. Cool. For frosting, cream the shortening and butter in a mixing bowl. Add vanilla. Gradually beat in sugar. Add milk; beat until light and fluffy. Frost cake. **Yield:** 12-16 servings.

Orange Taffy

"This taffy has a satisfying tang that hits the tongue just before the sweetness," reports Christine Olson, Horse Creek, California. *"It takes time to wrap all the little candies, but it's a fun way to get the kids to help in the kitchen."*

> 2 cups sugar
> 2 cups light corn syrup
> 1 can (6 ounces) frozen orange juice concentrate, undiluted
> Pinch salt
> 1 cup light cream
> 1/2 cup butter *or* margarine

In a heavy saucepan, combine first four ingredients. Cook and stir over medium heat until sugar is dissolved. Bring to a rapid boil and cook until a candy thermometer reads 245° (firm-ball stage). Add cream and butter; heat and stir until mixture reaches 245° again. Pour into a greased 15-in. x 10-in. x 1-in. pan; cool. When cool enough to handle, roll into 1-1/2-in. logs or 1-in. balls. Wrap individually in foil or waxed paper; twist ends. **Yield:** about 6 dozen.

Butter Pecan Crunch

" 'Elegant but easy' is the best way to describe this frozen treat my mother first sampled decades ago," says Julie Sterchi of Flora, Illinois.

> 2 cups graham cracker crumbs
> 1/2 cup butter *or* margarine, melted
> 2 packages (3.4 ounces *each*) instant vanilla pudding mix
> 2 cups milk
> 1 quart butter pecan ice cream, softened slightly
> 1 carton (8 ounces) frozen whipped topping, thawed
> 2 Heath bars (1.4 ounces *each*), crushed

In a bowl, combine crumbs and butter. Pat into the bottom of an ungreased 13-in. x 9-in. x 2-in. pan. Chill. In a mixing bowl, beat pudding mixes and milk until well blended, about 1 minute. Fold

in the ice cream and whipped topping. Spoon over crust. Sprinkle with crushed candy bars. Freeze. Thaw 20 minutes before serving. **Yield:** 12-16 servings.

Pecan Fudge Pie

"This fudgy pie is the perfect showcase for pecans. It's a special chocolaty twist on traditional pecan pie," states Jacquelyn Smith of Soperton, Georgia.

> 1-1/4 cups light corn syrup
> 1/2 cup sugar
> 1/3 cup baking cocoa
> 1/3 cup all-purpose flour
> 1/4 teaspoon salt
> 3 eggs
> 3 tablespoons butter *or* margarine, softened
> 1-1/2 teaspoons vanilla extract
> 1 cup chopped pecans
> 1 unbaked pastry shell (9 inches)
> Whipped cream, optional

In a large mixing bowl, beat the first eight ingredients until smooth. Stir in nuts; pour into pie shell. Bake at 350° for 55-60 minutes or until set. Cool completely. Garnish with whipped cream if desired. **Yield:** 6-8 servings.

Saucy Apple Cake

"This quick and easy cake appeals to everyone," notes DeEtta Twedt, Mesa, Arizona. *"Friends and family consider it one of their favorite desserts."*

> 1 cup sugar
> 1/4 cup shortening
> 1 egg, lightly beaten
> 1 cup all-purpose flour
> 1 teaspoon baking soda
> 1/2 teaspoon ground cinnamon
> 1/4 teaspoon salt
> 2 cups shredded peeled tart apples
> 1/4 cup chopped walnuts
> **VANILLA SAUCE:**
> 1 cup sugar
> 2 tablespoons cornstarch
> 1/2 cup light cream
> 1/2 cup butter *or* margarine
> 1-1/2 teaspoons vanilla extract

In a mixing bowl, cream the sugar and shortening. Add egg and mix well. Add the dry ingredients; mix well. Fold in apples and walnuts. Spread in a greased 8-in. square baking pan. Bake at 350° for 35-40 minutes or until cake tests done. For sauce, combine sugar, cornstarch and cream in a saucepan. Bring to a boil over medium heat; boil for 2 minutes. Remove from the heat. Add butter and vanilla; stir until butter is melted. Serve warm over warm cake. **Yield:** 9 servings.

Red, White and Blue Dessert

(PICTURED ON PAGE 62)

"Serving this rich, fresh-tasting dessert decorated like the flag is a great salute to the nation's independence!" reports Sue Gronholz, Columbus, Wisconsin.

        2 packages (8 ounces *each*)
          cream cheese, softened
    1/2 cup sugar
    1/2 teaspoon vanilla extract
    1/2 teaspoon almond extract
        2 cups heavy cream, whipped
        2 quarts strawberries, halved,
          divided
        2 quarts blueberries, *divided*

In a large mixing bowl, beat the cream cheese, sugar and extracts until fluffy. Fold in the whipped cream. Place a third of the mixture in a 4-qt. bowl. Reserve 20 strawberry halves and 1/2 cup blueberries for garnish. Layer half of the remaining strawberries and blueberries over cream mixture. Top with another third of the cream mixture and the remaining berries. Spread the remaining cream mixture on top. Use the reserved strawberries and blueberries to make a "flag" on top. **Yield:** 18 servings.

♥☎♥☎♥☎♥☎♥☎♥☎♥

Chocolate Potato Cake

"The secret ingredient in this moist rich chocolate cake is potatoes. It's a wonderful cake to make for a special occasion. The white frosting goes perfectly with the dark chocolate cake," assures Jill Kinder of Richlands, Virginia.

    3/4 cup butter *or* margarine,
          softened
    1-1/2 cups sugar, *divided*
        4 eggs, *separated*
        1 cup hot mashed *or* riced
          potatoes (no milk, butter
          or seasoning added)
    1-1/2 cups all-purpose flour
    1/2 cup baking cocoa
        2 teaspoons baking powder
        1 teaspoon ground cinnamon
    1/2 teaspoon salt
    1/2 teaspoon ground nutmeg
    1/4 teaspoon ground cloves
        1 cup milk
        1 teaspoon vanilla extract
        1 cup chopped nuts
FLUFFY WHITE FROSTING:
        2 egg whites
    1-1/2 cups sugar
    1/3 cup water
        2 teaspoons light corn syrup

    1/8 teaspoon salt
        1 teaspoon vanilla extract

In a mixing bowl, cream butter and 1 cup sugar. Add egg yolks; beat well. Add potatoes and mix thoroughly. Combine flour, cocoa, baking powder, cinnamon, salt, nutmeg and cloves; add to creamed mixture alternately with milk, beating until smooth. Stir in vanilla and nuts. In a mixing bowl, beat egg whites until foamy. Gradually add remaining sugar; beat until stiff peaks form. Fold into batter. Pour into a greased and floured 13-in. x 9-in. x 2-in. baking pan. Bake at 350° for 40-45 minutes or until cake tests done. Cool. Combine first five frosting ingredients in top of a double boiler. Beat with electric mixer for 1 minute. Place over boiling water; beat constantly for 7 minutes, scraping sides of pan occasionally. Remove from heat. Add vanilla; beat 1 minute. Frost cake. **Yield:** 16-20 servings. **Editor's Note:** Cake is moist and has a firm texture.

♥☎♥☎♥☎♥☎♥☎♥☎♥

Creamy Caramels

Marcie Wolfe of Williamsburg, Virginia writes, "I discovered this recipe in a local newspaper several years ago and have made these soft buttery caramels ever since. They're so much better than store-bought caramels."

        1 cup sugar
        1 cup dark corn syrup
        1 cup butter *or* margarine
        1 can (14 ounces) sweetened
          condensed milk
        1 teaspoon vanilla extract

Line an 8-in. square pan with foil and butter the foil; set aside. Combine the sugar, corn syrup and butter in a 3-qt. saucepan. Bring to a boil over medium heat, stirring constantly. Boil slowly for 4 minutes without stirring. Remove from the heat and stir in milk. Reduce heat to medium-low and cook until candy thermometer reads 238° (soft-ball stage), stirring constantly. Remove from the heat and stir in vanilla. Pour into prepared pan. Cool. Remove from pan and cut into 1-in. squares. Wrap individually in waxed paper; twist ends. **Yield:** 64 pieces. **Editor's Note:** It is recommended to test your candy thermometer before each use by bringing water to a boil; the thermometer should read 212°. Adjust your recipe temperature up or down based on your test.

♥☎♥☎♥☎♥☎♥☎♥☎♥

Freezer Pumpkin Pie

Vera Reid of Laramie, Wyoming suggests, "Put a cool twist on tradition with
this wonderful do-ahead dessert. Gingersnaps and pecans form the delicious baked crust for this pie's pumpkin and ice cream filling."

        1 cup ground pecans
    1/2 cup ground gingersnaps
    1/4 cup sugar
    1/4 cup butter *or* margarine,
          softened
FILLING:
        1 cup cooked *or* canned
          pumpkin
    1/2 cup packed brown sugar
    1/2 teaspoon salt
    1/2 teaspoon ground cinnamon
    1/2 teaspoon ground ginger
    1/4 teaspoon ground nutmeg
        1 quart vanilla ice cream,
          softened slightly

In a bowl, combine the pecans, gingersnaps, sugar and butter; mix well. Press into a 9-in. pie pan; bake at 450° for 5 minutes. Cool completely. In a mixing bowl, beat first six filling ingredients. Stir in ice cream and mix until well blended. Spoon into crust. Freeze until firm, at least 2-3 hours. Store in freezer. **Yield:** 6-8 servings.

♥☎♥☎♥☎♥☎♥☎♥☎♥

Apple Crisp Pizza

"While visiting a Wisconsin apple orchard bakery, I tried this tempting treat. At home, I put together this recipe. My family thinks it tastes better than the one used by the bakery," shares Nancy Preussner of Delhi, Iowa.

Pastry for a single-crust pie
    2/3 cup sugar
        3 tablespoons all-purpose flour
        1 teaspoon ground cinnamon
        4 medium baking apples,
          peeled and cut into 1/2-inch
          slices
TOPPING:
    1/2 cup all-purpose flour
    1/3 cup packed brown sugar
    1/3 cup rolled oats
        1 teaspoon ground cinnamon
    1/4 cup butter *or* margarine,
          softened
    1/4 to 1/2 cup caramel ice cream
          topping *or* caramel apple dip
Vanilla ice cream, optional

Roll pastry to fit a 12-in. pizza pan; fold under or flute the edges. Combine sugar, flour and cinnamon in a bowl. Add apples and toss. Arrange the apples in a single layer in a circular pattern to completely cover pastry. Combine the first five topping ingredients; sprinkle over apples. Bake at 350° for 35-40 minutes or until apples are tender. Remove from the oven and immediately drizzle with caramel topping or dip. Serve warm with ice cream if desired. **Yield:** 12 servings.

♥🍵♥🍵♥🍵♥🍵♥🍵♥🍵♥

Pecan Delights

(PICTURED ON THIS PAGE)

"Who can resist rich chewy caramel over crunchy pecans drizzled with sweet chocolate?" asks Linda Jonsson of Marion, Ohio. *"These candies have become a holiday favorite to both make and eat!"*

       2-1/4 cups packed brown sugar
           1 cup butter *or* margarine
           1 cup light corn syrup
       1/8 teaspoon salt
           1 can (14 ounces) sweetened condensed milk
           1 teaspoon vanilla extract
   1-1/2 pounds whole pecans
           1 cup (6 ounces) semisweet chocolate chips
           1 cup (6 ounces) milk chocolate chips
           2 tablespoons shortening

In a large saucepan, combine the first four ingredients. Cook over medium heat until all sugar is dissolved. Gradually add milk and mix well. Continue cooking until candy thermometer reads 248° (firm-ball stage). Remove from the heat; stir in vanilla until blended. Fold in the pecans. Drop by tablespoonfuls onto a greased waxed paper- or parchment-lined cookie sheet. Chill until firm. Melt chocolate chips and shortening in a microwave-safe bowl or double boiler. Drizzle over each cluster. Cool. **Yield:** about 4 dozen. **Editor's Note:** It is recommended to test your candy thermometer before each use by bringing water to a boil; the thermometer should read 212°. Adjust your recipe temperature up or down based on your test.

♥🍵♥🍵♥🍵♥🍵♥🍵♥🍵♥

Mocha Truffles

(PICTURED ON THIS PAGE)

"Nothing compares to the melt-in-your-mouth flavor of these truffles...or to the simplicity of the recipe," states Stacy Abell of Olathe, Kansas.

       2 packages (12 ounces *each*) semisweet chocolate chips

           1 package (8 ounces) cream cheese, softened
           3 tablespoons instant coffee granules
           2 teaspoons water
           1 pound dark chocolate confectionery coating
   White confectionery coating, optional

In a microwave-safe bowl or double boiler, melt the chocolate chips. Add cream cheese, coffee and water; mix well. Chill until firm enough to shape. Shape into 1-in. balls and place on a waxed paper-lined cookie sheet. Chill for 1-2 hours or until firm. Melt chocolate coating in microwave-safe bowl or double boiler. Dip balls and place on waxed paper to harden. If desired, melt white coating and drizzle over truffles. **Yield:** about 5-1/2 dozen. **Editor's Note:** Dark, white and milk chocolate confectionary coating is found in the baking section of most grocery stores. It is sometimes labeled "almond bark" or "candy coating" and is often sold in bulk packages (1 to 1-1/2 pounds). It is the product used for dipping chocolate. A substitute for 6 ounces of chocolate coating would be 1 cup (6 ounces) semisweet, dark or white chocolate chips and 1 tablespoon shortening melted together.

Fresh Peach Pie

Peach grower Judy Marshall enthusiastically shares this fruit-filled recipe she gives customers at her family's Schreiman Orchards near Waverly, Missouri. "This favorite recipe is reprinted annually in our cookbook," relates Judy.

           1 cup sugar
           2 tablespoons cornstarch
           1 cup water
           1 package (3 ounces) peach-flavored gelatin
           3 cups sliced peeled ripe peaches
           1 pastry shell (9 inches), baked
   Whipped cream, optional

In a saucepan, combine sugar, cornstarch and water until smooth. Cook and stir over medium heat until bubbly and thickened. Remove from the heat; stir in gelatin until dissolved. Cool. Arrange peaches in crust; pour filling over peaches. Chill until set, about 2 hours. Serve with whipped cream if desired. **Yield:** 6-8 servings.

DANDY CANDY. A platter of beautiful homemade candies like chocolaty Pecan Delights and Mocha Truffles (recipes on this page) is a tantalizing treat for the eyes...and tummies!

Fruit Pizza

(PICTURED ON THIS PAGE)

Janet O'Neal of Poplar Bluff, Missouri attests, "This pretty dessert has been a hit every time I've served it."

- 1 package (20 ounces) refrigerated sugar cookie dough
- 1 package (8 ounces) cream cheese, softened
- 1/4 cup confectioners' sugar
- 1 carton (8 ounces) frozen whipped topping, thawed
- 2 to 3 kiwifruit, peeled and thinly sliced
- 1 to 2 firm bananas, sliced
- 1 can (11 ounces) mandarin oranges, drained
- 1/2 cup red grape halves
- 1/4 cup sugar
- 1/4 cup orange juice
- 2 tablespoons water
- 1 tablespoon lemon juice
- 1-1/2 teaspoons cornstarch

Pinch salt

Pat cookie dough into an ungreased 14-in. pizza pan. Bake at 375° for 10-12 minutes or until browned; cool. In a mixing bowl, beat cream cheese and confectioners' sugar until smooth. Fold in whipped topping. Spread over the crust. Arrange the fruit on top. In a saucepan,

bring sugar, orange juice, water, lemon juice, cornstarch and salt to a boil, stirring constantly for 2 minutes or until thickened. Cool; brush over fruit. Store in refrigerator. **Yield:** 16-20 servings.

Banana Nut Layer Cake

(PICTURED ON THIS PAGE)

"This cake is the top choice of the 'birthday child' in our family," says Patsy Howard of Bakersfield, California.

- 1/2 cup shortening
- 2 cups sugar
- 1 egg plus 1 egg white
- 1 cup buttermilk
- 1 cup mashed ripe bananas
- 2 cups all-purpose flour
- 1 teaspoon baking soda
- 1 teaspoon salt
- 1 teaspoon vanilla extract
- 1/2 cup chopped walnuts

FILLING:
- 1/4 cup butter *or* margarine
- 1/2 cup packed brown sugar
- 1/4 cup all-purpose flour

Pinch salt
- 3/4 cup milk
- 1 egg yolk
- 1 teaspoon vanilla extract
- 1/2 cup chopped walnuts

Confectioners' sugar

In a mixing bowl, cream shortening and

sugar. Beat in egg and egg white. Add buttermilk and bananas; mix well. Combine flour, baking soda and salt; stir into the creamed mixture. Add vanilla and nuts. Pour into two greased and floured 9-in. round baking pans. Bake at 350° for 35 minutes or until cakes test done. Cool in pans 10 minutes before removing to a wire rack. For filling, melt butter and brown sugar in a saucepan over medium heat. In a small bowl, combine flour and salt with a small amount of milk; stir until smooth. Add the remaining milk gradually. Add egg yolk and mix well; stir into saucepan. Cook and stir over medium heat until very thick, about 10 minutes. Add vanilla and nuts. Cool. Spread between cake layers. Dust with confectioners' sugar. Chill. Store in the refrigerator. **Yield:** 10-12 servings.

Berry Good Topping

"The natural sweetness of fresh berries comes through in this sauce," assures Martha Balser of Cincinnati, Ohio.

✓ This tasty dish uses less sugar, salt and fat. Recipe includes *Diabetic Exchanges*.

- 1 pint fresh raspberries, *divided*
- 1/4 cup unsweetened apple juice
- 2 tablespoons unsweetened apple juice concentrate
- 2 teaspoons cornstarch
- 1/4 teaspoon vanilla extract

In a blender, puree 1 cup of the berries with apple juice. In a small saucepan, combine apple juice concentrate and cornstarch; stir until smooth. Add pureed berries. Cook over low heat, stirring constantly, until thickened. Cool. Add vanilla and remaining raspberries. Serve over yogurt, ice cream or pancakes. **Yield:** 8 servings (1-1/2 cups). **Diabetic Exchanges:** One 3-tablespoon serving equals 1/2 fruit; also, 35 calories, 1 mg sodium, 0 cholesterol, 8 gm carbohydrate, 1 gm protein, trace fat.

Cran-Raspberry Pie

"This is a treat our grown children enjoy when they come to visit," states Verona Koehlmoos, Pilger, Nebraska.

- 2 cups chopped fresh *or* frozen cranberries
- 1 bag (12 ounces) loose-pack frozen raspberries
- 1-1/2 cups sugar
- 2 tablespoons quick-cooking tapioca
- 1/2 teaspoon almond extract
- 1/4 teaspoon salt

Pastry for double-crust pie (9 inches)

SPREAD SMILES with delightful desserts like (clockwise from bottom) Fruit Pizza, Banana Nut Layer Cake (recipes on this page) and Chewy Brownie Cookies (recipe on page 98).

In a bowl, gently stir cranberries, raspberries, sugar, tapioca, extract and salt. Line pie plate with bottom pastry; add filling. Top with a lattice crust. Bake at 375° for 15 minutes. Reduce heat to 350° and bake 35-40 minutes more or until bubbly. **Yield:** 6-8 servings.

White Christmas Cake

(PICTURED ON THIS PAGE)

"White chocolate, coconut and pecans make this cake delicious," notes Nancy Reichert, Thomasville, Georgia.

    1/2 cup water
      4 ounces white confectionery
        coating *or* vanilla chips
      1 cup butter *or* margarine,
        softened
      2 cups sugar
      4 eggs, *separated*
      1 tablespoon vanilla extract
  2-1/2 cups all-purpose flour
      1 teaspoon baking soda
      1 cup buttermilk
      1 cup flaked coconut
      1 cup chopped pecans
FROSTING:
      1 package (8 ounces) cream
        cheese, softened
    1/2 cup butter *or* margarine,
        softened
      1 teaspoon vanilla extract
      1 box (1 pound) confectioners'
        sugar
      1 tablespoon milk

In a saucepan, bring the water to a boil. Remove from the heat; stir in confectionery coating until melted. Cool for 20 minutes. Meanwhile, in a mixing bowl, cream butter and sugar. Add egg yolks; mix well. Beat in coating and vanilla. Combine flour and baking soda; add to creamed mixture alternately with buttermilk. Mix well. Stir in the coconut and pecans. Beat egg whites until stiff peaks form; fold into the batter. Pour into three greased and floured 8-in. square baking pans. Bake at 350° for 25-30 minutes or until cake tests done. Cool in pans 10 minutes; remove to wire rack to cool completely. Combine frosting ingredients in a mixing bowl; beat well. Frost tops of two layers; stack on serving plate with plain layer on top. Frost top and sides of cake. **Yield:** 10-12 servings.

Cranberry-Almond Apple Pie

(PICTURED ON THIS PAGE)

"This treat is much better than everyday

FESTIVE FINISHES. Celebrate the tastes of any season with (top to bottom) White Christmas Cake, Cranberry-Almond Apple Pie and Washington Cream Pie (recipes on this page).

apple pie," reports Maxine Theriauit, Nashua, New Hampshire.

      1 cup sugar
    1/4 cup all-purpose flour
      3 tablespoons butter *or*
        margarine, melted
    1/2 teaspoon ground nutmeg
    1/8 teaspoon salt
      6 medium baking apples,
        peeled and thinly sliced
      1 cup fresh or frozen cranberries
      1 unbaked pastry shell (9 inches)
TOPPING:
    1/2 cup packed brown sugar
    1/3 cup all-purpose flour
    1/2 teaspoon ground cinnamon
      3 tablespoons butter *or*
        margarine
    1/3 cup sliced almonds, toasted

In a bowl, combine sugar, flour, butter, nutmeg and salt; mix well. Add apples and cranberries; stir gently. Pour into pie shell. In a small bowl, mix the brown sugar, flour and cinnamon; cut in butter until crumbly. Stir in almonds; sprinkle over filling. Bake at 350° for 1 hour or until apples are tender. **Yield:** 6-8 servings.

Washington Cream Pie

(PICTURED ON THIS PAGE)

Lyn Robitaille of East Hartland, Connecticut recalls, "My mom always made

this cake for my uncle, who shares his birthday with George Washington!"

      3 eggs
  1-1/2 cups sugar
      2 cups all-purpose flour
      2 teaspoons baking powder
    1/2 cup water
FILLING:
      1 cup sugar
      2 tablespoons cornstarch
      2 cups milk
      2 eggs, beaten
      2 tablespoons butter *or*
        margarine
      1 teaspoon vanilla extract
      1 can (21 ounces) cherry pie
        filling
Whipped cream

In a mixing bowl, beat eggs on high for 3 minutes; gradually add sugar. Combine flour and baking powder; stir into egg mixture alternately with water. Beat on low for 1 minute. Pour into a greased 9-in. square baking pan. Bake at 375° for 25-30 minutes or until the cake tests done. Cool. Split cake into two layers. For filling, combine the sugar and cornstarch in a saucepan; stir in milk. Bring to a boil; cook for 2 minutes. Stir a small amount into eggs; mix well. Return all to pan. Cook and stir for 1 minute or until thick. Remove from the heat; cool slightly. Add the butter and vanilla; cool completely. Spread between cake layers. Cut into squares; top with pie filling and whipped cream. **Yield:** 9 servings.

BOUNTIFUL AUTUMN BUFFET features (top to bottom) Pumpkin Cake (recipe on this page), Festive Fruit Salad (recipe on page 59), Wild Rice Harvest Casserole (recipe on page 70).

❤☎❤☎❤☎❤☎❤☎❤☎❤

Pumpkin Cake

(PICTURED ON THIS PAGE)

"A slice into this fun pumpkin-shaped dessert reveals a moist banana cake inside," relates Julianne Johnson from Grove City, Minnesota.

> 2 boxes (18-1/2 ounces *each*) banana cake mix
> 2 tablespoons butter *or* margarine
> 2 tablespoons all-purpose flour
> 1/2 cup light cream
> 1/2 cup sugar
> 1 teaspoon vanilla extract
> 1/2 teaspoon salt
> 1/2 cup chopped pecans

BUTTER CREAM FROSTING:

> 3/4 cup butter *or* margarine, softened
> 3/4 cup shortening
> 6 cups confectioners' sugar
> 1 teaspoon vanilla extract
> 2 to 4 tablespoons milk

Red, yellow and green food coloring
Ice cream cone *or* banana

Prepare and bake cakes in 12-cup fluted tube pans according to package directions; cool. For filling, melt butter in a saucepan. Stir in the flour to form a smooth paste. Gradually add cream and sugar, stirring constantly until thick. Boil 1 minute; remove from the heat. Stir in vanilla and salt. Fold in pecans; cool. Cut thin slice off bottom of each cake. Spread one cake bottom with filling; put cakes together with bottoms together. Set aside. In a mixing bowl, cream butter and shortening. Beat in sugar and vanilla. Add milk until desired consistency is reached. Combine red and yellow food coloring to make orange; tint about three-fourths of the frosting orange. Tint remaining frosting green. Place a small glass upside down in the center of the cake to support the "stem". Put a dollop of frosting on the glass and top with an ice cream cone or banana. Cut the cone or banana to the correct length; frost with green frosting. Frost cake with orange frosting. **Yield:** 12-16 servings.

❤☎❤☎❤☎❤☎❤☎❤☎❤

Apple Turnovers With Custard

(PICTURED ON BACK COVER)

"With the flaky turnovers and rich sauce, this outshines every other apple recipe I make!" writes Leora Muellerleile of Turtle Lake, Wisconsin.

CUSTARD:

> 1/3 cup sugar
> 2 tablespoons cornstarch
> 2 cups milk *or* light cream
> 3 egg yolks, lightly beaten
> 1 tablespoon vanilla extract

TURNOVERS:

> 4 medium baking apples, peeled and cut into 1/4-inch slices
> 1 tablespoon lemon juice
> 2 tablespoons butter *or* margarine, diced
> 1/3 cup sugar
> 3/4 teaspoon ground cinnamon
> 1 tablespoon cornstarch

Pastry for double-crust pie
Milk

Combine the sugar and cornstarch in a saucepan. Stir in the milk until smooth. Cook and stir over medium-high heat until thickened and bubbly. Reduce heat; cook and stir for 2 minutes. Remove from heat; stir 1 cup into yolks. Return all to pan. Bring to a gentle boil; cook and stir for 2 minutes. Remove from heat; stir in vanilla. Cool slightly. Cover surface of custard with waxed paper; chill. Place apples in a bowl; sprinkle with lemon juice. Add butter. Combine sugar, cinnamon and cornstarch; mix with apples and set aside. Divide pastry into eight portions; roll each into a 5-in. square. Spoon filling off-center on each. Brush edges with milk. Fold over to form a triangle; seal. Crimp with tines of fork. Make steam vents in top. Place on greased baking sheets. Chill 15 minutes. Brush with milk. Bake at 400° for 35 minutes. Serve warm with custard. **Yield:** 8 servings.

❤☎❤☎❤☎❤☎❤☎❤☎❤

Best-Ever Cheesecake

"I've passed this recipe on to dozens of friends," declares Lima, Ohio cook Howard Koch. "My daughter was so fond of it that she wanted it served for her wedding instead of cake."

> 1-1/4 cups graham cracker crumbs
> 1/3 cup butter *or* margarine, melted
> 1/4 cup sugar

FILLING/TOPPING:

> 2 packages (8 ounces *each*) cream cheese, softened
> 2 eggs, lightly beaten
> 2/3 cup sugar, *divided*
> 2 teaspoons vanilla extract, *divided*

Pinch salt

> 1 cup (8 ounces) sour cream

In a bowl, combine the graham cracker crumbs, butter and sugar; mix well. Pat evenly into the bottom and up the sides of a 9-in. pie plate. Chill. For filling, beat cream cheese and eggs in a mixing bowl on medium speed for 1 minute. Add 1/3 cup sugar, 1 teaspoon of vanilla and salt. Continue beating until well blended, about 1 minute. Pour into crust. Bake at 350° for 35 minutes. Cool for 10 minutes. For topping, combine the sour cream, and remaining sugar and vanilla in a small bowl; spread evenly over cheesecake. Return to the oven for 10 minutes. Cool completely on a wire rack. Refrigerate 3 hours or overnight. **Yield:** 8 servings.

♥☎♥☎♥☎♥☎♥☎♥☎♥

Ambrosia Dessert Bowl

(PICTURED ON THIS PAGE)

"This wonderful recipe uses fresh oranges. It's a nice light, refreshing dessert," shares Donna Morris of Weirsdale, Florida.

- 20 large marshmallows
- 2 cups heavy cream, *divided*
- 2 tablespoons sugar
- 2 teaspoons vanilla extract
- 1/2 teaspoon almond extract
- 1 can (20 ounces) crushed pineapple, well drained
- 1 cup flaked coconut
- 1 loaf (10-3/4 ounces) frozen pound cake, thawed and cubed (about 4 cups)
- 5 to 6 large navel oranges, peeled and sectioned
- 1/4 cup slivered almonds, toasted

Place marshmallows and 1/4 cup cream in the top of a double boiler; heat over boiling water until the marshmallows are melted and the mixture is smooth. Cool completely. Meanwhile, whip the remaining cream until thick. Add sugar. Fold into marshmallow mixture. Fold in extracts, pineapple and coconut. Place half of the pound cake cubes in the bottom of a 2-1/2- to 3-qt. clear glass bowl. Top with half of the orange sections. Top with half of the cream mixture. Repeat layers. Sprinkle with almonds. Chill until serving time. **Yield:** 10-12 servings.

♥☎♥☎♥☎♥☎♥☎♥☎♥

Pear Pie

"This pie showcases pears from our acres of fruit trees deliciously," says Jean Lauer, Summerland, British Columbia.

- 1 cup sugar, *divided*
- 2 tablespoons lemon juice
- 1/2 teaspoon grated lemon peel
- 1/4 teaspoon ground coriander
- 6 cups sliced peeled ripe pears
- 1 unbaked pastry shell (9 inches)
- 1/2 cup all-purpose flour

- 1/2 teaspoon ground cinnamon
- 1/4 teaspoon ground mace
- 1/3 cup butter *or* margarine
Vanilla ice cream, optional

In a bowl, combine 1/2 cup sugar, lemon juice and peel and coriander. Add pears and toss. Spoon into pie shell. In a bowl, combine flour, cinnamon, mace and remaining sugar; cut in butter until mixture resembles coarse crumbs. Sprinkle over pears. Bake at 400° for 45 minutes or until pears are tender. Serve warm or cold with ice cream if desired. **Yield:** 6-8 servings.

♥☎♥☎♥☎♥☎♥☎♥☎♥

Frozen Chocolate Torte

"In summer, this cool make-ahead dessert is one of my favorites," relates Tammy Neubauer of Ida Grove, Iowa.

- 1 package (10-1/2 ounces) miniature marshmallows
- 1 cup (6 ounces) semisweet chocolate chips
- 1 can (12 ounces) evaporated milk
- 1 cup flaked coconut
- 1/2 cup butter *or* margarine
- 2 cups graham cracker crumbs
- 1/2 gallon vanilla ice cream, softened

In a saucepan over low heat, melt the marshmallows and chocolate chips with milk. Remove from heat; cool. In a skillet, stir coconut in butter until browned.

Remove from the heat; stir in crumbs. Pat three-fourths into a 13-in. x 9-in. x 2-in. baking pan; cool. Spoon half of the ice cream onto crust. Top with half of the chocolate mixture. Layer with remaining ice cream and chocolate. Sprinkle with remaining crumbs. Cover and freeze for at least 2 hours. **Yield:** 12 servings.

♥☎♥☎♥☎♥☎♥☎♥☎♥

Ice Cream Sundae Dessert

"When you want a change of pace from heavy sweets, this creamy dessert fills the bill," assures Kimberly McKeever of Shoreview, Minnesota.

- 20 chocolate sandwich cookies, crushed
- 1/4 cup butter *or* margarine, softened
- 1/2 gallon vanilla *or* peppermint ice cream, softened
- 1 carton (8 ounces) frozen whipped topping, thawed
- 2 to 3 tablespoons chocolate syrup
- 1/4 cup chopped pecans

In a bowl, mix cookie crumbs with butter. Press into the bottom of a greased 13-in. x 9-in. x 2-in. pan. Carefully spread ice cream over crust. Spread whipped topping over ice cream. Drizzle chocolate syrup on top; sprinkle with nuts. Freeze until firm, about 2-4 hours. **Yield:** 12-16 servings.

CITRUS STARS in (clockwise, top left) Ambrosia Dessert Bowl (recipe this page), Glazed Chicken with Lemon Relish (p. 78), Sweet Broiled Grapefruit (p. 82), Grandma's Orange Rolls (p. 86).

Delicious to Taste...
Easy to Make...
Yours to Enjoy!

IF YOU LIKE the satisfying, home-style dishes in **The Taste of Home Recipe Book**, then you'll love *Taste of Home* magazine!

Every other month *Taste of Home* brings you treasured, "family-secret" recipes with the delicious taste your family will ask for again and again. That's because every *Taste of Home* recipe is contributed by our field staff of 1,000 country cooks or our millions of devoted readers. Which means each recipe is home-tested...and certified "a winner" by a family like yours. You get more than 85 of our "best-of-the-best" recipes in every issue!

Save Big on Great Family Recipes!

Now when you subscribe to *Taste of Home*—or give it to a friend as a "tasteful" gift—you'll save a bundle. With this special offer, you'll save up to **$12.00 off** the regular rate...and get 2 years of *Taste of Home* for only $10.98 per year! Just fill in, detach and mail one of these cards today!

With *Taste of Home*, you'll get:

- Cherished, never-before-shared family recipes!
- More than 85 home-tested recipes in every issue!
- Only recipes that use basic ingredients you have on hand!
- America's #1 cooking magazine—over 3 million subscribers!
- Cover-to-cover value...with **NO ADVERTISING!**